AMERICA'S OIL FAMINE

Also by Ruth Sheldon Knowles

THE GREATEST GAMBLERS
INDONESIA TODAY

AMERICA'S OIL FAMINE

How It Happened and When It Will End

by
Ruth Sheldon Knowles

COWARD, McCANN & GEOGHEGAN, INC.
NEW YORK

SBN: 698-10592-3
Library of Congress Catalog Card Number: 73-93769

Printed in the United States of America

To the pessimists of this world who are the burrs under our tail!
To the world's optimists who inspire us!
And to those, like my daughter, Carroll, who remind us that,
at times, the Emperor has no clothes on!

Contents

1

The Energy Bomb Drops

In Israel it was the morning of Yom Kippur, the Day of Atonement, October 6, 1973. The synagogues were filled with worshipers on this holiest of Jewish days. Suddenly, the quiet that enveloped the nation was shattered by wailing sirens, alerting a startled populace to the outbreak of the fourth Arab-Israeli war in twenty years. Egypt and Syria had simultaneously launched a massive invasion across the Suez Canal and on the Golan Heights.

The bloody fighting which ensued for three weeks before the United Nations arranged a cease-fire was not just another bitter chapter in the story of unresolved confrontation in the Middle East. It quickly became an international energy war when, within two weeks of the attack, the Arabs unleashed their ultimate weapon—their power to manipulate world affairs through economic action. By cutting back almost a fourth of the production of the world's greatest known oil reserves, and embargoing oil shipments to the United States and the Netherlands—and subsequently Portugal, South Africa and Rhodesia—they dropped a political and economic bomb whose spectacular fallout spread rapidly around the world.

When the war broke out, I was about to return to Saudi Arabia, where I had gone a few weeks earlier, to see King Faisal. I had been on a round-the-world research trip on the international oil situation, and the king was out of the country attending a crucial summit conference with other Arab leaders. His return was uncertain, so after seeing all the new oil developments in Saudi Arabia since my last visit, I kept a date to meet a new 250,000-ton supertanker, loaded with Saudi Arabian oil, at the superport of Milford Haven, England, where it discharged part of its cargo. I then rode it up the English Channel to Fawley, England, where it discharged the rest. Since superports and supertankers are very much a part of America's future, I wanted to see how they are handled and how people coexist with them.

I regret I did not see King Faisal, whom I had known since he was crown prince. I wanted to discuss his warnings to the United States government. The first had come in April, a good six months before

7

the oil embargo. He had warned that Saudi Arabia would find it difficult to raise its oil production to meet projected American needs unless the United States used its influence with Israel to bring about a political settlement in the Middle East that would be satisfactory to the Arabs.

Only a few in the U.S. government had taken him seriously. I knew, from having conferred with him at regular intervals since he became king in 1964, that he must always be taken seriously. As the most conservative of Arab leaders he has never played international diplomatic poker and would never stoop to a bluff. His warnings were particularly grave because he had consistently opposed the use of oil as a political weapon and was severely criticized by leaders of other Arab oil states as being too pro-American. These leaders had made fifteen different threats during 1972 to use their oil politically against their enemies, of whom they considered the United States Enemy Number One. The majority of Americans, in government and out, had pooh-poohed such threats. They counted on the traditional lack of Arab unity. They also were victims of the misconception that the Arabs needed to sell their oil more than other people around the world needed to buy it. This had been essentially true in the late 1960's, but beginning in 1970, the whole oil ball game, internationally and in the United States, had changed dramatically. King Faisal had emerged as the king of world oil, and the United States was heading toward an energy crisis of formidable proportions.

At that time I, like a latter-day Paul Revere, began writing and lecturing throughout the country, saying, "The oil crisis is coming!" As the world's greatest oil producer we had grown fat and prosperous, feasting on an abundance of energy. We were consuming one-third of world energy, although we account for only 6 percent of its population. Any thought that we might be forced to go on an energy diet was totally bewildering. However, owing to our zooming consumption and underdevelopment of our own great oil, gas and coal resources, predictions were that we would be importing 55 percent of our oil needs by 1985 unless our national policies changed. And the oil would come primarily from the politically unstable Middle East. It had been known since the end of World War II that the Middle East contained the major portion of the world's oil reserves, but this had never seemed particularly important before in connection with our own energy future. We are dependent on oil and gas for three-fourths of our energy, so the prospect of such enormous imports should have made us give priority attention to what was happening in the Middle East. The nose on our face is always more obvious to the other fellow than it is to us. And so it was in the case of ourselves and the Arabs.

Although, by and large, it went unnoticed in the United States, 1970 was the "Year of the Arab" in world oil. It marked the turning point for the course world events would take. For ten years, a cartel of Arab oil countries had been struggling to wrest control of their oil resources from the international oil companies to which they had given development concessions. In 1970 the host governments succeeded in shifting the balance of power from the companies to themselves and began a dizzying spiral of increasing their share of profits and also forcing up the price of international oil.

When I saw King Faisal in 1970 at his summer palace in Jidda, I asked him what he recommended I see in order to appreciate the progress the country had made since my visit a year earlier. "There has not been very much progress," he said with a sigh, "not as much as should have been made because of our support of the war against Israel and because our oil production has not increased." Yet three years later the king's money problem was the reverse. Saudi Arabia was making more money than it could absorb. As the result of a vast expansion program, it became the giant of world oil exporters, reaching a production of more than 8,000,000 barrels a day, almost equaling that of the United States, the world's largest producer. New Saudi discoveries and development of known reserves projected the capacity of a daily production of 20,000,000 barrels by 1982. The center of gravity of the world's oil future now lay in this otherwise barren kingdom of 6,000,000 people.

I knew, as did everyone who talked with him, that King Faisal was deeply unhappy about the steady deterioration of Arab-American relations. Each time I saw him following the six-day 1967 Arab-Israeli war, he was more sorrowful than the time before about America's pro-Israel policy in the Middle East. "Why can't Americans be evenhanded in their policy?" he would ask. "Don't Americans realize the danger of Communism and that by supporting the Zionists they are pushing other Arab nations into alliances with the Communists?" King Faisal, who will not permit a Communist to enter Saudi Arabia, felt bitterly alone as a last bulwark against the uprising influence of the Soviet Union. He is a deeply religious man. His stand against Zionist aggression is a holy cause because he is custodian of the sacred Muslim city of Mecca and the Moslem shrines of Jerusalem. However, he was tacitly willing to admit the existence of Israel as a state if the Israelis would withdraw from

Arab-occupied territories after the Arab-Israeli war of 1967 and if a peace settlement could be reached.

The international oil industry and those of us who professionally follow political and economic developments of the world oil situation knew that Middle East options had reached a critical point in early 1973. The Arab oil countries literally had more billions of dollars than they knew what to do with. They also knew that only the Middle East and North Africa, which were supplying 90 percent of international oil and have three-fourths of the world's proved oil reserves, could meet the soaring oil demands of all the consuming countries.

Obviously, the Arabs had been studying American energy surveys more closely than our own Congress. They knew, although the majority of the American public did not, the extent of the energy crisis in which the United States was already involved and how long it would take to solve it. The staffs of their governments and national oil companies are filled with young Arabs holding degrees from American, European and Middle East universities in economics, business administration and petroleum technical fields. They were and are aware of the vulnerability of the consuming countries. Japan imports almost 100 percent of its oil needs, Western Europe imports 93 percent and the United States 37 percent.

The Arabs' political target, of course, was the United States because of its all-out support of Israel. They knew that only 5 percent of American consumption was supplied by Arab oil, so an embargo could damage, but not wreck, the American economy. However, Arab oil supplied Western Europe with 73 percent of its needs and Japan with 45 percent of its consumption. By cutting back oil supplies to these countries, they hoped to force them to pressure the United States to influence Israel to withdraw from occupied territories and make a peace treaty.

Since 1970, King Faisal was under great pressure from other Arab governments to take up the oil weapon. During the six months before the Yom Kippur war he made every effort, through both public and private channels, to persuade the United States to change its Middle East policy. The sequence of events in this period was a bizarre episode in the history of American foreign policy. Seldom has an impending international disaster been so completely misjudged.

In April, 1973, King Faisal sent the Saudi Arabian Oil Minister, Sheikh Ahmed Zaki al-Yamani, and Deputy Oil Minister Prince

Saud to Washington with the first warning that Saudi Arabia might not increase its oil production, or even maintain current output, unless there was a "correction" in U.S. Middle East policy. The Nixon administration was polite, but unresponsive.

As a matter of fact, at the time the Saudi delegation arrived, President Nixon delivered a long-awaited energy message to Congress which was particularly revealing because of what it *didn't* say. The message was designed to be reassuring about America's growing oil shortage and stressed our capacity to avert any "genuine energy crisis" if we would "take the proper steps." Without giving specifics, the President stated that "it is clear that in the foreseeable future, we will have to import oil in large quantities" and urged building deepwater ports. He removed all tariffs on imported oil and products, suspended import controls and substituted a license-fee quota system. There was no mention of America's looming dependence on Middle East oil or the necessity of cooperation in any way with the Arab oil-producing countries.

The omission was deliberate. There had been a behind-the-scenes battle between those who favored speaking in terms of realities and those who felt it would be politically unwise to invite controversy at a time when Washington skies were being illuminated by Watergate fireworks. The "compromise" was that, like the fine print in an insurance policy, a paragraph appeared in the "Official Background Summary and Fact Sheet," issued by the Office of the White House Press Secretary, to accompany the text of the message:

> The projections are for large increases in imported crude oil and products, particularly during the next three to five years, primarily from the Middle East. In 1972, only about 1.4 million barrels per day, or about 30 per cent of total oil imports came from the Eastern Hemisphere (including countries besides the Middle East). This amounted to only 8 per cent of the total oil supply. By 1985, if present trends were allowed to continue, the U.S. would have to import from 50 to 60 per cent of its total oil supply and 30 to 40 per cent of this may have to be from Eastern Hemisphere sources. The President's energy initiatives can greatly reduce future foreign imports.

No mention was made of what imports of this magnitude could represent in terms of balance of payments, although then Commerce Secretary Peter G. Peterson had stated publicly a short time before that one of the "compelling dilemmas" in arriving at an energy policy was to find ways to reduce projected deficits in the energy trade balance. He estimated them as $15 to $21 billion by 1980, as contrasted with a $6 billion deficit in 1972.

The President advised Congress he had created a Special Committee on Energy, consisting of three Assistants to the President—John D. Ehrlichman, Henry A. Kissinger and George P. Shultz—"to protect and promote the interests of the people of the United States as energy users, and to coordinate the policies of the executive branch in this area." He also established a National Energy Office to report to him through the Special Committee.

The composition of the Special Committee did not offer the Arabs much hope that consideration of the Middle East problem would be high on its agenda. Within two weeks of the announcement, Ehrlichman, who had the most to say about energy matters publicly, resigned from Nixon's staff because of Watergate disclosures. Kissinger, then head of the National Security Council, had paid minimal attention to energy as a foreign affairs priority. China, the Soviet Union and Vietnam were his thing. Not until January, 1973, had he directed his staff to make a study of energy matters. When he was appointed Secretary of State in August, there was dismay throughout the Arab world that a German Jew would be at the American diplomatic helm. Any thought that he and Arab leaders would be kissing each other's cheeks before too long was preposterous. Treasury Secretary Shultz, as late as three weeks before the Yom Kippur war, told a foreign press club luncheon in Tokyo that the Arab oil-producing countries were "swaggering about a bit." But, he said, the United States effort to develop its own energy resources was "the one thing that tends to cool off the swagger."

Washington politicians and diplomats succeeded in shoving the Middle East problem aside during the critical months when something could have been done to prevent the war and the international energy crisis. They had little understanding of the emotionalism of Arab psychology. During my trips to the Middle East whenever I discussed the Arab-Israeli situation with Arabs, regardless of the logic of any economic or political arguments, they would inevitably sum up their point of view with a simple Arab proverb: "The friend of my enemy is my enemy." It was this philosophy that prevailed when the United States did nothing to implement its talk of "evenhandedness."

There were some in government who took the Arabs seriously. Chief among these was James E. Akins, one of Washington's most knowledgeable oil experts. He had been a Foreign Service officer in the Middle East from 1956 to 1965 and became director of energy policy for the State Department. Akins, who is now ambassador to Saudi Arabia, had repeatedly tried to alert the administration and Congress that the United States' oil crisis was a reality and that the Arab nations would use oil as a political weapon. When King Faisal announced his intentions to refuse to expand oil exports to the United States, Akins was in the forefront to warn that the king meant business.

When Washington turned a deaf ear, King Faisal told Standard Oil of California, Texaco, Exxon and Mobil, the owner companies of the Arabian American Oil Company, known as Aramco, which produces almost all of Saudi Arabia's oil, that he expected them to help get his message across. This posed a thorny government and public relations problem to the international oil companies. Nevertheless, in June Mobil took out newspaper ads detailing the United States oil stake in Middle East peace. The company stated that "it is time now for the world to insist on a settlement in the Middle East, backed by ironclad and credible guarantees from the United States and the Soviet Union, among others." This drew protests from Jewish organizations. The following month there were enraged organizational demonstrations when Standard Oil of California took the unprecedented step of sending a letter to the company's 260,000 stockholders and 40,000 employees, asking them "to urge our Government to work toward conditions of peace and stability" in the Middle East and to encourage the government to work toward "a course which recognizes the importance of these objectives to the future of all of us—a course which above all seeks a peaceful and just settlement of conflicting viewpoints." Protesters splashed paint on the company's headquarters, burned credit cards and threatened to boycott its products.

That same month the United States vetoed a United Nations Security Council resolution that strongly deplored Israel's continuing occupation of the Arab territory taken during the 1967 war. The U.S. position was that such a resolution "would have done irrevocable and permanent damage" to the 1967 UN resolution which provided that "the ending of occupation must be in the context of peace between the parties, that it must be in the context of all states in the area to live within secure and recognized boundaries."

Britain and France, which had voted for the resolution, took sharp issue with the United States. Western Europe was becoming impatient and exceedingly nervous about America's lack of correlation between its Middle East policy and the world energy problem. This was clearly brought out by a European study made by the U.S. General Accounting Office. After interviewing European government and industry officials, the GAO reported that there was "mistrust" of the U.S. and its motives. Europeans felt that the United States had brought its energy crisis on itself by mismanagement of domestic energy policy and that it was likely now to draw Europe into the crisis with it.

It was not until August that King Faisal's message and the potential world energy crisis became front-page news. During the summer of '73, America had squeaked through a much-heralded gasoline shortage. It had nothing to do with the Middle East but resulted from a shortage of refinery capacity in the United States. However, the communications media was on an energy alert and had been doing some homework in digging into the state of energy affairs and policy. King Faisal became the news "man of the hour" when President Sadat of Egypt secretly visited him. Reports leaked that the king had made a deal to back him financially if Egypt would not merge with Libya, ruled by the fanatic radical Colonel Muammar Qaddafi. This illustrated a major reshifting of power in the Middle East and showcased the king's key role in Arab politics. In an NBC documentary on *The Energy Crisis*, he demonstrated his key position in international politics. "We do not wish to place any restrictions on our oil exports to the United States," he stated, "but as I mentioned, America's complete support of Zionism against the Arabs makes it extremely difficult for us to continue to supply the U.S. petroleum needs and to even maintain our friendship with the U.S. As friends of the U.S. and in the interest of maintaining and cementing this friendship, we counsel the U.S. to change its one-sided policy of favoritism to Zionism and support against the Arabs."

On September 2 Libya nationalized 51 percent of all foreign oil companies, the majority of which were American. The U.S. government could no longer keep its head in the sand. On September 6 President Nixon for the first time publicly linked American oil needs to Middle East policy. In a press conference, on the day Congress returned from its August recess, he talked about the necessity of Congress' acting on his domestic energy proposals. He said that "if the Congress does not act upon these proposals —which, in effect, has [*sic*] as their purpose increasing the domestic capacity of the United States to create its energy, it means that we will be at the mercy of the producers of oil in the Mideast." When he was asked what he was doing to "meet these threats from the Arab countries to use oil as a club to force a change in our Middle East policy," he answered that it had been a "subject of major concern."

He went on to say, "The answer to the problem of oil that we presently depend upon in the Mideast—we depend on it not, of course, nearly as much as Europe; but we're all in the same bag when you really come down to it—the problem that we have here is that as far as the Arab countries are concerned, the ones that are involved here, is that it's tied up with the Arab-Israeli dispute. That is why in talking to Dr. Kissinger, both before I nominated him [as Secretary of State two weeks earlier] and since, that we have put at the highest priority moving toward making some progress toward the settlement of the dispute. That's one side of it."

If the President had stopped there, he might have given the Arabs reason to believe that, at long last, he was being responsive to their frustrations. He made the blunder of continuing and demonstrated his lack of understanding of both Arab sensitivities and economic realities. "The other problem, of course," he said, "are [*sic*] the radical elements that presently seem to be on the ascendancy in various countries in the Mideast, like Libya. Those elements, of course, we are not in a position to control, although we may be in a position to influence. Influence them for this reason. Oil without a market, as Mr. Mossadegh learned many, many years ago, doesn't do a country much good. We and Europe are the market. And I think that the responsible Arab leaders will see to it that if they continue to up the price, if they continue to expropriate, the inevitable result is that they will lose their markets and other sources will be developed."

The threatening mention of Mohammed Mossadegh, who became Premier of Iran in 1951, was a particularly inept reference to American undercover "diplomacy." Mossadegh, in connivance with Iran's Communist Party, nationalized the British-owned Anglo-Iranian Oil Company. The British and American governments mounted a secret operation to overthrow him, as London and Washington feared the Russians would acquire Iran's vast oil reserves. It was widely known that the American CIA organized and directed the 1953 coup that overthrew Mossadegh and kept the present shah, Mohammed Reza Pahlevi, then in exile, on his throne. The international oil companies had also successfully boycotted the sale of Iranian oil. Subsequently the British lost their oil monopoly, and an international consortium of British, Dutch, French and

American oil companies signed a forty-year pact with the shah for his oil.

In those days there was a surplus of world oil and buyers called the tune, but now the President was far behind the times. Since 1970 there has been a shortage of world oil. In view of the known years of lead time necessary to develop additional American or other international energy sources, the President's big talk about the oil-producing countries' losing their markets had all the menace of a toothless lion's roar.

Nevertheless, the President moderated his support of Israel, stating that "both sides are at fault" and that the United States would use its influence with Israel and "what influence we have with the various Arab states" to get negotiations for peace "off dead center."

There was no apparent sense of urgency to begin negotiations. As September ended, Kissinger, in a luncheon address to Arab foreign ministers at the opening fall session of the United Nations, advised them that the United States was ready to assist "to find ways" of creating a situation "with which you can live," but not to "expect the United States to bring forth miracles." A United Nations Middle East debate was scheduled for later in the year.

Arab leaders had their own ideas of how to get negotiations "off dead center." It was a gamble, but they felt that psychologically, economically and even militarily, conditions were favorable for the shock treatment of open warfare. If successful, it would give them more leverage at any negotiating table. At the worst, it would force the big powers to recognize that the Middle East stalemate was intolerable.

Even after the war began, King Faisal initially used his influence to prevent a drastic use of oil as a political weapon, hoping that the United States would not rush to the support of Israel, but would intervene diplomatically. On October 17, at an eight-hour meeting of Arab oil ministers in Kuwait to make a formal decision on how to use the oil weapon, the Saudis succeeded in convincing the others to take the relatively mild step of announcing a 5 percent monthly cut in oil exports every month until Israel evacuated the territories occupied in the 1967 war and restored the legal rights of the Palestinian people. The following day King Faisal received the news that President Nixon had asked Congress for $2.2 billion in emergency military aid for Israel to maintain the military balance and achieve stability in the Middle East. The camel's back broke. King Faisal announced a 10 percent slash in Saudi production and a total embargo on the United States, measures which were quickly adopted by other Arab oil countries. The embargo was then extended to the Netherlands because of Dutch pro-Israel policies. Within a few weeks Arab oil cutbacks reached 25 percent.

Throughout the industrialized countries, the immediate chain reaction to the Arab maneuver was astonishing. Like Alice, they suddenly fell down the rabbit hole and went through the looking glass. The militant problems of 90,000,000 people in the Middle East plunged the remaining 2.6 billion people of the free world into unexpected, painful difficulties and threatened their growth and progress. Stock markets plunged to new lows as analysts and economists predicted a world recession, bringing massive unemployment and rampant inflation. Factories closed for lack of fuel. Workers were laid off by the thousands in a startling variety of industries. Many countries began to ration gasoline and fuels. There were growing shortages in food, clothing, housing and manufacturing materials—all stemming from oil shortages. Airlines drastically reduced their flights. Everywhere the price of everything went up. Europe and Japan blamed the United States for what was happening. The Arabs had successfully splintered relations between the consuming countries. There was no common front. It was every country for itself.

In the United States, there was bewilderment, confusion and disbelief. Initially, people adjusted well to the conservation measures the government urged voluntarily or set arbitrarily. Gasless Sundays, lowered thermostats, reduced speed limits, going back on daylight saving time and turning off lights were all manageable things. But when fuel oil and gasoline shortages became realities instead of predictions and prices rose astronomically, the national mood changed sharply. It became ugly. Highways were blocked by protesting truck drivers. People were killed in angry demonstrations. There were fights at gasoline stations. The public was bitter and accusing.

The communications media covered "the energy war" with the zeal and dedication they had devoted to man's first landing on the moon. We suddenly heard more about energy than we had ever wanted to know or thought it possible to ask. We found ourselves awash in a tidal wave of conflicting opinions. There were those who said the crisis was only temporary. Others forecast that mankind could never again return to pre-Yom-Kippur-war affluence. There were those who claimed the crisis was not real but had been created by the oil companies to bring about higher prices. Some maintained it had been contrived by the government to divert attention from Watergate.

Nobody knew whom to believe. Credibility, in regard to the oil industry and government, was in as short supply as gasoline. Congress was flooded with Band-Aid bills. Every pertinent Congressional committee initiated hearings to determine what had happened and what to do about it. But there was no consensus or action. President Nixon tried to reassure the people that his Project Independence would make America self-sufficient in energy by 1980. The oil companies defended themselves in full-page newspaper ads. None of this was enough. Not even the lifting of the Arab embargo, five months after its imposition, and the easing of shortages satisfied the people. The nation's traumatic experience had posed vital questions. The people wanted them answered.

How did we get in this mess and why didn't we know what was going to happen?

Was the crisis real or did the oil companies conspire to create it to raise prices, make greater profits, put independents out of business, put through the Alaska pipeline and get rights to drill offshore?

How much is energy going to cost us and why?

How long will we have an energy problem?

How will it affect our jobs and life-style?

Are we really running out of energy? If not, why can't we have a crash program and solve our problems?

Does meeting our energy needs mean we will lose the gains we've made in protecting our environment?

What should the government do about our energy problem?

A nation addicted to instant coffee, fast food businesses, crash diets, wash-and-wear, five-minute news, direct dialing, air shuttles and all the timesaving, shortcutting gadgetry and techniques of our times expects quick and easy answers. There are none. Nor are there any instant solutions. However, there are real answers and real solutions. Some of the answers are tough. They involve sacrifices, higher prices and new mental attitudes. People won't like that. But we're basically a tough people and have weathered rough times. We can again. Some of the solutions will take more time than people would like to believe. They won't like that either. But we have good common sense and can figure out what's right, or wrong, or reasonable if we have all the facts. When the chips are down, what we really want to know is who the players are, what the stakes are and whether or not the deck is stacked.

Will Rogers once said, "Everybody's ignorant—only about different things." Most Americans have been blissfully ignorant about everything that lies behind their gallon of gasoline or fuel oil because it has always been abundant and cheap. Until now there has been little reason to ask any questions.

I have spent my life learning about energy problems as a journalist, petroleum specialist and consultant to governments and industry. As a child, before I ever found out that a wildcat was an animal, I knew it was a well drilled in search of oil. When we went on family picnics, instead of going to a park, my Oklahoma independent oilman father took us to wherever he was drilling his current wildcat, hoping to pay last month's bills with the oil he was going to find tomorrow. Later I found out how complex the vast energy industry is as I traveled all over the world, following the oil seekers and finders to deserts, jungles, mountains, oceans and the Arctic Circle, seeing oil fields, pipelines, tankers, refineries and research laboratories. I learned about the politics of oil, working with governments, studying petroleum laws, attending Congressional hearings and Arab oil congresses. Most of all, I learned about the people involved, from world leaders to oil field workers, and how and why the quest and thirst for oil affects the lives of practically everyone on earth.

The complexity of the national and international oil industry is why there are no quick and easy answers to many of the questions we want answered. It is also why there are so many misconceptions. Our energy problems did not develop overnight, nor were there any conspiracies to create shortages. When gas lines formed and prices soared at the very time that major international oil companies announced record net profit increases over 1972, that particular cause and effect derived primarily from improved profits overseas. To understand all this, we have to take a look at a lot of things: the nature of the oil industry and the difference between the handful of major oil companies and the 10,000 independent oil producers; the events that led to our becoming an energy-short nation; the role of price controls; the mistakes made by government and industry in underestimating consumption and which sources of energy would supply it; the effect of environmental legislation in curtailing the use of large sources of energy supply and preventing the development of others; why we didn't have a national energy policy, although we had been in an energy crisis since 1970; and how the Arab oil countries gained control of world oil prices, which, combined with their cutback, raised the price at the American gasoline pump.

We now know that there is no such thing as cheap foreign oil. The days of bargain basement prices for energy are gone forever. Yet we can hope to have reasonably priced energy when we develop our known resources and new types of energy. Our most difficult problem is to understand the role that prices and profits play in providing incentive and capital to do this on the big scale necessary to get the job done. Individually, we have a hard enough time swimming in our personal pools of credit cards, charge accounts, finance charges, interest rates, bank loans and tax returns. It is mind-boggling to breast the tidal waves of the vast amounts of capital investment, bond issues, debt-equity ratios, dividends to stockholders, domestic and foreign tax laws, costs and profits which compose the economic ocean navigated by the big enterprises providing a great proportion of our goods, services and jobs. When the energy crisis temporarily transferred the financial page to the front page, it became obvious that we need to know how big business really works and affects our pocketbooks. In hammering out a workable energy policy and legislation to implement it, understanding the economics involved is the most important, as well as controversial, issue.

We can be optimistic about the solution of our energy problem for many reasons. As a research scientist at Bell Telephone Laboratories once told me, "If you can define a problem, you have it half solved." Not only can we thoroughly define our problem now, but as the result of the multitude of scientific studies that have been made in the past four years, we know that we are the luckiest of all the industrialized countries. We have the physical resources and technology to become self-sufficient. We have enough potentially recoverable crude oil, natural gas, coal, uranium and shale oil to meet our needs for at least 200 years, at present consumption rates. The technological and economic problems of new energy sources, such as oil shale, the breeder reactor, geothermal power, solar power and nuclear fusion will ultimately be solved and conceivably could begin to become important power sources as the twenty-first century begins. Our real energy problem is immediate and short-term, not long-range.

However, as a 1972 joint government-industry energy study points out, until we can develop competitive synthetic fuels, the United States will have to rely on oil, natural gas, coal and nuclear power for 95 percent of our energy requirements. No crash program can solve our problem quickly, because of the long lead times necessary to develop new supplies of these fuels. It takes four to five years to find and develop an oil field, two to three years to build a refinery, eight to nine years to establish a nuclear electric generating plant, and two to five years to develop coal mines of all types. It will take ten years to develop a substantial synthetic fuel industry using oil shale or coal. Even if all lights were green now to launch a massive energy development program, we have a stupendous job ahead to meet our anticipated energy demand. To approach near self-sufficiency by 1990, we will need more than 500,000 new oil and gas wells; more than 60 new oil refineries; an equal number of plants for oil shale, and for coal gasification and liquefaction; more than 30 new nuclear plants a year during the mid-1980's, or a new plant every two weeks; more than 140 new coal mines, including a large number of small deep mines as well as high-capacity strip mines.

The next five to eight years will be our greatest period of stress, before our drive toward self-sufficiency begins to reduce our import requirements. It will also be our greatest testing period as to whether our recent experience has focused our attention on our real long-term problem or whether we are going to continue to live from one winter heating shortage and summer gasoline shortage to the next one. We demonstrated that we could cut energy consumption substantially when we had to. If we deliberately make conservation and efficient energy use a national way of life, while we are increasing our supply, we'll come out on top. One of the great benefits of the crisis was to make us aware of how much energy we waste in so many different ways, individually and industrially.

The industrial market consumes about 44 percent of our total energy as electric energy or for combustion processes, excluding that used for raw materials. The Du Pont company's Energy Management Services division has found, both working with its own plants and as advisers to outside firms, that efficient conservation efforts can achieve average energy savings of 10 percent in industrial plants. This means that all industry could trim its requirements by about 1,500,000 barrels oil equivalent per day, which represents the output of twenty-four average-sized refineries.

Higher energy costs are a strong immediate conservation motivation for both industry and individuals. Like everyone else, I nearly had a cardiac seizure when I found that my electric utility bill almost doubled from one month to the next. The price of gasoline makes us conscious of "Is this trip necessary?" Higher heating oil bills keep thermostats down. We are all concerned about a possible change of "life-style" owing to energy shortages, but that does not mean that in the long run it has to be for the worse. The public is already opting for smaller cars. There will be great improvements in mass transit. There will be energy-saving, rather than energy-consuming, devices and appliances. We are already changing our ideas about architecture and land use, such as placing homes close to work and trade. We are entering an exciting new era of putting technology to work in new ways. It is not a question of having to do without in order to "make do." However, it *is* a question of getting our priorities straight and being sure that we do not stifle growth through fear. Russell W. Peterson, chairman of the Council on Environmental Quality, at a recent Conference Board seminar on energy shortages, put forth the suggestion that we adopt a program "based half on growth and half on conservation." Since the energy we save can be put to work elsewhere, we can grow through conservation.

Perhaps the most emotion-charged question we are asking is whether an all-out effort to meet our energy needs means that we will lose the gains we've made and hope to make in protecting our environment. The answer is no. Since we became actively concerned about cleaning up our environment in the late 1960's, we have made great strides in doing so through environmental legislation, development of new technology and the expenditure of billions of dollars annually by industry and government. We have been learning that there can be neither 100 percent environmental solutions to problems at the expense of other social needs, nor 100 percent technological solutions at the expense of the environment. During the stress period of the next few years we may have to change the timetable of achievement of some environmental goals, but there is no reason to abandon them. The rapidity with which technology has advanced to meet environmental concern is progressively minimizing many risks connected with developing and utilizing energy sources of all kinds. Here again, by defining the problems we are hastening the solutions.

We Americans have been riding such a roller coaster of crises of all kinds for the past few years that we haven't taken time to catch our breaths and "look at the big picture," as we used to say. We've developed brain strain from looking at the small picture on the tube. There may be no such thing as a crisis to end all crises, but at least the energy crisis has opened our eyes to how connected everything is from the anklebone to the neckbone. Furthermore, it is high time that we realize that we are indeed the king sitting at the breakfast table with the magic crown on his head. We do not need to be intimidated by statesmen, politicians, academicians, scientists, environmentalists, industrialists, financiers or experts in any field. We can learn from them, but they are here to serve us and to woo us. They, like us, are people. None of us has the only correct road map. However, all of us, in our multiple roles of consumers, producers, taxpayers, voters and citizens, have the final say-so as to the direction we will take. You and I create the marketplace and fill the halls of Congress and the White House. Our track record may leave a lot to be desired at times, but we never need to clamor for "power to the people." We have it. What we want is what we get—good or bad.

When we ask what government should do about our energy problem, we are actually asking ourselves what we want. As we examine what has happened in the past few years, we will see why our government has no energy policy. It has responded to our demands for action on an uncoordinated, spot basis, seeking a remedy for the immediate pains we were complaining about the loudest. Now is the time for us to insist on a thorough health checkup. We have no mysterious, incurable disease. Primarily, we are suffering from mental malnutrition. Fortunately, we already have everything on the bathroom shelf to cure this, if we take time to read and understand the labels. The one thing we have to guard against is reaching for the wrong bottle and taking a panic overdose of quack legislative medicine.

For almost a century we Americans have been creating abundance for the many by setting and continually breaking every world's record in the development and use of energy. This has been our special genius—pioneering modern, industrialized society. Not only have we shown the rest of the world how to develop nature's energy resources, but to satisfy our own needs, we have spread out over the planet with our know-how and capital and developed other nations' resources for them. Our history books prate too much about political, social and cultural events, foreign policies and wars. But it is what we have done about energy that has changed our history, improved our lives and raised our expectations. In our unrestrained exuberance and pursuit of many goals we have suddenly created energy famine in the midst of plenty. We have now reached the point where we must do what Ralph Waldo Emerson calls "the hardest task in the world—*think!*" in order to continue pioneering and turn famine into plenty once more.

Dr. H. Guyford Stever, director of the National Science Foundation and chairman of the President's Advisory Committee on Energy Research and Development, tells a story that illustrates an important point about today's energy situation.

The famous creator of Sherlock Holmes, Sir Arthur Conan Doyle, once hailed a taxi in Paris, threw in his suitcase and got in after it. Before he could say a word, the driver asked, "Where to, Mr. Conan Doyle?"

The surprised author said, "You recognized me?"

"No," the driver replied, "I've never seen you or your picture."

"Then how do you know that I'm Conan Doyle?"

"Well," the driver said, "I read in the paper that you were vacationing in the south; I noticed you arrived on a train from Marseilles; you have a tan that comes from spending a week or more in the sun; from the inkspot on your middle finger I deduce you are a writer; you have the keen look of a medical man; and the cut of your clothes is English. Putting all this together, I felt surely you must be Sir Arthur Conan Doyle, the author of the great Sherlock Holmes stories."

Conan Doyle was amazed. "From the way you recognized me from all these small observations, you yourself are the equal to Sherlock Holmes."

"There's one more thing," said the driver.

"What's that?" Conan Doyle asked.

"Your name is printed on your suitcase."

Dr. Stever points out: "Related to our energy problem, as a nation we had to have the situation boldly spelled out for us before we believed what various clues told us was inevitable. Now in retrospect, we see clearly what we might have deduced sooner. But fortunately we have seen it soon enough—hopefully soon enough——to think and plan and act to avoid more serious consequences."

Our greatest danger is complacency. Once the headlines and the gas lines disappeared, there has been a growing tendency to believe that we don't have an energy problem—that the name on the suitcase is somebody else's.

2

From Energy Gap
to Energy Crisis

The Pileup

Our energy troubles seemingly erupted overnight in the summer of 1970. During a protracted heat wave, there were widespread power breakdowns. Utility systems throughout the Eastern Seaboard areas were forced to cut back services. New York City had to receive electricity help from as far away as Tennessee. Simultaneously, the federal government announced it had alerted its Emergency Petroleum Supply Committee to be ready for a possible world oil emergency. Then newspapers from coast to coast carried front-page stories that there would be a winter fuel crisis. They warned of shortages, higher fuel prices, industrial shutdowns, worker layoffs.

Government, industry and the public were caught by surprise. Although there had been warnings that we had an energy problem, few had paid attention. Suddenly a situation had developed which was like one of those disasters occurring on turnpikes in foggy weather when one car runs into another and soon there is a massive pileup. Actually, some of the events, both domestic and foreign, which came to a head so quickly had been in the making for years. There was no way to predict others. They merged to create a critical turning point in the nation's development—the end of energy abundance.

The root of our energy problem lay as far back as a 1954 Supreme Court decision, which made natural gas sold in interstate commerce subject to Federal Power Commission price controls. Natural gas is the cleanest, most efficient and environmentally desirable of all the fossil fuels. Since price regulations made it also the most inexpensive, demand skyrocketed. Ultimately, interstate pipelines were purchasing 70 percent of the nation's production. Natural gas provided one-third of all energy and supplied nearly half of the energy for industry and the residential market. Its cheapness depressed the market price of competitive fuels—coal and fuel oil.

This was responsible for the chain of events which led to a lopsided, unbalanced development of our energy resources and increased our dependence on foreign oil.

When refiners found that owing to competition from natural gas, fuel oil was selling at the refinery for less than the cost of the crude oil from which it was made, they converted more and more of each barrel of crude oil to the lighter products—gasoline, naphtha, kerosene and diesel oil—on which they could make a profit. They planned and designed new refineries to make these higher-priced products. Gasoline was the industry's bread and butter, accounting for half of all product sales and 18 percent of all the energy we consume.

In the 1950's we were also importing increasing amounts of cheap Middle East oil from fields the international companies developed after World War II. In the 1956 Israeli-Arab war we had an object lesson in the perils of becoming dependent on foreign oil. Egypt sank ships to block the Suez Canal, which was the artery for transporting oil from the Middle East. It remained blocked for six months, precipitating a crisis in Europe, which depended on the Middle East for three-fourths of its oil. Western Europe would have frozen that winter and been economically strangled if the United States had not saved it. We drew on all our own spare producing capacity, which then was 2,000,000 barrels a day.

The specter of the United States' one day becoming as vulnerable as Europe prompted President Dwight D. Eisenhower in 1959 to restrict oil imports for reasons of national security. His purpose was to encourage increased domestic production even though foreign oil was then cheaper than domestic oil because of the difference in production costs. An average U.S. well produces about 15 barrels a day and generally needs to be pumped, while the average Middle East well flows 5,000 barrels daily with no production assistance necessary. However, as the need for fuel oil increased and exceeded U.S. refining capacity to meet demand, fuel oil imports for the East Coast, which had the heaviest consumption, were exempted from controls in 1966. By 1970 domestic production of fuel oil was meeting only 30 percent of our requirements, but East Coast consumers depended on imports for 93.7 percent of their fuel oil. Furthermore, fuel oil supplied approximately 45 percent of the total energy consumed for commercial and industrial purposes on the East Coast. The East Coast was now almost as vulnerable as Europe.

What was happening concerning natural gas, refining and fuel oil imports was only part of the energy drama which was moving toward its climax. Government and industry forecasts for energy planning proved inaccurate. They anticipated neither the interaction of changing energy developments nor the big jump in consumer energy demand. To make matters worse, they put their bets on the wrong energy horse.

Electricity is really the name of the energy game to provide power for industry and the consumer's home consumption. The fuel mix to create electricity comes from oil, gas, coal, nuclear power and hydroelectric plants. The Federal Power Commission was created in 1930 to regulate hydroelectric projects and the transportation and sale of electric power. It was charged, in general, with fostering adequate service "at reasonable rates." The FPC's annual National Power Survey, predicting electricity demand and the availability of fuel sources to supply it, has traditionally been widely used by all energy industries in their production and development planning. In the last half of the 1960's the demand for electricity was greatly underestimated as no one expected consumer demand to increase as drastically as it did over normal annual growth rates. In addition, the growing role of nuclear power was greatly underestimated for unpredictable reasons. The 1964 power survey projected an average annual growth in U.S. electricity demand of 6.9 percent between 1965 and 1970. Instead, it averaged 8.1 percent, putting an unanticipated strain on the old workhorse fuel, coal, which was accounting for more than half of electricity-generating fuel. Utility companies were planning to put coal out to pasture in favor of the new glamor source, nuclear power. Only sixteen nuclear power plants were operating, producing less than two percent of the nation's electricity, but encouraged by the Atomic Energy Commission, which was spending $3 billion in research and subsidies, more than half of all new power plants ordered to meet rising consumption were nuclear.

The great nuclear rush began in 1963, when Jersey Central Power and Light Company ordered the first commercial atomic power plant. It issued a widely publicized analysis indicating that atomic power was already cheaper than coal and would become cheaper and cheaper. However, by 1969 the nuclear power program was in real trouble. With a lead time of eight to nine years necessary for new nuclear plants, construction was running two to three years behind schedule. There were unforeseen technological problems in perfecting high-capacity installations. There was a backlog in the manufacture of equipment. Construction costs, owing partly to a shortage of specialized labor, had doubled in the five years prior to 1969. Furthermore, the industry was encountering increasing public alarm and resistance in siting plants because of concern about potential radiation hazards and thermal pollution.

The nuclear power oversell had the effect of curtailing capital investment to expand coal development. Since it takes two to five years to develop a new mine, the coal industry had a slim margin of producible reserves when it was called on to provide 25,000,000 tons more in 1969 than the Federal Power Commission survey had estimated. The underestimate had also resulted in a shortage of railroad coal cars, cutting distribution by some 7,000,000 tons, as the railroad industry also used the survey for its production planning. Further aggravating the situation during 1969 was the loss of 20,000,000 tons of bituminous coal production through wildcat strikes in the industry. A new Coal Mine Health and Safety Act passed during the year forced many mines to close down operations as they could not comply with its provisions.

Increasing national concern over air pollution was another factor affecting declining coal production. We had been using the atmosphere as a garbage dump for industrial pollutants. The chief offender was sulfur dioxide from burning coal and oil with high-sulfur content. The first Clean Air Act of 1967 placed restrictions on sulfur emissions, and the Clean Air Act of 1970 contained even stiffer requirements. There was no incentive to open new mines containing high-sulfur coal when the technology for scrubbing excess sulfur from flue gases was not yet economically feasible. Nor was there an economic way to remove sulfur from coal directly. The bulk of the nation's undeveloped low sulfur coal reserves lie in the West, far from the consuming areas.

Owing to air quality standards, power plants were converting rapidly from coal to oil and were competing for low-sulfur oil with commercial and individual consumers. Most of this low-sulfur oil came from North Africa, either as crude oil imported to be blended with high-sulfur domestic and imported oil or as imported fuel oil from European refineries using North African crude oil.

The shifting energy situation and tight fuel oil supply caused some brownouts in 1969's summer heat wave. By the following winter it was touch and go to meet East Coast fuel oil requirements. Government and industry finally were aware that what was euphemistically being referred to as an energy "gap" and "shortage" was a serious long-range problem.

True to predictions, natural gas was now in short supply. Price control had reduced incentives to look for new fields, and reserves had declined for the second straight year. Gas companies were compelled to refuse new customers and alerted established users that their supplies would be reduced. Obviously, oil imports would have to be increased to meet rising East Coast requirements. The situation was now ripe for the full-blown "crunch" brought on when we got our first taste of the contemporary bitter brew of foreign oil overdependence and interdependence.

In May, 1970, a bulldozer in Syria accidentally cut Tapline, a pipeline carrying half a million barrels of oil daily from Saudi Arabian fields to the Mediterranean and crossing through Jordan, Syria and Lebanon. The Syrian government refused to let repairs be made until higher transit fees were paid. The pipeline would remain closed nine months. In the meantime, oil had to be shipped the long way around Africa to European and American markets, just as 3,500,000 barrels daily had been forced to do since the 1967 Suez Canal closing during the third Arab-Israeli shooting war. A world tanker shortage developed.

A month after Tapline was closed, the government of Libya, the free world's fifth largest oil-producing country, began cutting back oil production of American oil companies to a total of 600,000 barrels daily in a power play to force them to raise prices and the taxes paid to Libya. This cutback of North African oil on the Mediterranean intensified the tanker shortage, for additional Middle East production, to try to make up the Libyan loss, had to make the long haul. It took five times as much tanker tonnage as carrying oil from the Mediterranean had. The cost of getting a barrel of fuel oil from an overseas source to New York by chartered tanker more than tripled from the summer before. The cost of Middle Eastern and African crude oil at U.S. East Coast refineries had been almost one-third lower than U.S. oil delivered from the Gulf Coast. Now it was one-fifth higher. The Libyan cutback affected our air pollution control program as Libya was our principal source of imported low-sulfur oil, as well as low-sulfur fuel oil imports from European refineries.

What stunned government, industry and the public about the multiple collision of domestic and foreign events was that they could so *quickly* create the prospect of an immediate crisis. We were jolted out of our feather bed of abundance onto a bed of energy thorns.

There was a frantic flurry of activity in Washington. Congress scheduled emergency hearings. President Nixon appointed a White

power play through the crude cutback which had helped create the
fuel oil and tanker shortage. The major oil companies had given in to
Libya's demands for higher taxes and prices. Other oil-producing
countries were announcing negotiations for similar increases. The
real oil story of 1970 had shifted from Congressional hearing rooms
to Arab capitals.

As it finally turned out, people on the U.S. East Coast didn't go
cold. The much-touted fuel oil shortage of 1970–71 was averted by
industry and government emergency measures. Our reserve crude
production capacity had dwindled to about 1,000,000 barrels daily,
but producers drew on this. Refiners, with the incentive of increased
fuel oil prices, changed their product output and made up a great
part of the shortage. The government relaxed restrictions on
imported heating oil and crude from Canada. In January, 1971,
Tapline was reopened. As oil flowed to the Mediterranean, the
tanker shortage was alleviated. Prices went down.

We Americans are crisis-oriented and crisis-calloused. As soon as
the energy situation left the front page and nobody suffered, the
public began to lose interest. If anything, the "non-energy crisis"
confirmed the contention that the oil companies had created the
situation. After all, when prices went up, wasn't the product there?
Weren't electric utilities and electric appliance companies pushing
hard for new sales? Weren't oil companies promoting more travel to
burn up more gasoline? Weren't automobile companies turning out
fancier, bigger models that burned more gasoline with all their
gadgets and air pollution controls? What kind of energy crisis was
that?

Nevertheless, for those of us who had eyes to see and ears to
hear, the "non-energy crisis" had revealed the appalling vacuum in
which American non-energy policy was operating. The day of
reckoning had just been temporarily postponed. Hollis M. Dole,
then Assistant Secretary for Mineral Resources of the Department
of the Interior, summed up our predicament in a speech at Stanford
University in January, 1971:

> My concern is that having warned the public of an energy crisis that
> has not yet materialized, those who did so may now be accused of
> crying wolf. The wolf was indeed at the door earlier this winter; he
> has merely gone away for a time. But he will surely be back, and he
> may well bring the whole pack with him. For beyond this winter loom
> the peak load demands for electricity of next summer; the steadily
> diminishing capability of the gas industry to meet the demands upon

it; the ever-increasing dependency upon foreign oil, particularly along the East Coast; the tenuous supply of fission fuels available at reasonable cost for burner reactors; and the mounting constraints upon the use of coal in metropolitan areas.

Time and again we have been bailed out of difficulty by the facility with which the valve could be turned to increase domestic oil supply. After this is no longer possible, we shall feel—for the first time—the full force of foreign oil supply interruptions directly as they occur. This will be something totally new to our experience; to be dependent upon foreign oil sources not only for a substantial and growing part of our normal oil supply, but for *all* our emergency supply. Yet, ironically, it has been the failure of foreign oil supply that has been the cause of all our emergency needs for oil since the end of World War II!

New Political Uncertainties

For the next three years those in government and industry who advocated constructive action to prevent a genuine, four-alarm energy crisis spent most of their time talking to each other. It seems astonishing that there was no Congressional action on a problem of such national urgency. However, these were not ordinary political times. Profound changes had been taking place in the nation's living patterns, problems, mood and political structure.

The 1970 census told a great part of the story. It revealed the massive migration, regrouping and resettling of Americans which had occurred in a decade. In 1960, 15,635,000 Americans lived and worked on farms. By 1970 their numbers had been reduced by 38 percent to 9,700,000. The pattern of American life had been completely reversed. The first census of 1790 had shown that only 5 percent of Americans lived in towns or cities. In 1970, 95 percent did. Furthermore, three-fourths of America's 203,000,000 people were now living in congested metropolitan areas, and more than half of all Americans were living within fifty miles of the shores of the nation's oceans and Great Lakes. This concentration, of course, was a prime factor in accelerating pollution problems.

The average American was still not aware that we had an energy problem. However, *everybody* knew we were in the midst of an environmental crisis. Like the energy problem, it had been long in the making, and the two were interrelated. Concern over what we were doing to our environment as the result of our new technology with its outpouring of goods and tremendous consumption of resources had been increasing steadily since the early 1960's. The publication of Rachel Carson's controversial *Silent Spring* in 1962, with its eloquently grim account of the effects of DDT and other chemical pesticides on man, animals and plants, marked the beginning of a new ecological movement. However, it was not until 1969 that a dramatic occurrence ignited the fuse of an uneasy American conscience.

In late January, 1969, there was a blowout on a Union Oil Company offshore well drilling in California's Santa Barbara Channel, 5½ miles from the beaches of the famed resort community. Oil began erupting from the seabed, and before it was brought under control some months later, an estimated 10,000 barrels of oil had spilled into the channel, polluting beaches and over 200 square miles of ocean.

More than oil erupted at Santa Barbara. Intense press, television and national magazine coverage presented the event as a major ecological disaster. The sight of dead birds, fouled beaches and predictions of permanent damage aroused public opinion. The beaches were clean four months later, and an independent study by the Allan Hancock Foundation of the University of Southern California, involving about forty scientists, was conducted over the following eighteen months. The scientists found that the bird population had not been decimated, damage to sea life was not widespread, the area recovered environmentally, and all animals were reproducing normally. The channel fish catch was found to have been greater in a six-month period following the oil spill than in a comparable period the year before.

Nevertheless, Santa Barbara became the banner of an environmental crusade which quickly exploded into a dominant political issue.

The movement was part of a great change in American thinking which originated on college campuses. Professors and students alike were questioning American values as they had never been questioned before. In 1969 there were 7,500,000 students in the nation's 2,476 universities and colleges. Higher education was one of the country's biggest businesses and was a potent, active, political force.

Social protest was beginning to crystallize on both the professorial and the student levels in radical reaction to the Establishment —both political and industrial. There was a revulsion against a society which could produce material abundance and yet, seemingly, not solve social injustice; a society that could squander the lives of its young men and its natural resources in an undeclared war in

Southeast Asia and land a man on the moon, but had not won its war on poverty at home. There was mounting dissatisfaction with big business and big government in the broad area of "consumerism." There was increasing public suspicion and distrust of the concentration of business and the inefficiency of government, as well as the sincerity and motives of both. The time was ripe for a revolt against the technological age and the industries which produced it. The "environmental crisis" suddenly became a political issue comparable to Vietnam.

The public was jolted out of its complacency. We took off our blinders and were horrified by what we saw around us. We were not only polluting our air and water to an alarming degree, but were burying ourselves under a mountain of indestructible trash. Americans began clamoring in anger and fear for immediate action to prevent the catastrophes which the academic world was warning them would engulf mankind and perhaps destroy it.

Congress had passed a Federal Water Pollution Control Act in 1965 and an Air Quality Act in 1967, but little headway had been made in cleaning up either our water or our air. A large part of the authorized funds for environmental programs had been diverted by the government to other uses. Furthermore, there was no effort on the part of either Congress or the government to consider environmental problems as a whole. However, as 1969 became the vociferous Year of Environmental Awakening, government was spurred into action.

By the end of the year Congress passed the National Environmental Policy Act, of which Senator Henry Jackson, Democrat of Washington, was the principal author. The act made it national policy to "maintain conditions under which man and nature can exist in productive harmony, and fulfill the social, economic, and other requirements of present and future generations of Americans." Under the new law, the President appointed a Council on Environmental Quality to coordinate environmental matters at the federal level and serve as his principal advisers.

The act would have been just another noble statement of purpose except for a seemingly unimportant provision added to it, late in its legislative formulation. In the fine print in Section 102, Congress "authorizes and directs that, to the fullest extent possible: (1) the policies, regulations, and public laws of the United States shall be interpreted and administered in accordance with the policies set forth in this act." The same section further sets the requirement for all federal agencies to prepare a detailed statement of justification of "major federal actions significantly affecting the quality of the human environment." In effect, this meant that interested citizens can challenge in the courts any federal agency's ruling on a matter "affecting the quality of the human environment" on the ground that the ruling does not comply with the intent of the environmental act. It gave environmental action groups a powerful weapon which they would soon use in every area affecting energy development.

At the same time the Environmental Policy Act was being hammered out, Senator Gaylord Nelson, Democrat of Wisconsin, proposed that an Earth Day be held on April 22, 1970, to publicize nationally the perils of polluting our air, water and land. President Nixon officially proclaimed it. Senator Nelson and Congressman Paul McCloskey, Republican of California, served as co-chairmen of a nonpartisan national steering committee.

The idea was to mobilize the constructive energies of American youth in a massive campaign to halt accelerating pollution. The purpose was educational—to hold teach-ins on college campuses and in high schools. However, the new academic, ecological elite and politically militant students enthusiastically embraced the proposal as an opportunity to organize for political action involving a broad spectrum of campus radicals, liberals, moderates, administrators, faculty, politicians and businessmen. Never before had an "observance day" involved so much intense, highly organized, advance planning nationwide.

Two months before Earth Day, a series of accidents gave environmentalists more anti-oil banners for their crusade. An oil tanker ran aground in Nova Scotia during a storm and broke in half. It leaked 20,000 barrels of oil, polluting two harbors and some twenty miles of coastline. Another tanker ran aground in thick fog in Tampa Bay, Florida, spilling some 200 barrels of oil before the slick could be contained and the rest of the cargo offloaded. A fire broke out on a Chevron twelve-well offshore production platform in the Gulf of Mexico, seventy-five miles southeast of New Orleans. During the month it took to put the fire out, 1,000 barrels of oil a day flowed into the sea. Favorable winds and tides kept onshore pollution at a minimum. However, the psychological shock waves which these accidents set in motion were at a maximum. They equaled those set off by the Santa Barbara oil slick.

A Department of the Interior investigation of the fire determined that six of the Chevron wells lacked government-required safety devices called storm chokes, designed to cut off oil flow in the event of blowouts or fire. A federal grand jury began extensive hearings on violations of U.S. drilling and production rules by Chevron and other Gulf of Mexico operators, which ultimately resulted in Chevron's being fined $1,000,000 and three other companies' being fined $500,000.

During the first week of April, an indignant Congress quickly passed a tough bill, which President Nixon immediately signed into law, imposing stiff penalties for oil spills from tankers and industry facilities in navigable streams and coastal waters.

On April 13, nine days before Earth Day, environmentalists fired their first shot under Section 102 of the National Environmental Policy Act. It was a broadside. It stopped the building of a pipeline to bring oil from Alaska to the "lower 48 states." In 1968 Atlantic Richfield Company and Exxon had made the greatest oil strike in the history of America beneath the frozen tundra of Alaska's North Slope at Prudhoe Bay on the Arctic Ocean. The field was estimated to contain as much as 10 billion barrels, twice as much as the fabled East Texas, which had held the record. A score of major companies bid $900,000,000 for additional state leases to explore what promised to be one of the world's great oil provinces. Seven major oil companies organized a consortium, Alyeska Pipeline Service Company, to build an 800-mile 48-inch pipeline, from Prudhoe Bay to the ice-free port of Valdez on the Gulf of Alaska. From there it would be shipped in tankers to West Coast ports. Its original cost estimate of $1 billion made it the largest nongovernment construction project in history.

In 1969 the oil companies had complied with the then-existing environmental stipulations and imported a huge $300,000,000 mountain of pipe to begin construction. The completion target date was 1972 for a flow of 600,000 barrels of oil daily, eventually to be increased to 2,000,000. Under the new environmental act, three conservation groups—the Wilderness Society, Friends of the Earth and the Environmental Defense Fund—charged in court that the Interior Department had failed to make an adequate environmental impact review of the project. They claimed that the pipeline, in traversing 400 miles of frozen tundra, three rugged mountain ranges, seventy streams and rivers and one earthquake zone, would irreparably damage "the last great wilderness in the United States." They claimed it would adversely affect plant and animal life and result in disastrous oil spills caused by earthquakes and tanker accidents. A federal court granted them a temporary injunction enjoining the Secretary of the Interior from issuing a construction permit. The suit would delay beginning pipeline construction for almost five years while the national energy shortage continued to increase.

Earth Day, 1970, was a nationwide phenomenon never repeated, but its impact on public thinking and its political repercussions were immense. Carefully planned, highly organized teach-ins held in approximately 1,000 colleges and 2,500 high schools in all fifty states made environmental history. Their targets were government and industry.

The campus was the focal point for community action. Students prepared "dishonor rolls" and gave special awards to local polluters. They held environmental marches and rallies at pollution sites and mass phone-ins to polluters. They shone spotlights at night on belching smokestacks. They held mock funerals for the internal-combustion engine, buried cars—and then drove away in their own. At the University of Wisconsin they held a mock trial of the oil industry. Law students prepared lawsuits to restrain polluters legally. Local and national news and television media had a field day covering the colorful and controversial events. The public was urged to fight pollution, learn the issues, learn the laws and take political action.

Earth Day showcased a new type of scientific celebrity—the "prophets of doom" whose books have become environmental gospel and best sellers. Chief among these are Dr. Barry Commoner, biologist and ecologist, Washington University, author of *Science and Survival* and *The Closing Circle;* Dr. Rene Dubos, microbiologist and experimental pathologist, Rockefeller University, author of *So Human an Animal* and *Reason Awake;* and Dr. Paul Ehrlich, biologist, Stanford University, with *The Population Bomb.* Their common argument, in gloomy and frightening terms, is that time has run out for the human race. They maintain that science and technology have brought us to the brink of disaster, that we must choose between affluence and survival and that our problems can be solved only by drastic economic, social and political change. Dr. Barry Commoner, in testifying before the Senate Subcommittee on Intergovernmental Affairs in 1969, said that uncontrolled technology is destroying the country's "capital" of land, water and other resources, as well as injuring people. He asserted that the problems are so profound that they call for "not a new legislative base, but a new constitutional one."

Congress and the federal government were dismayed and shaken by the severity and universality of the criticism levied against them. They moved with haste to prove they were responsive to the public mood and its demands that "something has to be done." By the end of 1970 a master plan to control the American environment had been developed by the administration and approved by Congress. The Environmental Protection Agency, reporting directly to the President, was created to concentrate all government pollution controls of air, water, pesticides, solid wastes and radiation hazards into one body with policing authority over all states, industries and municipalities. The National Oceanic and Atmospheric Agency, a superior scientific agency clustering half a dozen separate bureaus in one body, was established to probe the problems and relationships of the ocean depths and the upper atmosphere, what man was doing to them and what he could do with them in the future.

On legal paper, at least, the piecemeal approach to environmental problems had ended. However, in the wave of emotional overreaction, little attention was paid to how much it would cost and who would pay for it. Nobody disputed the goals, but there was no realistic timetable to achieve them. There was inadequate research and technology available upon which to base reasonable requirements. This did not deter Congress.

The 1970 Clean Air Act, put through by Senator Edmund Muskie, Democrat of Maine, set such ambitious, comprehensive and strict standards that subsequently they would prove impossible to meet, such as the one requiring that all cars sold in the United States after 1974 must be near-zero polluters. Actually, in 1970 air pollution from cars had peaked out and was on its way down. Automotive research had improved engines to the point that all cars built in 1970 had carbon monoxide emissions already 62 percent below those of uncontrolled vehicles and 73 percent less hydrocarbon emissions. The arbitrary fixing of a date for near-zero pollution imposed the necessity of crash research programs with no consideration of dollars-and-cents cost to industry and consumers or what the cost in increased energy use might be. In addition, as subsequent research would prove, the standards set were not necessary to achieve the desired air quality.

The political pollution panic reached its apogee the following year when Senator Muskie introduced a bill calling for elimination of *all* pollutants in the nation's navigable waterways by 1985. The White House estimated achieving such a goal would cost government and industry $316 billion. Nelson Rockefeller, then governor of New York, testified in a hearing on the bill that his findings showed that it would cost New York State alone $230 billion and the nation anywhere from $2 to $3 trillion. However, the Senate passed the bill with a vote of 86 to 0, after only one day's debate, demonstrating the political temper of the times. The House subsequently modified the bill, and elimination of all pollutants was made a goal rather than required by a fixed date. Since even the modified version carried a $24.6 billion price tag, President Nixon vetoed it, but Congress overrode the veto.

The stringent new standards for both air and water pollution control meant multibillion-dollar investments in new equipment for factories, refineries, power plants and automobiles. A McGraw-Hill economic survey calculated that, based on the new 1970 standards, industry's investment in antipollution work would have to be $18.2 billion dollars from 1971 to 1976. Industry budgeted $3.64 billion for 1971. The oil industry had been the first to see the handwriting on the wall and, according to the Department of Commerce, was the leader of all United States industries in the amount of money expended for air and water conservation. It was spending a half billion dollars annually. Between 1966 and 1970 it had spent a total of $982,000,000 for air pollution prevention and $1.053 billion for water pollution prevention.

Obviously, the costs of cleaner air and water would have to be shared also by the consumer-taxpayer, both in higher prices for his commodities and in the amount of his tax revenues spent by government for pollution programs. However, in our haste to repent our sins, we weren't concerned with bookkeeping. Nor were we aware in 1970 that cleaning up and controlling the environment had any real relationship to the energy problem which erupted that year. It was a two-ring circus. Your viewpoint on what was happening depended on which ring you were watching. We didn't realize that we all were part of the act. We were the ones balancing on the high wire with no net under us.

During 1971 and 1972 the energy crisis for which the nation was headed continued to be a mystery, as far as the public was concerned. It was for this reason that in the spring of 1972 Representative Wayne N. Aspinall, Democrat of Colorado, chairman of the House Interior Committee, called energy-study hearings. Without understanding by Congress and the public, followed by action, Aspinall warned, "We will be caught up in a crisis of overwhelming proportions."

All government, industry and academic witnesses were in agreement that the nation had serious energy problems, but the dilemma was what to do about it. Interior Secretary Rogers C. B. Morton told the committee that he was receiving plenty of conflicting advice from conservationists, industry, consumers and some of the sixty-one departments and agencies of government which are concerned, in some form or other, with energy policy. All the advice could be summarized, he said, as follows:

> Give us an energy policy that is intelligent and concise and, above all, responsive to the interests of the nation as a whole. Give us a policy that can apply to the short term and to the longer term as well.
>
> Give us an energy policy, they say, that will provide the consumer with the type of fuel he wants, in the amounts he needs, at the time he must have it, and at the lowest possible price. Assure us this energy will be from secure and reliable sources.
>
> But don't drill offshore on my coastline, don't build any pipelines across my land, don't strip mine any coal, don't build any refineries or storage facilities in my area, abolish the oil-import program but don't move oil in by tanker for this might pollute our waters.
>
> Give us an energy policy that guarantees protection of the environment, where the use of energy does not intrude upon our esthetic values nor [sic] damage the ecology of the land. Give us an energy policy that will maximize national security and yet not impinge upon normal trade between nations.

Since there were no major disruptions of the flow of energy, those in government and industry who recommended action found they had no audience in high or low places. The years 1971 and 1972 were Presidential election campaigning years. Eighteen-year-olds were given the vote in 1971, adding 25,000,000 new voters to the electorate, which was now predominantly urban and young. Also, the electorate was untested and unpredictable. The opposition of environmental and consumer groups to energy resource develop- ment was political dynamite. It was safer for the federal government and Congress to stall and hope nothing happened to light the fuse.

Defining the Problem

Despite the fact that nobody was listening, a great deal was being done to define our problem. Government agencies and energy industry experts were jointly developing facts and proper analyses to show us what our options were.

In July, 1970, in the midst of trying to cope with power shortages, we received some extraordinarily good news about our domestic oil and gas resources. The National Petroleum Council, the official industry advisory group to the Department of the Interior, published a monumental study, *Future Petroleum Provinces of the United*

States. It had been two years in the making at the request of the Secretary of the Interior. Ira H. Cram, one of the world's leading petroleum geologists and former vice-president of Continental Oil Company, coordinated the research of 141 of the nation's most experienced petroleum geologists selected from major and independent oil and gas companies, state geological surveys and the United States Geological Survey. Their job was to evaluate the geology of the entire United States, including the continental shelf and slope, searching for areas with oil and gas potential.

It was critical to know how much oil and gas we could hope to find as U.S. and world consumption was expected to double between 1970 and 1980. In the 100 years of petroleum history a grand total of 225 billion barrels had been produced worldwide, of which almost half was produced in the United States. It would take another 225 billion barrels just to satisfy the predicted world demand of the 1970's, and the U.S. would consume a third of that. How soon would we run out of oil at this staggering rate?

The geologists came up with an unexpectedly reassuring answer. The total favorable area for finding oil and natural gas covers 3,200,000 square miles, of which approximately 43 percent lies offshore on the continental shelf and slope. Underlying this area are 6,000,000 *cubic* miles of sedimentary rocks which could contain oil and gas. The geologists pointed out that none of this area has been adequately explored. "Extensions to old fields and discovery of new fields at conventional depths and deeper are forecast for all regions," they stated. "The Atlantic, Florida, and Alaska continental shelves, and the entire continental slope, barely have been touched by drilling, and other prospective areas and depths on land and the continental shelf remain largely unexplored." They estimated that based on known yields of sedimentary rocks and known rates of recovery, if the ultimate petroleum potential of the United States is discovered and produced, "future production of crude oil would be 346 billion barrels (4.0 times past production); future production of natural gas would be 1,195 trillion cubic feet (3.6 times past production); and future production of natural gas liquids would be 38 billion barrels (3.5 times past production)."

For the first time, we had a detailed scientific appraisal of the huge petroleum resources we can expect to develop if we go about it the right way. However, the geologists deplored the drastic decline in exploratory and development drilling, especially onshore, which had been the trend of the past decade. "To the extent that policies of industry and government militate against accelerated exploration, particularly drilling, a high percentage of the petroleum resources of the United States is immobilized,'' they warned.

The geologists were concerned about what was happening because they know better than anyone how difficult it is to find oil. There is no direct finding method. Only a constant, vigorous exploration program can keep supplies of oil flowing and develop new ideas of where to look within favorable areas. The oil and gas you and I use today, someone had to start looking for from four to ten years ago.

Oil and gas finding is an art, a jigsaw puzzle and the world's most expensive gambling game all rolled into one. Finding a favorable area is just a starter. It is generally accepted that oil comes from the decomposition of marine animals and plants buried under successive layers of mud and silt over the floors of former seas for as long as 400,000,000 to 500,000,000 years ago. Heat and pressure changed this organic material to a complex mixture of hydrogen and carbon—oil and gas. So geologists study earth history in search of areas where buried marine, or source, rocks occur. However, oil and gas in the earth migrate. When compaction squeezes them out of source rocks, they travel—sometimes long distances—upward, sideward and downward through porous rock beds. Their travels stop when they run into a trap—a layer of impervious rock, shaped in such a way that it forms a seal, or cap, over the porous rocks. Unable to move farther, the oil and gas are imprisoned in porous rock between the cap rock above and the heavier brines, or fossil seawater, which permeate the rocks below. The tricky business of exploration is how to locate these traps.

In early days, men first found oil traps by drilling where oil had migrated to the surface through cracks or fractures. Then they followed oil trends or hunches, used divining rods and consulted fortune-tellers. By the end of World War I the infant science of petroleum geology determined that some underground traps, called anticlines, could be detected on the earth's surface where rock strata arched, or inclined in opposite directions from a ridge, like the roof of a house. By such techniques, almost all of the world's relatively easy-to-find oil was found by the 1930's. Since then the most important oil-finding tool is geophysics—the application of certain physical principles such as magnetic attraction, the pull of gravity, the speed of sound waves, the behavior of electric currents—to try to determine the shape of buried rock layers.

Locating a potential trap doesn't mean there is any oil or gas in it. You have to drill a hole to find out. The chances are about 1 out of 9 of finding some oil or gas. Only 1 in 50 is counted a commercial success. About 1 in 1,000 is a large field of 50,000,000 barrels or more. By 1970 the average cost of a well drilled onshore had risen to $70,000. An offshore well cost from $1,000,000 to $3,000,000.

Oil-finding results in the United States in 1969 typically demonstrated how risky this expensive hunt is. Approximately 6,000 new-field wildcats were drilled. Although 1 out of 11 was completed as a producer, only 1 out of 49 found enough oil to have an ultimate reserve in excess of 1,000,000 barrels of oil. These were considered "significant" discoveries. In 1970 the nation was gobbling up every day the equivalent of the total reserves of fifteen "significant" discoveries. However, what was really alarming was that while consumption was zooming upward, our efforts to find new oil were declining precipitously. From an all-time peak of 16,173 wildcats drilled in 1956, the number dropped to 7,693 in 1970, with a corresponding decline in oil reserves.

How could it happen that a nation with such tremendous undeveloped potential, as evidenced by the *Future Petroleum Provinces* survey, cut its oil and gas exploration efforts by half in a little over a decade? It wasn't because there was an increased emphasis on foreign exploration and development. On the contrary, domestic expenditures during that period were a little more than twice those for foreign. However, dollars don't tell the story—it is what the dollars find and who is spending them that is the heart of the American oil exploration effort. The nation's plight was, quite simply, the plight of its independent oilmen.

We Americans are so conditioned by the brand names of the gasoline we buy that we have a completely erroneous concept of the makeup of our oil industry. We tend to think of it as being the operations of a handful of big oil companies. There are, in fact, about 40,000 separate companies engaged in the exploration, production, refining, transportation and wholesale distribution of petroleum and petroleum products.

There are approximately twenty major integrated oil companies—"integrated" meaning that they operate in all branches of the industry. These majors include the five largest international oil companies—Exxon, Texaco, Gulf, Standard Oil Company of California and Mobil. Major oil companies dominate gasoline sales, holding about three-fourths of the gasoline market, with the largest single marketer accounting for only about 8 percent of all gasoline sales. About 95 percent of the more than 200,000 American service stations are operated by independent dealers who buy their supplies under contract from the major companies. In addition, there are 15,000 wholesale oil jobbers and 18,000 fuel oil and liquefied petroleum gas marketers. There are 127 companies operating 253 oil refineries in thirty-nine states with the largest refining company having less than 9 percent of total refining capacity.

However, the most basic oil industry group is the 10,000 independent producers, who traditionally have found, and continue to find, three-fourths of our new oil and gas. In addition to drilling three-fourths of the exploration wells, these wildcatting independents produce about a third of our crude oil. They operate some 350,000 "stripper" oil wells in twenty-seven states that average only 3.5 barrels daily, but account for an eighth of our oil production. The strippers represent a sixth of our total proved oil reserves, excluding Alaska. Independents range from individuals to very large firms that operate abroad as well as at home, but they are all a special breed of risk takers who have the courage, imagination and persistence to look for oil in unlikely places and find it. They also have to be able to raise the money to keep looking despite the great odds against them. One independent friend of mine was a fugitive from the law of averages. He drilled 200 dry holes before he finally hit a winner. There have been 700,000 dry holes drilled to date in America's search for oil. The reason we have found so much is that there have been so many thousands of gamblers who have had the incentive and optimism to keep drilling.

The United States is a "small-field" country with oil and gas being found in thousands of small, medium and large accumulations under a bewildering variety of geological conditions, rather than in a relatively few vast deposits such as those in the Middle East and Africa. World exploration results in 1970 illustrate the difference and the necessity for intensive multiple oil search in America. Although the nation's 7,693 exploration wells were an all-time low, they accounted for 72 percent of total free world exploration wells. However, even with a success rate of 16 percent, new discoveries did not replace oil produced during the year. U.S. oil reserves actually declined by more than 1 billion barrels. By contrast, with approximately the same success ratio, just 2 percent of free world new wells in Africa and the Middle East boosted oil reserves by more than 47 billion barrels.

The term "independents" is, in some respects, a misnomer. While independents are the backbone of the industry, they could no more exist without the major companies than the majors could exist without the independents. More than half the oil reserves found by independents have been sold to the majors, enabling the independents to continue their searches. Small operators rely on big companies to buy the oil they produce, to build the vast network of pipelines for its transportation, to build and operate the costly and highly specialized refineries and petrochemical plants that produce the myriad products we consume and, finally, to market these products on the tremendous scale the nation requires.

To finance their exploration, independent explorers and producers depend on the cash flow from the sale of their oil and gas production or properties and their ability to raise venture capital from outside investors. For this reason, they have been particularly vulnerable to the economic and political vicissitudes which have beset the oil industry since the mid-1950's. More than a third of the independent producers who were active at that time are no longer in business. All the decrease in domestic petroleum exploration and development since 1956 is due to the decrease in independent oilmen's activities. In 1956 independents spent $2.5 billion for domestic exploration and development. By 1971 they spent less than $1.2 billion. Major oil company domestic exploration and development expenditures remained constant, excluding lease bonuses to federal and state governments. During the same period the demand for oil doubled and consumption of natural gas increased 120 percent.

To begin with, the independent, like the rest of the industry, was caught in a cost price squeeze. Using the government's base years for measuring cost-price behavior, 1957–59, wages in the domestic oil- and gas-producing industry in 1969 were up 40.8 percent, oil field machinery up 24 percent, and oil well pipe up 17 percent. By contrast, the price of domestic crude oil was only 3.7 percent higher. At the same time the emphasis of major company exploration was shifting from onshore to offshore, having a profound effect on the amount of capital assistance major companies traditionally provided independents. One way in which an independent finances wildcats is to get dry hole or bottom hole money from major companies holding leases in the same area where he has assembled leases and decided to drill. Rather than test its own acreage, the major company agrees to contribute a certain amount of the cost of the wildcat if it is a dry hole or make a flat contribution, dry or not. If a number of majors hold acreage in the area, the independent can usually get contributions from all of them.

Another common practice is for independents to get farmouts from major companies that have blocks of acreage whose leases are about to expire and whose exploration budgets are committed to other areas or that hold acreage which they do not think is highly prospective. The majors checkerboard their leases in exchange for a test well and often also make a dry hole or bottom hole contribution. Some of the independents' best discoveries have been made on such deals. A former chairman of the board of Exxon, Eugene Holman, who was also a leading geologist, once told me that when he was promoted, his last duty as chief geologist for the company's U. S. operations was to classify all the domestic exploration projects according to the best prospects for the company to drill and those which should be farmed out. His colleagues never ceased to rib him about the results. All the company wells were dry holes, and the farmouts were discoveries.

The major companies shifted to offshore exploration to look for big fields. There were very few places left in the inland United States where they felt they could find giants—fields of 100,000,000 barrels or more. Between 1871 and 1919, the industry discovered 53 giant oil fields. During the 1920's and 1930's, with the development of the sciences of geology and geophysics, it discovered 135 giants, but in the 1940's giant discoveries dropped to 45, in the 1950's to 25 and in the 1960's to 13, excluding the Alaska discovery. By the mid-1950's it had become obvious that the place to go elephant hunting was offshore. A new exploration boom began.

Offshore oil poker was too high-stake for the vast majority of independents. Not only were drilling costs much greater, but obtaining state and federal leases involved huge bonuses. Offshore lease bonuses between 1958 and 1967 were about $2.5 billion more than normal expenditures for leases. This meant that much less exploration money to put into the ground. By 1970 there were approximately 12,500 offshore wells, producing about 15 percent of the nation's oil and 10 percent of its gas. This development cost $13 billion, including $6 billion in bonus, rental and royalty payments to state and federal governments. Although a number of giant fields were discovered, the industry had not recovered its investment, as the average rate of return was 7 percent and the investment payout period of a successful offshore discovery was estimated to take a minimum of ten years. Nevertheless, for those who could raise the price of admission, it was an exciting new theater of operations. Unfortunately for independents, it meant continued siphoning off of major company interest and assistance in onshore development.

There had been a major tax reform in 1969 to add to the indispensable independents' woes. It affected the entire oil industry but dealt a disproportionately cutting blow to independents' ability to raise wildcatting money. For more than half a century, our tax laws have provided special incentives to encourage oil and gas discovery and development. Chief of these is a percentage depletion income tax deduction. It recognizes that oil to an oilman is both his capital and his merchandise. He cannot depreciate oil over the years, as a manufacturer can his machines, and then go out and buy some more. Percentage depletion permits an oilman to recover the capital value of his oil and gas in the ground and helps provide risk capital to search for more oil. It does not apply to all of an oilman's or oil company's income—only to income from production. Up until 1969 an oilman, in the calculation of his income tax, could deduct 27.5 percent of the gross income from each producing property, but not in excess of 50 percent of the net income from the property.

The principle of percentage depletion applies to about 100 minerals ranging from 22 percent allowed for the production of sulfur, uranium and thirty other minerals down to 15 percent for iron ore, 10 percent for coal and 5 percent for sand and gravel. Oil and gas had the highest allowance because of the exceptionally high-risk costs of trying to locate new deposits.

Through the years, percentage depletion has been consistently attacked as a tax loophole with claims that the oil industry wasn't paying its fair share of taxes. Actually, oil companies have spent on exploration more than twice their annual tax savings from the depletion allowance, and a similar amount has been spent on development. However, in 1969 when the controversial issue was brought up in Congress, as it was every year, the percentage depletion allowance was reduced from 27.5 percent to 22 percent. Congress also added a 10 percent "minimum tax" on so-called tax preference items that include the percentage depletion deduction. This further reduced the effective oil depletion rate to approximately 18 percent.

Independents were the first to feel the effects of the new disincentive to investment resulting from the tax change. It reduced their risk capital from their own funds. It also discouraged investors in publicly offered drilling funds, which provided independents with about one-fourth of their exploration capital. Private investors who gambled on wildcats with the lure of a tax deduction if they hit, became supercautious in putting money into an industry with as many political problems as oil was developing. Overall, the tax reform cost the industry an additional $600,000,000 in taxes—but what it *really* cost was more than that. It meant an erosion of risk capital at a time when the industry needed it most to find new reserves to meet soaring demand.

Exploratory drilling continued to slide downhill in 1971, with the lowest number of wildcats drilled since 1947. Tom Medders, Jr., an independent oilman who was then president of the Independent Petroleum Association of America, warned that because of the government's failure to permit sufficient price incentives, beginning with the control of natural gas prices in 1954, the domestic petroleum industry "has just experienced its 15th year of dismantling its equipment and dispersing its skills."

The problems of oil and gas were of primary importance as they were supplying three-fourths of our energy needs. The National Petroleum Council, at Interior Department request, was undertaking a study of the petroleum outlook in the Western Hemisphere to the end of the century with emphasis on the role of federal oil and gas policies and programs in the future availability of supplies. However, the energy shock of mid-1970 made it apparent that our preoccupation with oil and gas was myopic. We needed to look at the whole energy situation. The Secretary of the Interior asked the National Petroleum Council to expand its study to take into full account all forms of energy. Consequently, for the first time in our mad energy-consuming rush we assembled a task force of 200 experts from the oil, gas, coal, nuclear and electric utility industries, government agencies and financial institutions to find out what was happening. Their pioneering assignment was to answer three basic questions: "How much energy do we need?" "Where are we going to get it?" "What changes in government policies or economic conditions would enhance our national energy posture?" Translated from the Washingtonese, the third question meant: "What should government do or not do to assure ample energy?" The answer to this one was bound to stir up a free-for-all.

Men and computers worked overtime. In July, 1971, a preliminary report was released, containing the bulk of the findings so that the government would be aware as soon as possible of the seriousness of the situation and have facts and figures to work with. The council warned that the major implication of the study was that "Continuation of present government policies and economic conditions would lead to significantly increased U.S. dependence on foreign energy resources, mostly in the form of oil from Eastern Hemisphere countries, and to an acute shortage of gas."

The historic study was finally completed in December, 1972. It gave us a clear, factual, detailed picture of our energy options.

However, the fact that neither the federal government nor Congress had acted on the basic findings of the preliminary report, issued a year and a half before, demonstrated how political our options were.

There was no doubt that we had ample resources to increase greatly production of all fuels and sustain economic growth at an annual rate of 4.2 percent a year to the end of the century. However, owing to the lead times necessary for development, there was no way to reverse the continuing severe deterioration of our domestic energy supply up to 1975. What happened after that depended on how quickly we changed our energy policies.

The study examined in detail U.S. energy demand, supply, logistics and financial requirements for the period 1971–1985. It analyzed trends for the balance of the century. It identified all economic and government policies which affect the energy situation and projected the effects of changes in these policies on the future energy situation. Case studies were made of overall supply and demand and of each energy source. The most favorable case assumed early resolution of environmental controversies, ready availability of government land for energy development, adequate economic incentives and better success ratio in exploration than in recent years. The least favorable case assumed environmental disputes will continue to delay development of energy resources, government policies will inhibit the energy industry, and finding rates will be lower than recent years.

The availability of government land was crucial At least 50 percent of the nation's remaining oil and gas potential, 40 percent of its coal, 50 percent of its uranium, 80 percent of its oil shale and 60 percent of geothermal energy sources are located on federal land.

The case studies revealed that if current trends continued, domestic supplies of energy would provide only 62 percent of U.S. requirements in 1985. Under the most optimistic supply situation domestic supplies could provide 89 percent.

Under present trends domestic oil and gas would contribute only 30 percent of our energy needs in 1985 but *could* provide as much as 56 percent. By comparison, domestic oil and gas met 64 percent of total energy requirements in 1970. There was no way to avoid oil imports' increasing by 1975 to 18 to 25 percent of energy requirements, which would amount to 42 to 51 percent of the total oil supply. However the options for 1985 offered a wide range. Under present trends, imports would be 33 percent of total energy supplies and 65 percent of total oil supply. Under optimum conditions they could represent only 6 percent of total energy and 18 percent of total oil supply. Imports of natural gas might reach 5 percent of energy needs.

In all case studies, coal and nuclear fuels could provide about 30 percent of energy requirements in 1985, up from 20 percent in 1970. If a greater proportion of the nation's energy needs could be met by electricity rather than by direct use of primary fuels, the combined potential supply of coal and nuclear fuels would be sufficient to meet up to 45 percent of 1985 requirements.

Although oil shale deposits are extensive, supply from this source was expected to make only a minor contribution to energy supply by 1985 owing to technological, environmental and economic problems. The same is true of synthetic oil and gas from coal.

Depending on developments, the nation's supply and demand balance in 2000 could range all the way from total national self-sufficiency in energy supplies to an alarming degree of dependency on imports. The dominant factor in energy growth between 1985 and 2000 will be energy requirements for electricity. By 2000 such requirements will account for nearly half the primary fuels consumed. Energy demand is expected to slacken in the last fifteen years of the century because of a number of trends: a lower rate of population growth; a more service-oriented economy; changes in social values and life-styles, including smaller families, increased multiple dwellings, smaller cars; greater use of mass transit; and higher energy costs.

New energy forms, such as fusion reactors, solar energy, magnetohydrodynamic units and hydrogen, are likely to still be in the research and development or working prototype stage as the twenty-first century begins. However, there are always possibilities of scientific breakthroughs.

The study concluded that costs of individual fuels will increase at rates of 2 to 9 percent yearly throughout the period of 1985, owing to technological, environmental and economic factors. During the same period total capital investment requirements will be in the range of $450 billion to $550 billion. This includes $200 billion to $300 billion to find, develop and process the primary energy supplies and about $200 billion for electric generation and transmission facilities.

We now had guidelines to the worst and the best that could happen to us and what it would cost. "The Nation must face *now* the fundamental issue of how to balance energy supply and demand most advantageously in the term beyond 1975," the study stated. "The major options involve (a) increased emphasis on development of domestic supplies, (b) much greater reliance on imports from foreign sources and (c) restraints on demand growth." The report evaluated the advantages, disadvantages and feasibility of each option.

Relying to a greater extent on imports "would not well serve the Nation's security needs nor [*sic*] its economic health because of uncertainties regarding availability, dependability and price. Greater reliance on imports would also result in major balance of trade problems that could adversely affect the value of the dollar."

Reducing demand growth is a complicated problem. As every woman knows, if you're an ample size 18, you can't fit into a size 9 dress without doing some major streamlining. The experts assumed that it was unlikely that growth in consumption would depart significantly from the average 4.2 percent annual rate during the 1971–1985 period.

Consequently, what the three-year study boils down to is that our most practical option is to increase domestic energy supplies of conventional fuels to get us through the critical period before alternative energy sources can come into play.

Now came the hard part: how to "enhance the national energy posture." The report made recommendations of fundamental steps to achieve increased supplies. Only three were noncontroversial. Nobody could quarrel with the statements that:

> . . . the United States must adopt a national sense of purpose to solve the energy problem; the security of the United States is dependent upon secure supplies of energy, and therefore healthy, viable and expanding domestic energy industries should be encouraged by government; both the government and industry should continue to promote energy conservation and efficiency of energy use in order to eliminate waste of our resources.

Most of the remaining recommendations concerned highly debatable issues, such as removing price control from natural gas; continuing tax incentives for discovery and development of primary energy resources; achieving a rational balance between environmental goals and energy requirements and minimizing delays of energy development; and accelerating leasing of federal lands, containing energy resources, to private enterprise for development.

The report's concluding recommendation was one of the most important of all: "the federal government should coordinate the many competing and conflicting agencies dealing with energy."

Much of the confusion and delay that now plague energy suppliers stem from conflicts among the more than sixty federal organizations having specific responsibilities for various fuels. State and local agencies also have authority. There is little consistency. All too often one agency may encourage an action while another agency prohibits it. For example, standards set forth by the Environmental Protection Agency promoted increased use of natural gas because it burns cleanly, while Federal Power Commission policies inhibit an increase in natural gas supplies.

Old Political Strategies

Although many of the National Petroleum Council's recommendations were highly controversial, the facts succeeded in focusing Washington's attention on the seriousness of the long-range energy problem. The prospect of the spectacular outflow of billions of dollars for oil imports unless something was done could no longer be ignored. The rate of energy consumption in 1972 increased more than twice as fast as in 1971. Imports were soaring. European demand had also been increasing steeply, and oil was in tight supply worldwide.

What really prodded the Nixon administration and Congress into action was an onslaught of protests and demands from their constituents. Fuel shortages during the winter of 1972–73 were severe enough to hit every part of the country in one form or another. Workers were laid off when plants and factories couldn't get enough gas or heating oil. Schools and universities closed from New England to Colorado to Texas. Grain rotted in Western silos for lack of heat. Major airlines were forced to ration jet fuel at Kennedy Airport. Furthermore, refiners predicted that there would be a critical spring and summer gasoline shortage, with rationing becoming a possibility.

An irate, baffled public demanded to know what the crisis was all about *this* time! When the Ninety-third Congress convened in January, 1973, a flood of bills were introduced by Congressmen from almost every state. Federal officials also began saying publicly that "energy is our Number One domestic problem." President Nixon announced plans to form a Council on Energy Policy and to deliver a major energy message to Congress. It took almost four months to prepare the Presidential energy message. It went through nine drafts. Nobody kept count of the number of arguments. The final version, delivered in April, was the result of so many trade-offs that in trying to please everyone, it didn't please anyone. A White House aide commented privately, "Everything had to give a little—national security, environmental quality, supply, price."

The only actions taken by the President were to abolish import quotas and replace them with a tariff system and to order a triple increase in the amount of federal offshore acreage to be offered for oil exploration leases. He urged Congress to pass legislation which would provide incentives to increase domestic energy supplies. It was the first comprehensive effort of the federal government to come to grips with the nation's energy problems. Meeting these problems would now depend on how Congress, industry and consumers responded.

Congress was engaged in a hostile showdown with the President over legislative and executive power. It was determined to assert its independence by deciding on its own energy legislation. As a matter of fact, the important Senate Interior and Commerce committees began hearings almost two months before the President's message was delivered. From January to September, 1973, thirty-two Congressional committees and their subcommittees collectively held more than 650 days of hearings on more than 1,000 energy-related bills and resolutions. However, next to energy, the nation's biggest shortage remained a shortage of action. Congress busied itself more with trying to fix the blame for shortages than in considering what should be done to prevent continuing shortages.

The confusion surrounding the energy crisis was deepened by events during the summer of 1973. By May the nation seemed headed for a gasoline shortage of major proportions. Supplies were so short that more than 1,000 service stations were closed by Memorial Day. Congressmen were besieged with complaints from independent station owners and marketers that they could not obtain supplies. Major company suppliers cooperated with the government in a voluntary allocation program seeking to divide available supplies equitably among all consumers. There was intense publicity about the prospects of summer rationing. However, in June the oil industry managed to turn things around. Refiners ran their plants flat out. They operated at levels believed impossible. They recommissioned obsolete equipment. In addition, the new import policy permitted foreign crude oil and gasoline to pour into the country.

The prodigious refining effort stopped the shortage, but it didn't solve the problem. As a matter of fact, it made it more difficult to understand the problem. The oil industry was attacked more severely than ever before on charges that the major companies had rigged the shortage to raise prices and put independents out of business.

The biggest brickbats came from Senator Henry M. Jackson, Democrat of Washington, who is recognized as the most powerful legislator in shaping energy policy. As chairman of the Senate Interior Committee he had been conducting an energy study for two years. In June, although he personally refrained from charging conspiracy, he asked the Federal Trade Commission to make a crash thirty-day study of charges that oil companies conspired to create the shortage. A week later he announced on national television that the Senate Permanent Investigations Subcommittee on Government Operations, which he also heads, would investigate the possibility that the gasoline shortage was a "premeditated plan."

Yet Senator Jackson had long been on record that the energy crisis was real. Only a few months before he had called it "the most critical problem—domestic or international—facing the nation today." However, in May something else had happened besides the gasoline shortage. The nationally televised Senate Watergate hearings had run the soap operas off the air. It was open season for 1976 Presidential election campaigning—two years ahead of normal time. Senator Jackson, who had lost out to Senator George McGovern in the nominating campaign of 1972, was in a position to use the energy crisis for political maneuvering. His staff, which had estimated that he was recognized by less than half the American voters, advised him that attacking the President and the oil industry was the quickest way to television network exposure.

In his letter to the Federal Trade Commission requesting the crash study, Senator Jackson wrote:

> On the basis of available evidence, I do not charge or allege conspiracy. I do, however, charge that corporate self-interest, acting in response to friendly, timid, and often incompetent administration policy, has led to a situation in which oil industry corporate managers—without meeting, without collusion, without conspiracy—are led, invited and encouraged: (1) to squeeze out the independents; and (2) to force the price of gasoline and other petroleum products up and up.

Representative Les Aspin, Democrat of Wisconsin, was less polished in his allegation. "There is little doubt that the so-called gasoline shortage in the Midwest is just a big, lousy gimmick foisted

on consumers to bilk them for billions in increased gasoline prices,"
he charged.

Senator James Abourezk, Democrat of South Dakota, wrote
President Nixon that "Our energy 'crisis,' I believe, is deliberately
contrived by the major oil companies to achieve a number of
objectives they are seeking." In addition to the possible motives
given by the other Senators, he listed passage of legislation
authorizing construction of the Alaska pipeline, easier environmental rules and additional tax loopholes.

Denials played second fiddle to such charges. Public distrust and
suspicion of the major oil companies was rampant. The root causes
of the gasoline shortage were so complex that the oil companies
found it rough going, if not almost impossible, to try to explain what
had happened. Nobody had believed what they had been explaining
about the complexities and interrelationships of our energy use
since the first phase of the energy crisis erupted in the electricity
shortage of mid-1970. Now gasoline demand outstripped supply.
That was a simple fact. But the answer to *why* went all the way back
to the 1954 Supreme Court decision on natural gas prices as we have
already seen in unraveling the tangled ball of yarn which the energy
crisis had become.

Not only had we been running short of energy since 1970, but
gasoline demand had been spurting ahead of supply at a record rate.
In 1968 the number of passenger cars, trucks and buses on American
highways and streets passed the 100,000,000 mark and traveled 1
trillion miles. However, in 1973, 96,000,000 passenger cars *alone*
traveled 1 trillion miles and an additional 275 billion miles were
driven by more than 22,000,000 trucks and buses. Furthermore,
because of devices required to meet air pollution standards, the
25,000,000 passenger cars produced since 1970 got anywhere from 5
to 35 percent fewer miles to the gallon. Because of the increasing
number of cars and their decreasing performance, gasoline demand
began to rise 6 to 7 percent yearly instead of 4 to 5 percent. To
illustrate the difference a percent can make, 1 percent of 1972
gasoline consumption was more than 1 billion gallons.

During our many years of oil abundance, we had become
accustomed to cheap gasoline. Gasoline wars and service station
sales giveaways of everything from glasses to cut-rate wigs were a
traditional part of the American scene. Gasoline had never risen in
price at the rate of other commodities. According to the
government's Consumer Price Index, between 1961 and 1972, the

price of gasoline increased 20.4 percent as compared to 35.4 percent for all commodities. When the 1973 gasoline shortage caught up with us, domestic crude oil prices had increased. Foreign imports were even higher than domestic crude. There was no surplus refinery output to be offered at lower prices. Gasoline discounts disappeared, and during the first half of 1973 gasoline prices increased an average of 4 cents a gallon. We were beginning to head in the direction of $1-a-gallon prices of import-dependent Europe.

Members of Congress, in calling for investigations of the gasoline shortage, noted pointedly that the earnings of the five biggest oil companies "jumped by 26 percent between the first quarters of 1972 and 1973, and profits of 27 smaller oil companies jumped by 32.1 percent." That wasn't the whole story. A broad survey of 655 nonoil companies made by the *Wall Street Journal* showed that average business profits for the first quarter of 1973 were 27.8 percent higher than the year before.

The charges of conspiracy were based mainly on allegations that in order to make higher profits, the major oil companies were determined to force independent marketers and refiners out of business. Small dealers and service station association representatives testified before various Senate and House committees that the big, integrated companies should be broken up so that independent dealers could stay in business. On the other hand, independent refiners testified that there was nothing to the charge that the majors had contrived the gasoline shortage.

The refiners said that there were three reasons why refining capacity had not kept up with demand: lack of assured supplies of crude oil; low profits; and environmental opposition to refinery siting. Refineries had to use more foreign crude oil because of declining domestic oil supply and the delay in the development of Alaskan reserves. Imports of crude were controlled by federal regulation, but there was no overall government energy policy. Consequently, there was no solid basis to plan new refining capacity with assurance of long-term foreign supply. At the same time, the decontrolling of fuel oil imports encouraged the building of refineries in the Caribbean, where there were no environmental restrictions, to supply U.S. demand. These imports were not price-controlled. In the United States prices for refinery products were controlled and distorted by competition from the artificially low regulated prices for natural gas. Environmental protests also discouraged and prevented building of new refineries. All these factors added up to the undesirability and risk of building refineries costing an average of $250,000,000 each. This unfavorable political and economic climate applied to both independents and majors.

In spite of all this testimony, one branch of the government, the Federal Trade Commission, concluded that the eight largest integrated oil companies in the United States had combined or agreed to monopolize refining, to maintain monopoly power over refining and to maintain a noncompetitive market structure in refining. In an antitrust complaint aimed at breaking up the companies, the FTC said the results of these alleged violations had been higher prices to consumers, higher profits to companies, crude and product shortages for independent refiners and marketers and a general lessening of competition.

The complaint was filed against the Exxon, Texaco, Gulf, Mobil, Standard Oil of California, Standard Oil of Indiana, Shell and Atlantic Richfield companies. No specific charges were made. Rather, the FTC said, "These major firms, which consistently appear to cooperate rather than to compete in all phases of their operation, have behaved in a similar fashion as would a classical monopolist: they have attempted to increase profits by restricting output." The complaint alleged that their failure to build refining capacity to meet demand was to squeeze the independents and had nothing to do with environmental problems or the unprofitability of refinery operations.

All the major companies which were named vigorously asserted that the accusations were completely unfounded. A Texaco spokesman said, "It is nonsense to contend that the petroleum industry is noncompetitive. With over twenty large integrated companies operating in one or more of the various activities of producing, refining, transportation, and sales, the petroleum industry is among the most competitive of U.S. industries. No company has as much as 12 percent of the crude production, refining capacity, or product sales in the U.S."

Senator Philip A. Hart, Democrat of Michigan and chairman of the Senate Antitrust Subcommittee, who had requested the FTC to initiate the study three years before, commented delightedly, "The day many predicted would never come is here! I feel like we've won the Irish Sweepstakes!"

However, the Treasury Department's Office of Energy Advisers stated flatly that "many of the facts in the FTC report are inaccurate" and that "the FTC report is biased." The Treasury Department's critical analysis concluded:

As a result of this bias, the FTC's final conclusions are incorrect or misleading at best, regarding: (a) the charge that the majors control the output of the independent crude producers, (b) the charge that the majors have engaged in exclusionary practices in their use of exchanges, (c) and the conclusion that the independent sector's welfare is dependent on the well-being of independent refiners. Integration of the producing, refining, transporting, and marketing of the crude oil and petroleum products has proven to be an efficient method of operation.

Furthermore, the Treasury Department study found that the FTC complaint, if successful, "would cause considerable adverse impact on future domestic energy supplies" and that "the FTC report's implication that the current shortages of petroleum are deliberately contrived by the major oil firms is incorrect." The study called upon the FTC to withdraw its complaint.

The FTC complaint established a legal basis for a protracted trial to be held which would be presided over by an FTC examiner. It also provided instant ammunition for a barrage of antitrust suits against the majors. The State of Connecticut filed a federal lawsuit against twenty integrated oil companies asking divestiture of producing and transportation facilities and treble damages of $675,000,000 for alleged monopolistic practices. Florida filed an antitrust suit against fifteen companies. A Los Angeles federal grand jury launched a probe of marketing practices in the West.

Lewis A. Engman, an ambitious young lawyer, who had moved to the Federal Trade Commission chairmanship from an obscure junior White House staff position, was using the energy crisis to showcase his reform policies for the agency. "One of my general views of the commission's role is that we should be more aggressive in enforcing the antitrust laws," he stated. With the strong backing of Ralph Nader and other consumer groups, he had lobbied for Senator Jackson's amendment to the Alaska pipeline bill to force the nation's 500 largest manufacturers to disclose information on sales and profits, as well as costs for such items as advertising and research, by industrial categories rather than on a companywide basis or by generalized categories. As part of his efforts to challenge the accuracy of industry data reporting, he and Senator Hart got into a battle with the Federal Power Commission over the natural gas shortage at the same time the FTC antitrust complaint was filed. The interagency confrontation provided sensational headlines.

John Nassikas, Federal Power Commission chairman, earlier in the year had sponsored the first independent gas supply study conducted by the U.S. government in cooperation with the U.S. Geological Survey, the U.S. Naval Petroleum and Shale Reserves Office, the Office of Management and Budget, the Census Bureau and the regulatory agencies of the major gas-producing states. It was made to ascertain the accuracy of industry figures to provide a basis for independent judgment of supply for rate making and energy policy planning. Opponents of higher gas prices argued that FPC's only supply data came from industry, implying that industry manipulated figures to influence FPC to raise gas prices at the wellhead. The survey, made by teams of government scientists, found that the gas shortage was actually worse than industry figures indicated. Their figures were nearly 10 percent lower than the estimates of the American Gas Association. Nassikas had originally opposed deregulating controls over the price of natural gas, but the study made him change his mind. Senator Hart's Antitrust Subcommittee and the Federal Trade Commission questioned the study's reliability as basic data were provided by seventy-nine gas-producing companies.

The subcommittee requested the data for examination. The Federal Power Commission refused on the basis that it had promised confidentiality to the producers and the release of such information would benefit their competitors. The subcommittee then served a subpoena on Nassikas. Such subpoenas on federal officials are often threatened but seldom served. An angry Nassikas appeared and still refused to turn over detailed data but delivered a breakdown of information without identifying companies. He insisted that there was a genuine natural gas shortage and that "workable competition" existed among gas producers.

Senator Hart remained skeptical, saying, that "information we have seems to point in the other direction." He called James Halverson, director of the Federal Trade Commission's Bureau of Competition, to appear. Halverson claimed that the FTC's investigations showed theat producers had been underreporting their reserves to the Federal Power Commission. He said their procedure of reporting reserves through an American Gas Association committee composed of employees of major producers "could provide the vehicle for a conspiracy" among the companies to falsify data. Based on these charges, Senator Hart expressed his doubts about the natural gas shortage's being real and said that Halverson's statement "could lead reasonable men to think a hoax" had been perpetrated.

Although Halverson did not name companies, two producers

involved—Gulf and Continental—denied any understatement of reserves. They pointed out that there is a difference between "proved" reserves figures, used publicly, and "probable" reserves figures, which are used as the basis for variable management decisions in planning and obtaining financing. Reserve estimates constantly undergo changes depending on development and economics.

On other Congressional battlefronts, some legislators, with Senator Jackson in the lead, were calling for direct development of oil and gas reserves on public lands by the federal government. Jackson also introduced legislation to create five government-industry corporations to develop technology for new energy supplies.

Congress had not been entirely inactive in regard to energy legislation in the midst of the multitude of conflicting proposals and contentious hearings. After five years of litigation and completion of the most exhaustive environmental impact studies ever carried out in history, both the Senate and House voted in September, 1973 to exempt the trans-Alaska pipeline from further court review under the National Environment Policy Act of 1969. Although it would be four years, at the earliest, before the pipeline could be completed, the nation's greatest oil discovery could eventually begin supplying 2,000,000 barrels daily of the oil the nation so badly needed.

However, as the month ended, a roundup of prospects for other Congressional energy action showed that little was planned to be done until the following year. Although the FPC estimated that curtailments of natural gas supply to committed customers would be 18 percent larger in the coming winter than the year before, the Senate Commerce Committee, which would shape any natural gas legislation for the Senate, did not plan even to get started on hearings until time to adjourn for the year. The House Commerce Committee planned no hearings until 1974. Senator Jackson postponed any consideration of the creation of a Department of Natural Resources and Energy until 1974. Congress was too busy trying to prove that the shortages were not real to be concerned about increasing supply or developing a master energy policy.

In July, 1973, Interior Secretary Morton had released a preliminary report, titled "Emergency Preparedness for Interruption of Petroleum Imports into the United States," which went largely unnoticed—except by Arab producing countries. The report, prepared by the National Petroleum Council, which he requested by July, advised that if an emergency should commence on January 1,1974, when the United States would be importing about 42 percent

companies who obtained concessions to explore for and develop oil. Prior to this law, companies had always got the lion's share. It was a bitterly fought battle between the Venezuelan government and the oil companies. The government won its terms, after threatening an embargo, because its oil was essential to fuel the World War. Those of us advising the government were more concerned about assuring the flow of oil for victory than we were about any precedent that a bigger government take of oil profits would set. At that time not even the oil companies realized that they had hit the world's oil jackpot in the Middle East. However, after the war, the interrupted development of newly discovered Middle East big oil fields resumed. The first order of business for Middle East governments was to follow Venezuela and negotiate new tax agreements with the companies. Fifty-fifty profit sharing became universal.

World War II had brought about the demise of colonialism, and a new kind of nationalism was sweeping the world. Developing countries not only demanded control of their own political destinies, but were determined to be free of economic colonialism in all its forms. In the oil-producing countries, fifty-fifty profit sharing, although brand-new, was no longer enough. The two leaders who were dedicated to obtaining much, much more were Perez Alfonso and Tariki.

These two men, with such totally different backgrounds and heritages, were unlikely collaborators in a plan which would ultimately change the course of world economic history. Pérez Alfonso, a lawyer, came from the Venezuelan elite. Tariki, an American-educated geologist and petroleum engineer, came from a desert bedouin tribe. However, both men were more similar than dissimilar. Each was a philosopher, an idealist and an odd sort of mystic. They were tough and gentle at the same time. Each put country and cause ahead of self. Each had vibrant charisma and was persuasively articulate. Because of their passionate belief in their cause, their followers were ardent. Neither of them was politically ambitious, nor did they play to the crowd, which is why their influence became so great. The events they precipitated mushroomed and outpaced them so that each became a legend in his own living time. But OPEC was the lengthened shadow of these two men.

In Tyler, Texas, when they confided in me that they were going to organize the foreign oil-producing countries to control the price of world oil, I was horrified. I had teethed on respect for antitrust laws and the evils of cartels and monopolies. In expressing my immediate reaction, I told them, "You kids are up to no good." I then displayed the cloudiness of my crystal ball by saying, "How on earth do you expect to control world oil through an organization in which the United States doesn't participate? After all, we are the biggest oil-producing country in the world. You will never be able to do this."

They patiently pointed out to me that the whole point was to organize *without* the United States, because American oil companies were primarily in control of their resources and called all the shots in the marketplace. At this point in 1960, neither Pérez Alfonso, Tariki nor I realized that what would really call the shots and make their dream a reality within a decade was the increasingly voracious appetite of American energy consumers and the unpredictable developments in the American political scene concerning environmental problems.

Following the Texas meeting, Tariki went to Venezuela with Pérez Alfonso where they put the finishing touches to their plans. Within three months they would have an unusual opportunity to launch OPEC on the basis of "necessity" rather than "desire."

In August, 1960, the international oil companies cut the posted prices of Middle East crude between 2 and 5.25 percent because there was a world oil surplus. Traditionally, the prices of international oil and products roughly followed prices in the U.S. Gulf of Mexico, the only place where consumers could get large-scale continuing supplies. An international marketer couldn't hope to get more than that price but didn't need to sell for less. Consequently, the international oil companies publicly "posted" such comparable prices for Middle East oil, and they were used as the official basis to figure the payments of royalty and income taxes to the host governments. If a company actually sold its oil at a discount, it did not affect the government.

At the time of the price cut, the Iraq Petroleum Company, whose owners were most of the international companies, was having difficulties in negotiating oil issues with the new military revolutionary government of Iraq, which had overthrown the monarchy in 1958. For Sheikh Abdullah Tariki, the time, the reason, and the place had suddenly merged for the formation of the Organization of Petroleum Exporting Countries which he and Petroleum Minister Pérez Alfonso had been planning. He visited Baghdad, and the Iraqi government promptly announced that the governments of the five countries that were supplying 80 percent of all the oil moving in international trade—Iraq, Iran, Kuwait, Saudi Arabia and Venezuela—would meet to protest the price cuts. Within four days OPEC was formed "for regular consultation amongst its members with a view to co-ordinating and unifying the policies of the members."

OPEC's first resolution was the Magna Charta of oil exporting countries. The governments agreed:

> That members can no longer remain indifferent to the attitude heretofore adopted by the Oil Companies in effecting price modifications;
> That members shall *demand that Oil Companies maintain their prices steady and free from all unnecessary fluctuation;*
> That members shall endeavor, *by all means available to them,* to restore present prices to the levels prevailing before the reductions; that they shall *ensure* that if any new circumstances arise which in the estimation of the Oil Companies necessitate price modifications, *the said companies shall enter into consultation with the member or members affected* in order fully to explain the circumstances;
> That members shall study and formulate a system to ensure the *stabilization of prices by, among other means, the regulation of production,* with due regard to the interests of the producing and the consuming nations, and to the necessity of securing a steady income to the producing countries, an efficient, economic and regular supply of this source or energy to consuming nations, and a fair return on their capital to those investing in the petroleum industry.

The emphasis which I have supplied above denoted a whole new concept of the international oil business. However, international oil companies and consuming countries did not tremble in their boots at these words. International commodity cartels had been tried before and seldom worked. But a Pandora's box had been opened which would never be shut again. A few weeks later, at the Second Arab Petroleum Congress in Beirut, Sheikh Tariki presented a paper on "The Pricing of Middle East Crude Oil and Refined Products." He accused the seven international oil companies controlling Middle East production of having swindled their "partners," the host governments, out of almost $3 billion over seven years by keeping Middle East posted prices artificially low. His arguments were too complex to offer any valid picture of international oil economics or collusion. However, he blew the first trumpet blasts to announce the belligerent entry of Middle East governments as performers on the stage of world economic history.

OPEC did not succeed in getting posted prices back to their previous levels. They couldn't agree on any formula for prorating production. However, they succeeded in preventing prices from being lowered again despite a continuing world surplus. The operating companies did not want to risk stirring up a hornet's nest of renegotiating concession contracts by further reducing government revenues. They preferred taking a profit squeeze by realizing less on actual sales.

Many companies and international observers scoffed at the idea of OPEC's becoming a potent pressure group because of the historical and political differences and conflicts among its members and countries. The prevailing view was that the need of each OPEC country for a market for its oil would prevent any agreement on cutting back production to try to raise prices. Nevertheless, the problem of how profits from oil development are shared between most countries and international oil companies was one of the most controversial ingredients in the explosive, international witch's brew mixed in the Middle East caldron.

The struggle with OPEC in which American oil companies abroad were about to become involved was of scant interest to Americans at home. Ironically, the circle of history had come full round. We would be forced to become concerned about foreign oil for the very reason American oil companies had first gone in search of it—a shortage of oil in the United States. Few people realized that the major companies originally began to explore for foreign oil in the 1920's under a mandate from the U.S. government to go out and find oil resources because we were afraid we were running out of oil.

World War I marked the world shift from coal to an oil-based economy. "The Allies floated to victory on a sea of oil," Lord Curzon, Britain's Foreign Secretary, proclaimed. eighty percent of that oil came from America. The use of oil revolutionized warfare and pioneered development of tools to revolutionize the postwar world. It was a war of fast oil-burning ships, planes, tanks, trucks, tractors, cars, ambulances and even taxicabs, a fleet of which saved Paris in 1914 by rushing troops and supplies to repel the Germans. At the same time, war production made America the greatest industrialized country in the world. Oil was replacing coal for ships, railroads and the generation of electricity. The number of passenger cars and motor trucks quintupled. Farm tractors tripled. The aviation industry had been born.

The war drain on American oil resources was so tremendous that we were now consuming more oil than we produced. Between 1920 and 1922 we became a net oil-importing nation, drawing on Mexico's new fields. The threat of an oil famine was considered an impending national catastrophe. The nation panicked over the prospect.

Congress quickly passed the depletion allowance tax provision and opened the public domain for oil leasing to encourage oil exploration at home. Democratic and Republican parties and government officials urged American citizens to acquire and develop oil properties abroad. But there was a huge stumbling block. Great Britain, France and Holland, which also realized the importance of oil, were determined to keep American oil explorers out of the Middle East and Far East. Iran, under concession to the British Anglo-Iranian Oil Company, was the only major oil-producing country in the Eastern Hemisphere. However, Iraq, which had been part of Turkey, was known to have great oil prospects. Under an agreement in the League of Nations, to which the United States did not belong, all the oil rights to the former Ottoman Empire were given to the Iraq Petroleum Company, jointly owned by the British, French and Dutch. American public opinion was inflamed by this "closed door policy," and an international diplomatic war began.

Immediately after becoming Secretary of Commerce in 1921, Herbert Hoover called in seven of the largest American oil companies and persuaded them to form a joint American company to seek a concession in Iraq. Under extreme pressure from the American government, the British, French and Dutch ultimately backed down and the American companies won a 23.75 percent interest in the Iraq Petroleum Company, which would soon develop one of the most lucrative oil areas in the world.

The "closed door policy" war spilled over into the Dutch East Indies, now Indonesia, which was the principal oil-producing country in the Far East. American companies were excluded, but the Dutch buckled under and let them obtain concessions after the Royal Dutch Shell's American subsidiary was refused permission to lease oil lands of the Creek Indians in Oklahoma. An irate Congress had passed the Minerals Leasing Act of 1920 authorizing the Secretary of the Interior to reject lease applications on public lands to citizens of foreign countries that deny "similar or like privileges to American citizens or corporations."

There was great popular backing for a bill introduced by Senator James D. Phelan, of California, to incorporate the "United States Oil Corporation." With the sanction and backing of the government the company would develop foreign resources. American oilmen and oil companies would provide the capital, and the government would have prior right to any or all oil produced on payment of the market price. The bill was not passed because the government finally decided direct participation would create too many foreign relations problems. However, the government gave strong diplomatic support to American oil companies as they fanned out across the world, looking for new oil resources.

When American companies began their drive for foreign oil in 1919, the bulk of their $400,000,000 investment abroad was in refining and marketing. By 1925, forty American companies had invested $1 billion in exploration and development in Central and South America, the Middle East, Far East and Africa. However, by that time, fears of U.S. oil shortages had disappeared. Tax incentives and the high price of oil had triggered such intense successful exploration at home that oil gushers became the trademark of the Roaring Twenties. By 1923 oil production had doubled from 1918. By 1929 it had tripled and passed the billion barrels' annual production mark for the first time. The flood of new American oil assumed Biblical proportions in 1930 when the spectacular East Texas oil field was discovered, which would hold the American record for reserves of a single field until the discovery of oil on Alaska's North Slope in 1969. East Texas oil deluged the nation. The field had a production capacity of 26 times more than the entire world could consume daily. America's problem now was to reduce physical and economic oil waste through overproduction by state and federal proration and conservation laws.

The largest oil companies that had responded to the U.S. government's call to find oil in other parts of the world continued to expand their holdings and their search abroad. They wanted to protect their earlier investments, and despite world overproduction, prospects of finding big new oil fields were alluring. From 1930 to the beginning of World War II the international oil game turned into a horse race between British-Dutch oil companies and American majors competing for concessions worldwide. It was almost a photo finish as far as their respective control of foreign oil production was concerned. But American companies captured what would turn out to be the biggest plums in terms of total reserves.

Standard Oil of California, known as Socal, was among the major companies that had joined the campaign to find foreign oil. However, by 1930, it had drilled thirty-seven dry holes in six countries and explored in a dozen others without finding anything. Then, its luck turned. It acquired an option from Gulf Oil Corporation for a concession on the small island of Bahrein in the Arabian Gulf, just off the coast of Saudi Arabia. Gulf was unable to exercise its option because it was part of the American group which the U.S. government had helped obtain participation in the Iraq Petroleum Company. These companies had agreed that none of them would act independently in a prescribed area which included a large part of the Middle East. The British government controlled Bahrein's external affairs, and only after considerable pressure by the U.S. State Department did the British validate Socal's option and permit it to obtain a concession.

When Socal discovered oil in Bahrein in 1932, its success persuaded King Ibn Saud of neighboring Saudi Arabia to give the company an exclusive oil concession on all of eastern Saudi Arabia for sixty-six years. Meanwhile, the Gulf Oil Company obtained an option on a British concession in Kuwait, which adjoins Saudi Arabia and was outside the Iraq Petroleum Company restricted area. Again, the State Department had to intervene before the British would permit Gulf to become an equal partner with the British Anglo-Iranian Oil Company in the Kuwait Oil Company. The American camel had now nosed all of itself into the Middle East tent.

In 1932, when Socal first approached King Ibn Saud for a concession in Saudi Arabia, he called the Royal Council of members of the ruling family to consider the proposal. The council opposed permitting the Americans to enter the country on the grounds that its offer of 4 shillings gold or its equivalent in dollars or sterling, per ton royalty was too little. The king overruled their objections, saying, "The Koran says on fertile land, a tithe of one-tenth, on unfertile land, one-half as much. The Americans are offering about one-fourth. Are you unsatisfied with one-fourth when God is satisfied with one-twentieth?" However, once the land became fertile, the philosophy quickly changed.

Saudi Arabia was so isolated from the so-called civilized world that the first American geologists arrived wearing beards and Arab dress in order to avoid attracting attention. Few Saudis had ever seen a Westerner. Socal had found oil in the neighboring island of Bahrein, but it was five years before Socal and its new partner, Texaco, found oil in Saudi Arabia. When World War II broke out in 1939, Saudi Arabia was producing only 10,000 barrels a day. The oil was so strategically located and urgently needed that the U.S. government made scarce material available to double production. Three more oil fields were found. The U.S. government sent a group of experts to the Middle East to estimate proved and probable oil reserves. The mission was headed by E. L. De Golyer, world-famous geologist and appraiser of oil and gas reserves, and Dr. W.

E. Wrather, director of the U.S. Geological Survey. They reported the startling and sobering fact that "The center of gravity of world oil production is shifting from the Gulf-Caribbean areas to the Middle East, to the Persian Gulf Area, and is likely to continue to shift until it is firmly established in that area." At that time such a conclusion was as momentous as Columbus' proclaiming the world was round, not flat.

Immediately following the war, such enormous capital investments were needed to develop Saudi Arabia's oil and build a refinery and a pipeline to the Mediterranean that Socal and Texaco obtained two new partners—Standard Oil Company of New Jersey, now Exxon, and Socony Vacuum, now Mobil. The new company was named Arabian American Oil Company, known as Aramco. All four Aramco owners had Venezuelan subsidiaries which had accepted the 1943 fifty-fifty profit-sharing law. Consequently, when Saudi Arabia demanded more money, negotiations were concluded on a fifty-fifty profit-sharing basis. The agreement reached in 1950 was the first one in the Middle East. Similar agreements were soon made by companies operating in Kuwait, Iraq, Turkey, Bahrein and Qatar. Oil income to governments was more than doubled.

Profit sharing in Iran became a pawn in a political struggle, involving riots, bloodshed, international intrigue and oil nationalization which almost bankrupted the nation. The British Anglo-Iranian Oil Company, in which the British government owned the controlling interest, held the monopoly on Iranian oil. After the war, and before the Saudi agreement, the company offered to increase royalty payments, but not on an equal sharing basis. By the time it offered a fifty-fifty deal in 1951 it was too late. A Communist-backed campaign to nationalize the oil industry was in full swing led by a fanatic Prime Minister, Dr. Mohammed Mossadegh, who wrested power from the shah. Mossadegh was overthrown in 1953, but he had unleashed such a frenzy of nationalism that it took a year for the shah to find a politically acceptable solution to the oil dispute which also would put Iran back in the oil business. The "cold war" was hot, and the United States government was deeply concerned that unless Iran got back on its feet financially, it would fall an easy prey to the Soviets. Russia historically had always wanted to take over Iran. It would be an even greater prize for the Soviets with its huge oil and mineral resources and its access to the Persian Gulf and Arabian Sea.

Iran had resumed diplomatic relations with Great Britain, but the two nations were at an impasse over the question of Iran's right to nationalize the oil properties. For the Iranian government to survive, the properties would have to stay nationalized. Any effort to put a figure on how much financial compensation Iran owed Anglo-Iranian would also be fatal. With the assistance of the U.S. government, a new, politically acceptable international oil group was formed to which Iran transferred full operating rights to the properties of the "former oil company" for a term approximating that of the old concession.

Anglo-Iranian, which became British Petroleum, retained a 40 percent interest in the Iran consortium, each of five American companies—Exxon, Mobil, Socal, Texaco and Gulf—had 8 percent interest, totaling 40 percent; Royal Dutch Shell took 14 percent; and Compagnie Française des Pétroles, controlled by the French government, took 6 percent. At the stipulation of the American government each of the five American companies gave up 1 percent so that a group of nine independent American companies received 5 percent interest. The newcomer companies paid British Petroleum $600,000,000, partly payable on a per barrel basis over a period of years. The National Iranian Oil Company, which was given ownership of the former concession area, would receive 50 percent of the profits under an operating agreement to last until 1994. It also agreed to pay British Petroleum $70,000,000, in installments, for its physical assets.

Some international companies feared that the agreement to operate the nationalized Iranian properties without ownership rights, which up to then had been inherent in a concession, would set dangerous precedents. However, head consortium negotiator Howard W. Page, vice-president of Exxon, pointed out that the consortium agreement provided rights which were just as effective as ownership. "Instead of a contract giving us ownership of the properties for a long period of time," he explained, "we have a contract giving us full rights to exclusive use and complete management of those properties for the same period of time and on the same financial terms."

There was one ludicrous episode in the round of Middle East profit-sharing agreements. Oil was not discovered until 1958 in Abu Dhabi, a tiny sheikhdom and former British protectorate on the Persian Gulf. Almost simultaneously, Abu Dhabi Petroleum Company (owned by British Petroleum, Shell, Compagnie Française de Pétrole, Exxon and Mobil) struck oil on land, and Abu Dhabi Marine Areas Ltd. (owned by British Petroleum and Compagnie Française de Pétrole), which held the offshore concession, found oil under the waters of the Persian Gulf. Sheikh Shakhbut was absolute ruler at the time. As fields were developed and oil royalties began to pour in, Sheikh Shakhbut viewed his new wealth as though it were a modern plague for which there was no antidote. He was bewildered and bitter about the influx of thousands of poverty-stricken people from other sheikhdoms and from Jordan, Pakistan, Iran and India—seeking jobs. He felt his people were threatened. He saw little merit to modern customs. The British wanted to establish a post office, but he refused. He said his people had not had a post office for 200 years; therefore, they did not need one. Nor would he spend any of his oil income on development.

When the original concession for Abu Dhabi was negotiated in 1939, the standard royalty agreed on was about 9 cents a barrel. In view of all the fifty-fifty profit-sharing agreements which had been made, the oil companies were actually embarrassed to pay so little, especially when production figures and payments began appearing in various newspapers and trade journals. For two years they tried to get Sheikh Shakhbut to revise the concession to share profits equally. He adamantly refused. During one discussion he told the company representative that he was not interested in the money and he would be perfectly happy if they would take their half of the oil and go away, leaving his half under the ground. Finally, in late 1965, the members of the ruling family pressured him into accepting profit sharing. The following year they persuaded him to turn over the rulership to his brother, Sheikh Zayed bin Sultan al-Nihyan.

When I visited Sheikh Zayed in Abu Dhabi, I found that this wise desert ruler considered himself "an agent of God" in putting his country's oil wealth to work for his people and leading them into today's computer world. His desolate 25,000 square miles of desert, bypassed by history and civilization since the mid-eighteenth century when his tribe settled there, now ranks seventh in proved oil reserves of free world countries. The 35,000 Abu Dhabians are outnumbered by 75,000 foreigners, who have flocked to participate in the country's overnight development. Including the foreigners, Abu Dhabi's per capita income from oil alone is five times the per capita income of the United States and next year will increase to ten times.

"God did not put this wealth in the earth just for me or my people," Sheikh Zayed told me. "He put it here for all of us. God did not intend for people to be miserable and unhappy. He wants people to be happy, and he created abundance. He intended some people to be more responsible than others and to help others. I have always wanted to help the people, and even before the wealth came, I have done everything I could. I borrowed money when I had no collateral to help them have water and make farms. I was like a man in chains. Now I am unchained, and I can help the people."

Sheikh Zayed has created a modern country so quickly that it seems like a desert mirage—skyscrapers, hotels, schools, hospitals, airports, seaports, paved highways across the country, agricultural projects, small industries, public parks and even a remarkable national zoo. Although he has no formal education, Sheikh Zayed has given education priority and pays the bedouins to keep their children in school. Sheikh Zayed believes in sharing with his neighbors. He has been the leader in establishing the United Arab Emirates, a federation of the autonomous Persian Gulf sheikhdoms of Abu Dhabi, Dubai, Ras al-Khaimah, Sharjah, Ajman, Umm al-Quaiwan and Fujairah. Sheikh Zayed is federation president and bears 90 percent of the costs. Oil wealth is creating a new nation of 300,000 people, uniting tribes that have been warring for centuries.

Kuwait is another anomaly representing the Walter Mitty dreams of every person who speculates, "What would *I* do if I had all that money?" Before oil was discovered in 1938, it was a desert, the size of Connecticut, sparsely inhabited by bedouin nomads and a fringe population of fishermen and pearl divers on the Persian Gulf.

Today it is the second largest oil country in the free world in terms of proved oil reserves, surpassed only by Saudi Arabia. With a total population of only 750,000, half of whom are foreigners who immigrated to get in on the oil boom, Kuwait has developed a near-perfect social welfare state. There are no income taxes. Almost everything is free—health services, education through the university, telephones, utilities. Low-cost housing is available for everyone, but most Kuwaitis live in luxury homes and apartments. Kuwait City, where the majority of the population clusters, is one perpetual, solid traffic jam. There are 200,000 cars registered, and everyone drives around in circles as there is literally no place else to go.

The bridge from the stark poverty of nomadic life to sudden extreme wealth and instant civilization has not been easy to cross. Kuwaitis are still in a state of cultural shock. I spent one afternoon listening to a unique debate between the sixty-five white-robed members of the National Parliament, which is an elected body. They were reviewing the annual report of the emir, Kuwait's hereditary ruler. One sentence stated: "The people are given land by the generosity of the government." The truth of this was argued fiercely for several hours. A group of older Kuwaitis maintained that generosity comes only from God, not individuals. A younger group protested that individuals also could be generous "as the agents of God." The rest of the session was occupied with a discussion of the meaning of various passages of the Koran and whether or not Kuwaitis were following the teachings of their religion.

Rapid development of Middle East oil has meant more than royalties and tax revenues to the governments of the oil-producing countries. It has meant the transfer of advanced technology into their economies, employment, upgrading skills, reinvestment of foreign profits, development of new businesses and services. Furthermore, in the postwar developing world, oil companies had a new management philosophy of enlightened self-interest and social responsibility. They were concerned about avoiding nationalizations such as those in Bolivia, Mexico, Brazil and Argentina prior to the war and in Iran immediately following it.

Saudi Arabia is a prime example of the new oil company approach. After the war Aramco had 12,000 people, mostly Saudi Arabians, in a company-created oasis on the shores of the Persian Gulf. Practically all food and goods had to be imported. Since no one in this backward, isolated country was equipped or trained to render needed services on the scale required, the company had to build houses, hospitals, schools, establish grocery stores, laundries, shoe repair shops, banks—in short, run a town. The company did not want to perpetuate artificial company camps. It wanted to divest itself, as soon as possible, of nonoil activities. So it began helping Saudi Arabians develop the necessary skills to become entrepreneurs.

Initially, a contractor was simply a nomad with a camel to haul stones. Aramco helped local citizens buy machinery to build houses, roads and pipelines. Soon Saudi contractors were running multimillion-dollar firms. Aramco's Arab Industrial Development Department made guaranteed or direct loans to Saudis who had feasible ideas for starting such businesses as cement plants, power plants, fishing industries, clothing factories and small manufacturing industries. Aramco hired Dr. Grover F. Brown, chief agronomist of the U.S. Department of Agriculture, to develop agriculture, which was then limited almost entirely to the date palm. He showed Saudis how to grow dozens of varieties of vegetables and raise poultry. Soon they were supplying the entire country and exporting vegetables and eggs to neighboring countries.

"The best way to help people is to teach them how to make a profit," Abdullah Matrood, one of the new Saudi entrepreneurs, told me as he showed me though his modern $750,000 laundry and dry-cleaning plant and adjoining dairy—Saudi Arabia's first. He started his laundry at age fourteen with a borrowed iron, soliciting business from Aramco employees. Aramco lent him a small building. By the time he was supervising eighty employees he asked the company for a loan to build his plants which now service most of eastern Saudi Arabia.

Aramco's aid program provided a solid base for the government to carry out nationwide projects so that all Saudi Arabians can benefit from the country's new wealth. Originally with Aramco's technical assistance, and later with that of international consulting firms, the government has used its oil revenues to build schools, hospitals, communication systems, roads, harbors, airports. It has developed water resources, agricultural projects and new industries.

King Faisal is a strong believer in free enterprise as the bridge between feudalism and democracy. He has laid down the policy that he wants the public to have private ownership in government projects. On the first such experiment—a $23,000,000 fertilizer plant using natural gas as raw material—the government offered the public 49 percent of the stock. To encourage small investors, a purchaser was limited to 300 shares, and this class provided 95 percent of the total subscription. "In every case, we hope that ultimately the people will be able to take over stock ownership completely," King Faisal told me.

The concept of "planting petroleum"—or plowing back oil profits into national development was not confined to Saudi Arabia. It has been applied in every country where oil companies are operating today. Since World War II more than a billion dollars a year of private capital has been poured into petroleum development, amounting to 40 percent of total private capital investment in all developing countries.

As I have traveled through all the oil areas in developing countries, I have found that it is not the discovery of oil alone which benefits a country. It is the political climate in which it is produced. Wherever a government has fostered the private enterprise efforts of its own nationals combined with the expertise of private enterprise oil companies, maximum progress is made. The initiative of the people of a developing country is already there. It simply needs opportunity and incentive in order for the people themselves to "plant petroleum" in ways which no government can ever achieve.

Iraq and Algeria offer good examples of how to retard

development. Each has great oil resources, being respectively the seventh and tenth largest oil exporting countries. However, they are in dire economic straits, and their people have benefited relatively little in comparison with the majority of oil-exporting countries. The socialist Iraqi and Algerian governments, which nationalized their oil industries, have been constantly involved in disputes with the international companies which originally developed their oil. These governments have lacked the benefit of a businesslike approach permitting the principles of free enterprise to encourage the initiative of their people.

The same is true of the socialist-minded Shah of Iran, who has played such a devious role in the manipulation of international oil prices. Iran, which has been an oil producer since 1908 and is the world's second largest exporting country, has twice nationalized its oil industry. Yet it is still unable to feed itself. The shah prides himself on being a champion of land reform and modern industrial development. However, 70 percent of the people are illiterate, and 60 percent live at subsistence level. At the same time, since 1965, the grandiose, ambitious monarch has siphoned off more than $5 billion to buy modern arms in his obsession to restore the ancient grandeur of Persia and become the military "guardian" of Middle East oil.

Debacle at Teheran

Once the Middle East fifty-fifty profit-sharing agreements became universal, the major international oil companies did not anticipate further revisions. They did not reckon on the effects of competition. The international oil industry was controlled by the so-called seven sisters—the American Big Five companies, British Petroleum and royal Dutch Shell. These seven majors controlled 90 percent of international production, refining, transportation and marketing. Although they competed among themselves, it was not classic textbook competition in the sense of a marketplace created by many companies. Nevertheless, since the majors were fully integrated companies operating in consuming and producing countries, they were vulnerable to pressures in both marketplaces. Consumers and producers view prices from opposite ends of the telescope. Furthermore, there is no birth control in the oil industry. The seven sisters were beginning to feel the competition of a great many new international brothers who were helping make the oil market overflow.

At the end of World War II only twenty-eight American oil companies were active in seventy-eight countries, but by 1958, 190 American companies were operating in ninety-one countries. Ente Nazionali Idrocarburi (ENI), the Italian state oil company, had become a powerful competitor of the majors in exploration, refining and marketing. The Japanese Arabian Oil Company struck oil in offshore Kuwait. Although the Russians were not engaged in exploration or production outside the Soviet Union, they were becoming an increasingly disruptive factor in the international market. They were using oil as a political weapon in their cold war strategy. By dumping cheap oil in European and Asian markets, they were attempting to gain political influence in consuming countries. Their tactics had been part of the reason for the 1960 cut in Middle East posted prices.

The biggest shove to upset the seven sisters' applecart came from the newcomers in exploration. They succeeded in making the fifty-fifty profit-sharing principle obsolete almost as soon as it was established. They were so anxious to get in that they didn't mind paying a higher price of admission. Also, since they didn't have interests all over the world, they didn't have to play the international domino game of being worried about how a new agreement in one country would affect old agreements in other countries.

The first breakthrough came in Iran in 1957 and 1958 with offshore concessions to two newcomers: Pan American Oil Company, a subsidiary of Standard Oil of Indiana, and SIRIP, an offshoot of ENI. Each concession was owned half by the foreign company, as operator, and half by the state National Iranian Oil Company. The foreign company had to bear all exploration expenses and, once oil was found, share profits fifty-fifty with the government on the foreign company's half. In effect, this meant a seventy-five to twenty-five profit split. Concessions were to run only twenty-five years with renewal options and provided for relinquishment of unexplored areas within time limits. In 1958 Saudi Arabia and Kuwait granted separate offshore concessions on their jointly owned Neutral Zone to the Japanese Arabian Oil Company for exploration in the Persian Gulf. The concessions provided for a 56 percent profit take to Saudi Arabia and a 57 percent take to Kuwait. The governments were given options, which they subsequently exercised, to purchase 10 percent of the stock of the companies once production began.

On the other side of the world in Indonesia, Pan American made an even more precedent-shattering upheaval of the old concessionary oil pattern. Under President Sukarno, Indonesia passed an oil and gas law in 1960 which nationalized the oil industry, providing that only state enterprises could develop oil and gas, but foreign companies could work as contractors. Pan American promptly signed a Contract of Work on a formula of sixty-forty profit sharing at realized market prices. This posed a monumental problem to the established producing concession owners: Caltex, jointly owned by Socal and Texaco; Royal Dutch-Shell; and Stanvac, jointly owned by Exxon and Mobil. Becoming contractors, to conform to the new law, meant giving up both management control and the exclusive right to set oil prices and a great increase to the government in profit sharing. The companies' basic fear was the effect on their Middle East operations. Their negotiations with the Indonesian government were in a three-year deadlock until tensions mounted to the breaking point. In 1963 President Sukarno issued an ultimatum that unless new agreements were reached within seven weeks, the government would take unilateral action.

This bombshell ricocheted in capitals around the world. If American, British and Dutch interests were ousted, it would mean that Indonesia would turn to the Soviets for petroleum development and technology. Sukarno was already being swept into the Communist orbit, and this would be a major break with the Western world. President Kennedy was so deeply concerned that he offered to help mediate the dispute, as far as the American companies were concerned, through a team of U.S. government advisors. President Sukarno agreed and suggested a meeting in Tokyo which he would personally attend. Wilson Wyatt, lieutenant governor of Kentucky, represented President Kennedy. The rest of the team included Howard P. Jones, U.S. ambassador to Indonesia; Walter J. Levy, an internationally known oil consultant; and Abram Chayes, legal adviser to the Department of State. The American companies sent attorneys, and Royal Dutch Shell, which obviously would have to go along with whatever was decided, sent observers. The three-year controversy was settled in three days. All three companies gave up their concessions and became contractors. They were given contracts on new exploration areas. A gradual take-over of their existing marketing and refining facilities with compensation to be paid, was agreed upon. There was no way to speculate on what might happen now in the Middle East.

The majors already had suffered a severe setback in Iraq, the fourth largest Middle East producing country. Its erratic military dictator, General Abdul Karim Kassem, had reversed Iraq's pro-Western policy. He wanted the Iraq Petroleum Company, with its British, French and American ownership, to relinquish the majority of the area of its monopoly oil concession which had been converted to a fifty-fifty profit-sharing basis. The company offered to give up 75 percent over a period of time. This was not to General Kassem's taste. With no further ado he proclaimed a law which deprived the company of 99.5 percent of its concession area, retaining only its producing oil fields. At the same time he created the Iraq National Oil Company to develop the rest of the country. Thus began the longest, strangest deadlock in oil history, lasting until Iraq nationalized the company in 1972. Iraq Petroleum continued to produce and profit-share while the national company did nothing, during a series of revolving-door radical revolutions and international political uncertainties. All during this period, every major and independent oil company representing almost every country in the world—including Iraq Petroleum—paid court to the government, trying to do business on an undeveloped north end of an oil field it had taken away from the company. The probable reserves were estimated at more than 5 billion barrels.

Although, like Humpty Dumpty, the old way of doing business with oil-exporting countries lay in pieces, OPEC was still struggling to assert itself in the mid-1960's. As yet there was no such thing as an Arab Oil Policy. Sheikh Tariki, who was too much of a firebrand for the conservative Saudis, was dismissed from his ministry. He became a consultant to radical Arab governments. He was calling passionately for nationalization of the entire Arab oil industry as "a national necessity." "The foreign companies have full control over the destiny of the Arab nation and realize tremendous profits out of the Arab natural wealth," he told the 1965 Fifth Arab Oil Congress in Cairo. "These profits are exported abroad and even accumulated so as to be used in ventures for the exploration for new oil prospects in other areas of the world that may become a source of new competition for the Arab countries and, consequently, weaken the latter's bargaining power and compel them to agree on the reduction of prices."

Tariki airily brushed aside the idea that there would be any difficulties resulting from nationalization. He considered production operations routine, which could be carried out by Arab technicians. Refining, transport and marketing were "mere commercial transactions." The fact that the oil companies, from their own share of profits, made heavy international investments in these areas to develop them and keep them running was beside the point. He considered such costs to be the financial responsibility of consuming countries.

Tariki's oratory appealed to Arab emotionalism, and he was constantly interrupted by applause. The congress' final resolutions did not reflect his views, and I asked Tariki if he had accomplished what he expected. He smiled cryptically and said, "Of course. Even more. Now everybody is talking about nationalization. This reaches the people through radio and newspapers. This puts the pressure on the rulers. Also, this reaches the oil workers."

More moderate Arab leaders did not disagree with Tariki's thesis that Arab oil should be controlled by Arabs. But they advocated going the route of obtaining an increasingly greater share of profits, being given a direct participation in the foreign operating companies and strengthening the Arab national oil companies so that they eventually would be able to take over all operations.

OPEC's problem in getting Arab unanimity to achieve these goals was that of trying to get a litter of kittens into a basket. As soon as it had gathered a few, while it was chasing the others, the first ones would hop out. The most recalcitrant kitten was the newest member—Libya. It was also another Horatio Alger story and would shortly become the nemesis of the seven sisters and the rest of the international oil industry as well.

In 1951 the United Nations declared the former Italian North African territory of Libya an independent nation. It was the first state to emerge from colonialism and chose to be a constitutional monarchy. Bordering the Mediterranean, it had no known resources, and 90 percent of the country was barren desert. The new nation was almost completely dependent on aid from the United States, Great Britain and the United Nations. However, geologists considered it a likely place to look for oil, and there was a scramble among majors and independents for concessions. Millions of dollars had to be spent finding and detonating thousands of mines laid in the desert, across which some of the fiercest battles of World War II had raged. In 1959 Esso Standard of Libya, a subsidiary of Exxon, discovered the first oil. In 1961 it began exports of 40,000 barrels daily. Discovery succeeded discovery by all companies. By 1969 exports had soared to 3,000,000 barrels daily, making Libya the world's third largest oil-exporting nation, even exceeding Saudi Arabia by 100,000 barrels a day.

Libya got an immediate grip on the European oil market because of its geographical closeness. Also, Libyan independent oil companies heavily discounted their oil in competition with Middle

East major company oil in order to break into the market. When the Suez Canal was closed during the 1967 Arab-Israeli war, Libyan oil was at a premium as Middle East costs went up owing to the long tanker haul around Africa. Furthermore, Europe was becoming pollution-conscious, and Libya's low-sulfur oil was sought by all countries. By 1969 Libya was supplying Germany with 45 percent of its requirements, Italy 28 percent, the United Kingdom 22 percent and France 17 percent.

Then the unexpected happened. Riding straight out of the pages of the Koran came a fiery, young zealot to change commercialism into a cause. On September 1, 1969, Libya's ailing eighty-year-old King Idris was at a European spa. In Tripoli, the Libyan capital, a group of young army officers gave a party for the senior officers of the king's loyal national police. At the end of the evening the army officers arrested them, proclaiming Libya a republic with twenty-eight-year old Colonel Muammar Qaddafi as head of state and commander in chief. This was no Balkan musical comedy revolution. It was a deliberate, long-planned coup by a nomad's son who believes himself to be a "sword of Islam," destined to unite 100,000,000 Arabs. He is the extreme Arab nationalist, a revolutionary and puritanical reformer.

The unknown Qaddafi caught the outside world by surprise. His first moves were to close all nightclubs, bars and casinos and change all street signs from English into Arabic in Tripoli, which resembled a West Texas oil boomtown more than an Arab city. He then ousted the Americans and British from their air bases and expelled the 25,000 descendants of Italian colonialists still living in Libya. Qaddafi's new civilian Cabinet members made vague, soothing statements that Libya would honor its oil concessions and that although "no spectacular changes" would be made, its policy would include "more effective control" on petroleum production. This made the oil companies and European consuming countries highly nervous.

Four months following the coup, Oil Minister Ezzedin Mabruk summoned the twenty producing oil companies to a general meeting to announce that the government would start discussion with individual companies on demands for higher crude oil tax prices. Shortly after the meeting started, the oilmen were startled when Colonel Qaddafi strode into the room. He erased all doubt concerning the tough posture he would take in negotiations. "People who have lived for five thousand years without petroleum are able to live without it even for scores of years in order to reach their legitimate right,'' he warned them sternly.

This was no idle puffery. The Spartan young man spent his life in his father's desert tent and in military barracks. As a devout Muslim, he neither drank nor smoked. His guiding precept was: "The Arabs need someone to make them weep, not someone to make them laugh." One of his first acts was to restore the practice of amputations for thievery, according to Koranic law. Simple theft meant the loss of the right hand. Armed robbery involved the additional loss of the left foot. Qaddafi could do what he pleased as he had few political pressures. Libya's population was less than 2,000,000, and 75 percent of the people were either small farmers on the thin strip of fertile land along the Mediterranean or nomads in the vast desert. Furthermore, the government had $2 billion in hard currency which could comfortably see an austerely governed small nation through hardships.

This was a situation in which no modern economic arguments concerning growth and development could carry any weight. I had an insight into the frustrations of the oil negotiations a few months later when I was in Libya and talked with Omar Muntasser, director of the Oil Ministry's Department of Economics. Negotiations on tax prices had been dragging, and as a reminder to the oil companies that he meant what he said, Qaddafi shut down Esso Libya's new $350,000,000 liquefied natural gas plant while a tanker was loading the initial cargo of "frozen gas" to deliver to Italy. The government claimed its share of profits was too low. I asked Muntasser why the government didn't permit shipments to be made to fulfill the sales contract while they discussed profit split. I pointed out that the government was losing money by not selling gas. "You don't understand," he said. "They will only negotiate if *they* are losing money. The government isn't losing any money, because before the plant was built, the gas was flared in the fields and we didn't make any money on it then. So we aren't losing any money by not selling the gas now. Besides, we don't need the money. Do you see?" I felt like Alice in Wonderland when the White Queen tested her on mathematics by asking what was the answer to the problem "Divide a loaf by a knife."

Following the course of Libya's negotiations with the oil companies from February to September was like watching the strategy of a bunch of coyotes attacking a herd of sheep. First they cut off the lambs and weak ewes, one by one, and then they baited the old rams into a cul-de-sac from which there was no escape. Saudi Arabia, Kuwait, Algeria and Iraq were on the sidelines, cheering and openly supporting the maneuvers. Whatever Libya gained they would, too.

The government was negotiating separately with each of the twenty companies. For almost three months, all of them maintained there was no justification for a price rise, while some argued that prices, in fact, were already too high. Colonel Qaddafi had two answers to that. First, the charismatic leader delivered a dramatic public speech exhorting the Libyan people to mobilize for the "coming fight with the oil companies" which he linked with "world Zionism and local forces of reaction," Secondly, he clamped a 128,000 barrels daily cutback on an Occidental Petroleum Company oil field. Occidental, with 800,000 barrels daily production, was providing 21 percent of Libya's total output.

Occidental was an ideal first choice for a pressure victim. Although it was a $2 billion corporation, it was a newcomer to both the oil business and the international oil business and most of its barrels of oil were in one country—Libya. It was a one-man show run by Dr. Armand Hammer, a character as curious as Qaddafi. His father was a Jewish doctor who had left czarist Russia because he was a socialist. Armand made his first million in the pharmaceutical business while he was getting a medical degree from Columbia University. He went to Soviet Russia in 1921 with a mobile hospital he purchased from Army surplus, but decided the Russians needed food more than medical assistance. He traded a million bushels of American wheat for Russian furs, hides and caviar. Lenin took such a liking to him that he asked Hammer to take over an abandoned asbestos mine. Hammer parlayed that into representing Ford and thirty-seven other American equipment companies and opening Russia's first pencil factory. When he left Russia, the government let him take his profits out in czarist art treasures and jewels, which made him a multimillionaire when he opened the famous Hammer Art Galleries. After successful ventures in whiskey making and cattle ranching, in 1958 he took over a dying Los Angeles oil company, Occidental, and began building it into a worldwide company. However, the successful trader Hammer met his match in the successful negotiator Qaddafi for a simple reason. Qaddafi wasn't interested in quick profits.

Occidental officials protested that cutting back production would cause a permanent loss of around 55,000,000 barrels of recoverable oil—equal to $60,000,000 in government tax revenues—for the wells would be flooded with water if they were not continually produced. Libyan authorities contended that Occidental was critically overproducing its fields. They hinted ominously that other cutback orders might follow soon. Tantalizingly, they didn't say which fields or companies. When Occidental tried to make up its lost production by producing more from its other fields, the government promptly slashed its total production by 300,000 barrels. Occidental was forced to begin rationing its international customers.

A week later Libya nipped at the heels of the major companies. It ordered Amoseas, jointly owned by Texaco and Socal, to cut its output by 120,000 barrels daily for "conservation" reasons. Europe was feeling a real pinch as Libyan supplies began to dry up. Contracted tankers were routed out of the Mediterranean to the Arabian Gulf to haul spare oil around Africa, and an acute tanker shortage developed. The shortage had begun a month earlier when Syria closed the 500,000-barrels-daily Trans-Arabian pipeline to the Mediterranean.

A month later Libya flushed another company out of the herd, cutting 125,000 barrels daily from Oasis, jointly owned by Continental, Marathon, Shell and Amerada Hess, which was producing 31 percent of Libya's oil. And just in case all the companies hadn't gotten the full message, the government nationalized the marketing operations of Esso, Shell and ENI with no indication when they would consider starting discussions in regard to compensation. Marketing operations were unimportant, but the Libyan oil industry, with $2 billion invested in production, shuddered collectively.

By mid-August, 1970, the government had hit Esso, the country's largest producer, with a 110,000-barrel cut, Mobil with 55,000 barrels, and taken another bite of 60,000 barrels out of Occidental. The pressure was heavy. It was too heavy for three companies. When exploration and drilling lagged, after the talks started, the government had issued a "drill-up or give-up" directive. Gulf Oil, which had spent $32,000,000 in exploration, now notified the government it was pulling out entirely, leaving 30,000-barrels-daily production behind. Atlantic Richfield and Grace Petroleum gave up a jointly held concession, on which they had drilled some dry holes, rather than face increased exploration rentals and all the uncertainties.

Libyan production was down almost 800,000 barrels daily. The entire world oil supply situation had been disrupted and was in a turmoil. The U.S. government alerted its Emergency Petroleum

Supply Committee to be ready to reactivate for a possible world oil emergency. At the same time, it warned that the United States no longer had the capability to assist other countries as it had in 1967 in the aftermath of the Arab-Israeli war. Newspapers throughout the United States carried front-page stories about a possible winter fuel crisis with industrial shutdowns and worker layoffs.

In a five-month period the individual oil companies in Libya had reportedly tripled their tax price offers. Each time the government expressed dissatisfaction. It was really after bigger game. It concentrated negotiating pressure on Occidental and Esso. On August 30, the eve of the first anniversary of the September 1 revolution, Occidental buckled, reportedly under threat of a take-over. The strange contest between Dr. Arnold Hammer and Colonel Muammar Qaddafi came to an end. Dr. Hammer flew to Tripoli with an extraordinary package deal, which the government accepted. It scuttled forever the principle of fifty-fifty profit sharing between governments and oil companies.

Occidental agreed to cancel its fifty-fifty agreement with the government in favor of a 58 percent tax rate and to raise the posted prices on which the tax rate is figured by a whopping 30 cents a barrel. The government immediately restored Occidental's full production rate. Libya then told the other companies to "take it or leave it." One by one, the companies capitulated. Some of the tax rates varied, but the basic rate for government profits in Libya was now firmly established at 55 percent.

As the last details were being settled in October, the weary American negotiators, who had been sweating it out in Tripoli for ten months, couldn't believe the news from home. In Washington, Congressional investigations were in full swing to determine if the threatened winter fuel oil shortage, precipitated by all these events in North Africa, was real or if it was a conspiracy by the major oil companies to raise prices to the American consumer.

The major oil companies needed no crystal ball to predict that the Libyan settlement would prompt a new round of negotiations in Middle East countries. Nobody disappointed them. Even before they had actually signed the new Libyan accords, the Prime Minister of Iran demanded its income tax rate be increased to 55 percent and an increase in posted crude prices. Within a month the majors had agreed to the 55 percent income tax rate in all the Middle East producing states. The question of how much posted prices would be increased was postponed until after the semiannual OPEC meeting to be held in December 1970, in Caracas, Venezuela.

The OPEC countries were jubilant at the beautiful price vistas Libya had opened for them. Then, two days before the Caracas meeting opened, the Venezuelan Congress extended the view. The government had been under mounting political pressure to put the squeeze on the oil companies to make up increasing government budget deficits. Venezuela, then the second largest oil-exporting country, next to Iran, already had the highest profit sharing of any country, with total taxes giving the government 70 percent. The oil industry was stunned when the Venezuelan Congress raised the income tax rate to 60 percent from a maximum 52 percent. This meant that adding other taxes, the government would receive 80 percent of the profits. To make things tougher, the Congress made the new rate retroactive to the beginning of the year. It also provided that the government could unilaterally set tax reference prices for crude oil.

The OPEC resolutions passed in Caracas left no doubt that the revitalized organization now knew how much muscle it had and was determined to use it. Their objectives were to view 55 percent as a "minimum" income tax rate, to eliminate all tax advantages the companies had and to establish a "uniform general increase" in the oil tax prices in all member countries. The revolt of the petroleum-exporting countries was now in full swing. The battle with the companies was set for January 12 in Teheran, Iran, with a team from Iran, Iraq and Saudi Arabia to represent the six Persian Gulf exporting countries. Furthermore, OPEC threatened that there would be "concerted and simultaneous action by all member countries" to enforce their objectives if they were not attained in negotiations on a fixed timetable of approximately three weeks after negotiations began. The companies were left to guess whether "action" meant embargo or nationalization.

There are some years you might just as well stay in bed. For the international oil industry, 1971 was one of these. On January 3 the local Libyan representatives of the oil companies were suddenly summoned to the offices of Major Abdul Salam Jallud, Deputy Prime Minister. He presented a set of new demands of such magnitude that they were tantamount to putting the companies out of business. The new tax and price increase demands were three times as costly as the demands Libya had made, and obtained, only three months before. The companies were told that if they did not comply they would be forced to shut down oil production or they would be nationalized.

Libya was obviously upstaging its partners in OPEC before the

Teheran conference could start. However, something more serious was in the making. Major Jallud frankly stated to the company representatives that Libya's new demands were intended to "hurt" the companies to force them to put pressure on the United States to change its pro-Israeli policy. In addition to American companies, there were British, Dutch, Italian, French and German interests operating in Libya. He told them all that they must be made to feel the "effects of Zionist aggression" in order to press Western governments to change their Middle East policies to be more favorable to the Arab cause. "When companies suffer," Jallud stated, "they may be impelled to do something to alter United States policy." For the first time, oil prices and policy were openly being used as a political weapon.

With this move, Colonel Qaddafi proclaimed himself the political successor to Egypt's Gamal Abdel Nasser, who had died three months before. Nasser was Qaddafi's hero. He had been moved to tears when Nasser told him, "You remind me of myself when I was your age." Now, Qaddafi was obsessed with the goal of achieving what Nasser had failed to do—unite 100,000,000 Arabs and destroy Israel. He was determined to devote his oil and money to that end alone.

Colonel Qaddafi put his money where his mouth was. He supplied hundreds of millions of dollars of aid to Egypt and Syria. He financed, and still does, the Palestinian guerrillas. He bankrolled the countries of sub-Sahara Africa, particularly those with large Moslem populations. He poured millions into Uganda, Mali, Chad, Niger and Congo-Brazzaville to get them to break with Israel, which also had wooed them. He even lent the U.S. Black Muslims $3,000,000 until he decided they were not true believers in Islam. He is so prorevolutionary that he proudly announced that he had helped finance the Irish Republican Army. His reason? "There is a history of English dealings with the Arabs which goes back for decades, even before my birth," he told an interviewer for the French *Le Figaro*. "So the reason for our support of the Irish guerrillas is justified. It is a little country which has taken up arms to defend its rights and freedom. We have given it our support."

The governments of the United States and Western Europe could no longer view the situation as an economic matter concerning only oil companies and host governments. The threats by OPEC and Libya to cut off oil struck at the heart of the economies of all industrialized nations. The United States and British governments decided to undertake an active and public role to assist the companies at the January Teheran meeting with OPEC countries.

The first problem solved was obtaining U.S. Department of Justice permission for the American companies to form a solid negotiating front to equalize, as much as possible, their bargaining powers against the oil governments acting in concert. American antitrust laws prevented joint company consultation and action without legal permission. Similar waivers had been made during the war and for purposes of government advisory committees. A solid front, it was hoped, would prevent the companies from being picked off one by one as Libya had done and was now trying to do again. Libya was concentrating its new attack on the already-battered Occidental and other independents that were the most vulnerable because of their dependence on Libyan crude. In addition, it was considered essential by the Western governments and companies to negotiate with all OPEC countries at once to prevent the kind of leapfrogging that was going on between Libya and the Gulf producing countries.

There was a prodigious scurrying of company and government officials back and forth between Washington, New York and London to consolidate viewpoints and prepare actions to meet OPEC and Libyan deadlines. Cable and telephone wires hummed. Hours, not just days, counted. On January 11, executives of thirteen major and independent companies met in the New York law offices of John J. McCloy, who represents leading major oil companies before the State Department. The companies were drafting a "Message to OPEC." In an adjoining room were James E. Akins, then head of the State Department's Office of Fuels and Energy, and Dudley Chapman, of the Justice Department's Antitrust Division. As the oilmen finished each portion of the message, it was given to Akins and Chapman for review and comments.

The final approved document was historic. It was the first worldwide approach to oil negotiations. Cleared by the Justice Department on January 13, it was transmitted to OPEC governments on January 16. The companies' proposal called for stability in financial arrangements with producing governments and for a simultaneous settlement with all of them. It asked for an "all-embracing negotiation" between the companies and OPEC and invited other oil companies to join the proposal. Later, eleven more did. The settlement the companies offered included: a revision of posted prices in all OPEC countries, with provision for moderate annual adjustments "against the yardstick of 'world-wide inflation' or similar criterion"; a further temporary transportation adjustment for Libyan crudes with appropriate adjustments for other "short haul" crudes; no further increase in the tax rate percentage "beyond current rates," no retroactive payments and no new obligatory reinvestment; and the agreement to hold firm for five years from date of settlement, when terms would be subject to review.

The companies asked for OPEC's reaction as soon as possible. They offered to meet OPEC representatives "whenever and wherever" the producing governments wished. Meanwhile, they asked for postponement of negotiations demanded by individual OPEC member countries.

Simultaneously with the delivery of the message, on President Nixon's instructions, Undersecretary of State John Irwin and James Akins left to present personally the U.S. government's deep concern to the Shah of Iran, the King of Saudi Arabia and the ruler of Kuwait. "In these talks," Akins relates, "Secretary Irwin explained that the United States took very seriously threats to cut off oil deliveries to America or her allies, and that any country which took such action would find its relations with the United States severely and adversely affected. In reply, all three monarchs assured him that the 'threats' had been misunderstood, that they were directed solely against the companies, and that the oil would be made available to consumers even if the negotiations with the companies broke down." Secretary Irwin also requested an extension of the negotiations deadline and assurance that agreements reached with the companies would be honored for their full terms. The monarchs agreed to both requests.

At the same time the "Message to OPEC" was drafted, a special "Libyan Producers Agreement" was signed by the original thirteen OPEC agreement company signatories. It also was approved by the State and Justice Departments, but its contents were kept highly confidential for three years. Libya had already singled out Occidental and Nelson Bunker Hunt, a Texas independent with 236,000-barrels-daily Libyan production, as the chief sheep for their new coyote hunt. Both companies were in favor of joining a solid company front, but they wanted an insurance policy to enable them to withstand the thumbscrew pressures they were certain the Libyan government would apply to punish them for taking a stand with the majors.

Majors and independents met together and separately. The majors proposed that if any company having Libyan production were cut back for refusing to meet government demands, the other companies would share their Libyan production pro rata with the victim. If they were restricted by the government from doing this, then they had the option to pay the victim 25 cents a barrel. Companies with Persian-Gulf crude would supply the victim with oil on a barrel-for-barrel basis. If Gulf OPEC governments prevented this, they had the option to pay 10 cents a barrel. The independents fought strenuously against the option clause because oil was worth much more than 10 to 25 cents per barrel. The Gulf producers refused to give up the option but wrote into the agreement that it was their "intention" to provide oil. The independents were successful in getting the majors to agree that it was also the "intention of the parties that they will endeavor, before making an agreement with the Libyan Government, to include a requirement that the Libyan Government accept an offer on comparable terms . . . from all other concessionaires." This reassured the independents that, as G. Henry M. Schuler, Hunt's Libyan representative, put it, "the lead-off batter need not fear that he would be left holding the bag if he resisted unreasonable demands which others later accepted."

The united front, with diplomatic support, caught all OPEC countries by surprise. Libya fumed and ranted about the "Message to OPEC," which Major Jallud called a "poisoned letter." He proclaimed that "Libya will defeat the consuming countries and also the oil companies!" On January 19 he ordered Occidental and Hunt to "take your name off the OPEC letter or face government action" and gave them until January 24 to report back.

When the negotiating ministers of Iran, Saudi Arabia and Iraq met with company representatives in Teheran on January 19 to discuss the message, they publicly stated that they responded favorably to the proposal "in principle" but that they would want some "amendments." What the OPEC ministers said in public and what they did in private were opposite ends of the pole. The scenario of the following hectic two weeks before the OPEC meeting was a Machiavellian behind-the-scenes power struggle which ended in disaster for the companies. Everything came apart at the seams before they were even sewn.

When the representative of the oil companies' operating consortium in Iran presented the OPEC message to Finance Minister Jamshid Amuzegar in Teheran on January 16, he immediately objected to OPEC-wide negotiations. He had taken the lead in the OPEC Caracas meeting to prevent such an approach when other member countries suggested it. He told the consortium representative that OPEC could not stop Libya from making "crazy demands" and that if Libya were included, the companies would end up with an agreement in which the most radical demands would be the common denominator. On January 18, the day before the OPEC ministers were to meet with the company representatives, Undersecretary of State Irwin and U.S. Ambassador to Iran, Douglas MacArthur, Jr., met for two hours with the shah and Dr. Amuzegar. Following the meeting, Ambassador MacArthur briefed the British, Dutch and French ambassadors and the company representatives. Although the shah did not specifically make any threats, the suave, wily Cornell-educated Dr. Amuzegar told the American diplomats privately that the joint approach was a "dirty trick" against OPEC which would result in the entire Gulf's being shut down and "no oil would flow."

January 19 was D-Day in reverse. Ambassador MacArthur forcefully recommended to Washington that the companies should negotiate with the Gulf countries and Libya separately. The British ambassador so advised his country. Only the Dutch ambassador angrily warned that such a retreat from the "Message to OPEC," delivered three days before, destroyed the whole strategy. In Washington, Secretary of State William Rogers backed down and advised John McCloy, the companies' lawyer, to tell his clients they should hold separate discussions with the Gulf countries and Libya. Back in Teheran that afternoon, when the company negotiators tried to push the joint approach with the three OPEC ministers, Dr. Amuzegar told them, "If you think you have a problem with your governments, I am quite confident that they will agree to a regional or Gulf approach." The ministers then gave the companies a forty-eight-hour deadline to agree to "Gulf countries only" negotiations. They threatened that if the companies refused to abandon the global approach by January 21, a full OPEC conference would be held to decide whether the countries would legislate individually or jointly obtain the high terms which Venezuela had already decreed unilaterally.

The following day, while the shah was telling the British ambassador that he understood the Americans had accepted the "Gulf only" procedure, the companies formed the London Policy Group, representing all signatories to the OPEC message, to regroup on strategy. Neither U.S. nor British government officials fully understood the danger that separate settlements could lead to further leapfrogging. The group concluded they could salvage the situation by agreeing to hold "separate but necessarily connected" meetings with the Gulf countries and Libya. The negotiating team would be split in half but would make it clear that their purpose was to get all the countries to agree to the same terms and that neither half of the team could act on its own.

At the forty-eight-hour deadline conference the OPEC ministers continued to insist on "Gulf only" negotiations but agreed to a one-week recess. Both sides promptly made a play for the press. The London Policy Group made an announcement: "The oil companies' objective remains the achievement of an overall settlement covering the producing countries concerned. The companies reaffirm that any settlement with the oil producing governments concerned must be reached simultaneously."

The shah grandstanded and got more coverage. He held a two-and-a-half-hour press conference to torpedo the companies. "The oil companies grouped together and there was even news that the governments of industrial countries had decided to support the oil companies or to use their influence to bring pressure in favor of the oil companies," he stated. "If this proves to be correct, obviously it will be a precise example of what is called economic imperialism and neocolonialism, which during the course of history has on several occasions influenced the thoughts and ideas of responsible leaders in the world." He threatened an embargo of Gulf production if the companies persisted and stated categorically that no matter what happened in the negotiations, "the oil companies . . . or those holding concessions should in my opinion be removed." This made good press copy to build up a battle between the have-not producing nations and the have consuming nations.

The shah was confident that he had made the U.S. government withdraw its support of the global approach. Furthermore, the week before, an emergency meeting of a high-level group of the Organization for Economic Cooperation and Development, representing the United States, the United Kingdom, France, the Netherlands, Germany, Italy, Japan, Denmark and the commission of the six-nation European Economic Community, had been held in Paris. They had concluded and announced that the negotiations in progress between oil companies and producing countries were commercial, not political. They made it clear they didn't want to get involved.

The London Policy Group then adopted a more conciliatory attitude toward the negotiations. They were still trying to keep a "necessary" connection between Gulf and Libyan discussions. On

January 25 they split the team, with British Petroleum's Lord Strathalmond heading the Teheran group and Exxon's senior vice-president, George T. Piercy, heading the Libyan group. On January 27 Piercy arrived in Libya, having requested a conference with Major Jallud to present the companies' proposal. Jallud refused to see him. When Piercy saw Oil Minister Mabruk, he denounced the oil company "cartel" and refused to receive the proposal. Piercy then sent it to him with a covering letter. Mabruk sent it back. It went without saying that Libya was waiting until the Teheran negotiations were concluded so that it could make even greater demands in accord with its determination to continue "hurting" the oil companies until U.S. government Middle East policies changed. Piercy had no choice but to send another letter to the minister advising him the team was returning to London.

In Teheran, things were going just as badly. Every attempt by the companies to obtain agreement on favorable terms as a basis of negotiation met a stone wall. The Gulf states did indicate that they would be agreeable to some reasonable assurances against future leapfrogging, once an agreement was reached. However, on January 28 they warned that if negotiations broke on January 31, OPEC would hold a full meeting on February 3, followed by a worldwide shutdown of oil production to prove "solidarity."

On January 30 the Teheran and Tripoli oil company teams met in London. They might just as well have met at Waterloo. They agreed to abandon the "Message to OPEC" and to recognize the total separation of Gulf and Libyan negotiations. The confident air of "diamond cut diamond" with which the companies had delivered their assertion of a united stand on January 16 had vanished. It was now "diamond cut butter." The OPEC governments no longer had to bluff. They knew they held all the aces, and the companies, their governments and the consuming countries were playing a losing game.

For the next two weeks during the Teheran "Gulf only" negotiations the companies put up a valiant struggle. They started off with an unexpected psychological disadvantage. On the first day of preliminary negotiations a copy of a key cable from London, detailing what the team should demand, was either lost or stolen at a press conference given by the team's public relations man. It was published verbatim in Teheran newspapers and caused an uproar because the companies were offering far less than the Iranian government had led the people to expect. The companies were offering 15 cents-a-barrel increase in posted prices, whereas the Gulf countries were demanding 54 cents a barrel.

On February 2, the day before the full-scale OPEC conference assembled in Teheran, the companies announced that they had failed to reach agreement with OPEC representatives on financial items or "to obtain adequate assurances that a sufficient volume of oil will be made available for the needs of consuming countries." They "greatly regretted" the breakdown of talks and were willing to resume negotiations "at any time and place."

In the opening OPEC session the shah declared the best course of action now was unilateral tax and price legislation by the Gulf countries, but he would be agreeable to continuing negotiations if OPEC so voted. It did but issued a no-choice ultimatum. If the companies did not "voluntarily" accept OPEC demands by February 15, the countries would legislate. If the companies did not accept the legislation, OPEC would "take appropriate steps including total embargo." Only Indonesia abstained from the total embargo vote.

Despite such whip-cracking, when the companies resumed negotiations, they were able to win some points and compromise others. They persuaded the Gulf countries to agree that the settlement would last five years with guarantees against either further price whipsawing or cutoff of supplies. They managed to fight off any retroactive application of the higher prices, as well as any forced reinvestment of profits. Finally, they were assured that the Gulf countries would not support demands other OPEC members might make for terms higher than those in the Gulf settlement. In return for these assurances, the Gulf countries got almost everything they had been demanding. They got an immediate 35 cents a barrel increase in posted prices; 5-cents-a-barrel increase on June 1, 1971, and on January 1 of 1973, 1974, and 1975, plus a 2.5 percent increase on the same dates to compensate for world inflation; and a fixed tax on profits of 55 percent, not to rise if higher rates are achieved in other countries. Overall, the agreement would bring more than $10 billion in added payments to the six Gulf countries during the five-year period. In prior years the countries had been receiving about $4.4 billion a year. By 1975 they would be getting $7.5 billion.

The agreement was signed in Teheran on February 14 by the chief negotiators for both sides with flashbulbs recording all the usual jolly smiles, although some were jollier than others. Not represented at the signing table were the sure losers of the conflict just ended—the consumers, large and small, whose energy costs would now take a sharp jump upward. Also, the governments of the consuming countries, which had pulled out the diplomatic rug from under the companies, could now sit down and count up how much the fray would cost them in foreign exchange balances: $240,000,000 for Britain; $200,000,000 for Italy; $250,000,000 for the United States. Developing countries without oil or money could gloomily wonder how to meet the new misery.

The Arab Take-Over

Now the Libyans had the stage to themselves. After Teheran, attempting to decide what terms to offer Libya in countering their demands was like trying to figure out how to win an earthquake. Nevertheless, the Libyan team of majors and independents painstakingly put a package together which they thought was reasonable and had a chance. When Occidental and British Petroleum presented it on March 7 to Major Jallud, he didn't even bother to read it. He demanded to know the financial breakpoint at which they "would walk out of Libya." He told them that if the companies' final offer was too low, Libya would nationalize them and pay compensation. He threatened an embargo, saying Libya didn't care what happened to Europe. He instructed them to report their acceptance of Libya's terms by 10 A.M. March 9.

The scenario was heating up like Teheran; only this time there were no phony Marquess of Queensberry rules such as prevailed when Dr. Amuzegar would get tough at the conference table and then charm his antagonists on weekends while showing them the beautiful antiquities of ancient Persia in Isfahan. The Libyans preferred Queen of Hearts rules—"Off with their heads!" With the delighted support of other OPEC countries, Libya was using iron knuckles.

On March 8 all the other Libyan oil companies submitted offers identical to those of Occidental and British Petroleum to demonstrate their support. Libya flexed its own support muscles. On March 11 the Deputy Prime Minister of Syria flew to Tripoli to announce his stand against the oil companies, which implied that Syria would again stop the flow of Arabian oil in the Trans-Arabian pipeline to the Mediterranean if that would help. On March 12 Nigeria, which had suddenly become an important oil-producing country, announced its intention to become a member of OPEC and sent a delegation to Tripoli "to coordinate respective positions in the face of foreign oil companies." On March 13 the Oil Minister of Algeria, which had just nationalized all the foreign oil companies operating there and had been working hand in glove with Libya, arrived. On the same day the Iraqi Oil Minister, who had helped head the Teheran negotiations, arrived. The traffic jam at the Tripoli airport was not ended. Saudi Arabia's Oil Minister was due in on March 15.

On March 13 the Libyans demonstrated the penultimate of their arrogance. With the approval of the whole negotiating team, Texaco and Socal raised the offer on posted prices. Major Jallud threw the proposal at the representatives' feet and threatened action if no change was made by midnight.

The posted price of Mediterranean oil was of concern to Saudi Arabia and Iraq since both had pipeline outlets to this sea. In Teheran they had refused to discuss any price settlement on this oil without reaching an agreement with Libya and Algeria. The Saudi, Iraqi and Algerian ministers gave Libya their blessing and a free hand to get the highest price possible. The ministers also promised that if the companies refused the minimum demands, they would meet again in Tripoli to discuss retaliatory measures, including an oil stoppage. The companies had hoped that the Saudis would not support this but learned that they were afraid that if they didn't, the Libyans would pay Palestinian guerrillas to blow up the Trans-Arabian pipeline. Libya had Iraq in its pocket because it promised to pay Iraq for any revenue losses from an embargo. Before Saudi Minister Yamani left Libya, he told Piercy that the situation was so explosive that he had appealed directly to Colonel Qaddafi to overrule Major Jallud's insistence on immediately nationalizing the companies. Jallud wanted to use Algeria's take-over formula of seizing 57 percent control.

In Europe, oil companies and governments quietly began stockpiling oil in anticipation of a Libyan shutdown. There was no publicity in order to avoid public alarm.

The companies were caught between a rock and a hard place. If they settled, they would avoid nationalization, still be in the picture and keep the oil flowing. On the other hand, meeting Libya's demands might jeopardize the Teheran agreement. There was no assurance Libya would stay put, and giving in would be a signal to other countries to act Libyan style. However, they decided they had reached the point of no return. They would have to make a settlement and try to mix as much orange juice with the bitter medicine as possible.

Libya had kept up the pretense that it was dealing with the companies individually, but the companies kept their united front and nobody fell out of bed. The real miracle was that after all the acrimonious arguments and rude treatment by the government an agreement was finally reached. On March 21 all the companies submitted an identical proposal with a covering letter stating that the proposal was a "complete package" and should be considered "as a whole in recognition of the interdependence of its parts." On April 2, the Ministry of Petroleum informed each company that the Revolutionary Command Council "has agreed to your stated offer" as "proposed in your letter dated March 21."

For a man who didn't care about money, Colonel Qaddafi did pretty well. He didn't get as much as he originally demanded, but he got far more than the oil companies agreed to in Teheran because he took that as a starting point. Instead of the Teheran 35-cents-per-barrel posted price increase, he got 64.7 cents, plus another 25 cents "temporary" freight premium, reflecting the higher profitability of Libyan oil compared to Middle East crude because it didn't have to be hauled around Africa. Posted prices were escalated upward by another 48.5 cents per barrel over the next five years to compensate for world inflation. The cumulative package gave Libya $3.9 billion in additional revenues over the next five years. All the increases added up to Libya's receiving $1 billion more annually than it would have received on the same production a year earlier.

The companies managed to win three highly controversial points which Libya had flatly maintained up until the last moment were nonnegotiable. The industry insisted that the settlement should be valid for five years. The government refused to make such a guarantee. The government insisted that the freight premium should go all the way back to the Suez Canal closure in June, 1967. It also insisted on a 25-cents-per-barrel obligatory profit reinvestment in Libya. The government finally agreed to the five-year duration and not to make the freight premium retroactive, in return for the companies' adding an extra 2 cents to the posted price package. In lieu of the 25-cents-per-barrel obligatory reinvestment, they accepted the companies' guarantee to maintain six exploratory rigs active in the country for the duration of the five-year deal. If they had no prospects to drill, they would spend an equivalent amount on secondary oil recovery or gas utilization.

Shotgun weddings seldom augur well for a happy married life. Only a month after the Tripoli agreement was signed Major Jallud was already building up a case to terminate it if Libya so chose. At a press conference in Tripoli he said the escalation clause to counter inflation was too low. If it did not balance the increase in import prices for Western goods, "this would mean the agreement would not live." He also stressed that the five-year life of the agreement would depend on new investments by the oil companies and that the exploratory obligations in the agreement were only a minimum. He said Libya was "intransigent" on reinvestment of part of the companies' profits and that if they failed to cooperate and continued only to exhaust the oil fields, "then the agreement will not last long."

The Tripoli agreement struck sparks in Teheran that also boded trouble for the future. Dr. Amuzegar told the consortium that the shah was "incensed" that the companies had given Libya so much more than they gave the Gulf countries. He said that if the consortium did not concede more benefits to Iran, then Iran would support the "radical" members of OPEC in their next moves.

Nigeria could hardly wait for the dry ink on the Tripoli agreement to get the oil companies producing its 1,500,000 barrels daily to "agree" to the same terms given Libya. Its new oil development, resumed after a lengthy civil war, was making it one of the most important exporting countries.

Libya had ushered in 1971—the Year of the Arab—with its maverick demands which had helped make such a debacle out of the companies' efforts to assume a united front. It ended the year with another bombshell. On December 7 it unexpectedly nationalized all of British Petroleum's rights and assets in a concession jointly held with Nelson Bunker Hunt. On the surface, the move apparently had nothing to do with oil economic maneuvering, but was Colonel Qaddafi's enraged lashing out against the British for not preventing Iran from a military take-over of three tiny islands in the mouth of the Persian Gulf.

Although Iran collaborated with the Arab countries in OPEC, there were bitter rivalries, jealousies and fears constantly rumbling and churning under the surface. The shah is determined to assert his sovereignty over the Gulf, which Iran historically claims as its own. The decision of the British to give up their military protectorates of the Gulf Arab sheikhdoms in 1971 played into his hands. The day before British withdrawal was official, Iran landed troops on the islands, which were claimed by the rulers of Sharjah and Ras al-Khaimah. As the self-appointed champion of the Arab cause Colonel Qaddafi called in the British ambassador, worked himself up to a blind fury, accused the British of conspiracy with Iran and announced the nationalization of British interests.

Libya watchers were convinced that Qaddafi's tantrum was merely a preliminary strategy. It virtually assured the 51 percent nationalization of all oil companies whenever Qaddafi wanted to show his displeasure with the U.S. government in the Arab-Israeli conflict. Nelson Bunker Hunt, co-owner of the nationalized field, nervously conferred with the other Libyan oil companies to get them to reinforce the original "safety net" agreement which Libyan independents had made with the majors to protect them in a united stand. The agreement was confirmed, but the stage was being set for ultimate trouble between the companies involved.

If the international oil companies had expected a five-year period of "stability" in the Middle East oil picture, as their press releases cheerfully indicated following Teheran, they were quickly disillusioned. An elated OPEC, well aware that the balance of power had totally shifted from oil companies to host governments, was now ready to zero in on bigger gains than those achieved by taxes and tax reference prices. They wanted participation in the operating companies. Kuwait Oil Minister Abdel Rahmon Atiki put it more bluntly. "Participation is a tame word," he said. "Its true connotations are nationalization or take-over. What we call phased participation is in fact phased nationalization. Oil companies should gladly accept this gradual approach, since our resources cannot continue indefinitely to be developed by other than our own citizens."

Immediately after Teheran, OPEC countries began discussing their ideas among themselves and hiring economic and technical specialists to advise them. In January, 1972, the Gulf producing countries summoned the oil companies to Geneva to settle two issues: a dispute over revising the Teheran agreement to compensate for devaluation of the dollar and readjustments in other world currencies, government participation in oil company subsidiaries and, by far the more important, operating in their countries. The monetary dispute was quickly settled with an agreement to boost Gulf crude prices by 8.49 percent, amounting to $700,000,000 more annually in taxes and royalties.

When discussions began on participation, the companies played a listening game. They were completely in the dark about what the demands would be. They expected the worst, particularly since

Saudi Oil Minister Yamani, in a London interview two days before, had fired some opening guns by saying, "If I were a consumer looking down the road to 1980, I would feel rather scared . . . scared that sometime in the 80's I wouldn't be able to find enough energy around to keep my industries going." Yamani predicted the world soon would be "crying for oil," and the only way the West could have security of supply would be to participate in its exploitation by partnership with the Arabs. He said he believed British and French companies were resigned to accepting this, but that the real stumbling block to participation was "American stubbornness."

The companies no longer had even the semblance of a united front. Twelve oil companies had twelve negotiators at the Geneva meeting. They made no commitment about participation but agreed to discuss it as individual companies. OPEC appointed Yamani, who had been advocating participation since 1968, to negotiate with them on behalf of all Gulf producing countries. Yamani announced that he would seek 20 percent participation as the "minimum of minimum" and that compensation would be determined solely by the book value of their investments. It would not include any allowance for proved oil reserves for the simple reason that "the oil is ours."

Sheikh Ahmed Zaki al-Yamani emerged as one of the shrewdest and most devious oil negotiators in the world. He became "Mr. OPEC." As such, he took the play away from the imperious, tricky Shah of Iran and had no qualms about battling him on principles and policy. Yamani had his own ambitions. Although he is tough, when I first visited him in Saudi Arabia I was impressed with his disarming, soft manner. Dressed in Arab robes and looking like a twin to Omar Sharif, he fondled his pet Pomeranian dog in his lap and talked about the changes in modern Arabia. He is an outstanding bridge between the old and new. Born in Mecca in 1930, he is the son of a distinguished religious judge. Yamani obtained a doctorate in international law at New York University and a degree from Harvard Law School. He became a legal adviser to Saudi Arabia's Income Tax Department and cut his professional teeth on studies of Aramco's tax returns. He is thoroughly at home with Westerners. He is also totally loyal to his king and shares with him the sense of Saudi Arabia's destiny to resolve the Arab-Israeli conflict.

Sheikh Yamani logically began the first participation discussions with Aramco. It was the biggest company and the one he knew most about. He was also on its board of directors. Aramco tried to stave off participation with an alternative proposal to negotiate a separate venture with a 50 percent share for the government in several established but undeveloped discoveries on its acreage. But King Faisal became impatient with the lack of progress and sent a message to Aramco through Yamani warning the companies that the Gulf governments would resort to legislation if the companies failed to agree to participation. OPEC members met in emergency sessions in Beirut in March. The night before the meeting opened, the owner companies of Aramco delivered an eleventh-hour letter to Yamani accepting 20 percent participation in principle. An immediate confrontation was averted, but companies and countries were still far apart on compensation and terms.

By July negotiations were deadlocked. Yamani accused the owner companies of Aramco of "procrastination and evasiveness" in the participation negotiations. He told them that his government was determined to take all necessary measures to achieve its participation goal. In October, Yamani and the companies came to the final, momentous agreement in New York. Surprisingly, it provided for 25, instead of 20, percent government participation in established Gulf producing countries. It would escalate gradually to 51 percent in 1983. The controversial issue of compensation was calculated on an "updated book value," which in the case of Aramco came to around $500,000,000 for the initial 25 percent and another $500,000,000 for the four other Gulf producing countries. Each government's share of oil production would be divided into three categories: some for direct sale by state companies; some to be sold back to the companies under long-term contracts; some to balance out fluctuating amounts taken by oil company partners. The companies would pay varying prices for the different categories. They would lose about half the future profits on the production turned over to the states which they otherwise would have made under full ownership of output.

By this time Yamani was representing only Saudi Arabia, Kuwait, Abu Dhabi, Qatar and Iraq. Each state would negotiate the same agreement separately with the companies operating in their territories. As usual, Libya was waiting to see what happened, so it could top it. Iran had bowed out of participation since the shah said they had already long ago nationalized the oil companies. He also was playing games.

When the companies originally protested that participation should not be discussed until 1976 because the Teheran agreement guaranteed the concessions in their existing form for five years, the

U.S. State Department supported their position. American ambassadors made representations in Iran, Saudi Arabia and Kuwait, but to no avail. However, according to James Akins, the State Department's energy chief, when the companies began negotiations, "the United States played one major role, forcefully noting that it would have to consider compensation based on 'book value' as confiscation. In the discussions, it was pointed out that many of the OPEC countries themselves would soon be investing large sums abroad; any principle that meant in practice no compensation might later apply to their own investments."

With participation settled—at least for the time being—Saudi Arabia gave the U.S. government and the oil industry a shock. Immediately upon signing the participation agreement in New York, Yamani went to Washington to attend the annual conference of the Middle East Institute. The theme was "World Energy Demands and the Middle East." Minister Yamani proposed, in a sensational speech, that Saudi Arabia be given exclusive rights to quota and duty-free deliveries of crude oil in the United States. In return, he said, Saudi Arabia would invest "huge amounts" of surplus oil revenues in domestic U.S. downstream oil industry operations "right up to the gasoline pumps." "In the last resort, there will never be a substitute for Saudi Arabia in the field of oil," Yamani declared, "as, indeed, there will never be anything to parallel its friendly policies towards this country."

Such an idea was revolutionary. To implement it would have required sweeping changes in U.S. government policy and precipitated an international scramble, pitting consuming governments against each other to make deals with producing governments. However, this proposal in the fall of 1972 anticipated the necessity of planning for the raging international debate which began in 1974: What would the oil exporting countries do with their enormous profits and world money power vis-à-vis the interests of consuming and developing countries?

At the same meeting, State Department's Akins repeated his warning of a few months earlier that the United States and other major consuming countries must see to it that the Arab producing countries found good, solid investment opportunities abroad; otherwise it was questionable whether or not they would produce oil in the amounts the consuming countries needed.

Unfortunately, there were too few on the American political scene who recognized, even at this late date, the importance of moving U.S. policy toward the Arab countries in a more "evenhanded" direction. Nor did they read as carefully as the Arabs already had done the U.S. energy reports, which were now pouring out, showing the magnitude of our future dependence on Arab oil. In the fall of '72, the United States was preoccupied with the Presidential election and, along with other consuming nations, had relegated the international energy problem to a "study" being carried out by the twenty-four-member-countries Organization for Economic Cooperation and Development. In the vacuum created by consuming countries' "nonaction," momentum began to accelerate toward the further erosion and collapse of the oil companies' positions in the exporting countries.

In the United States all these events were as far removed from the American consumer's consciousness as though they had been occurring untelevised on another planet. However, the domestic energy facts of life had finally caught up with us in the critical 1972–73 winter fuel oil shortage with the accompanying world tight oil supply. We saw little connection between what was happening politically and economically in the Middle East and the flood of Congressional energy bills and the President's April, 1973, energy message. This, of course, was because nobody made the connection for us or heeded King Faisal's warnings. As we squeaked through the summer without a major gasoline shortage, we paid scant attention to the major oil upheavals which now occurred in Iran and Libya.

While Yamani was negotiating participation with the oil companies, the Shah of Iran grabbed the spotlight by announcing in a highly publicized press conference in London that he was going to extend until 1994 the agreements with the international oil company consortium which were due to expire in 1979. He spoke glowingly of "a new kind of relationship, between free partners" that "will eventually open a new page in the relations of producing countries and the oil companies." However, when he saw what Yamani finally got, he couldn't stand being a political "loser." He promptly reversed his position and began negotiations for an immediate full take-over of the consortium. The twenty-year agreement, concluded in July, 1973, gave Iran 100 percent ownership of all oil and facilities and reduced the companies to oil customers, with the preferred right to buy and distribute Iran's oil. Complicated formulas provided for prices and certain compensations. The companies agreed to advance oil prepayments up to 1980 for 40 percent of the funds Iran requires for annual budgeted expenditures. Although the National Iranian Oil Company nominally took over all operations, the government signed an agreement with a service company, wholly owned by the consortium companies, to continue oil field technical operations. The shah translated nationalization into Iranianization.

Libya, naturally, could not be bothered with niceties. Nationalizations were very much in style since the companies had no way of fighting back and little home government support. During participation negotiations, Iraq had blithely nationalized the northern fields of the Iraq Petroleum Company. The only consequence was that the company finally agreed to settle this nationalization plus all previous nationalizations. Although British Petroleum had tried to penalize Libya by boycott and international lawsuits for the 1971 nationalization of the lucrative field which it owned jointly with Nelson Bunker Hunt, Libya had not suffered. It made Communist-bloc barter deals for its nationalized oil. In the "prestige leapfrogging" which was going on between individual Arab countries and Iran as to who could slice off the biggest chunks of oil company salami the quickest, Colonel Qaddafi waited to take the center of the stage until he was sure the world crude oil situation was so tight he could call all the shots.

In May, 1973, Qaddafi delivered an ultimatum to the oil companies to accept 100 percent Libyan control of oil operations. It would pay only net book value for the take-over and sell the oil back at market prices with no guarantees. He cracked the whip a little by cutting Esso's production by 60,000 barrels a day. He waited until June 11 to fire a big gun at a celebration, attended by President Sadat of Egypt and President Amin of Uganda, commemorating the third anniversary of the expulsion of "U.S. imperialist forces" from Wheelus Air Base. Colonel Qaddafi announced to an enthusiastic multitude that he had expropriated the properties of Nelson Bunker Hunt to give the United States "a big hard blow on its cold insolent face." The official decree proclaimed that it was a "warning to the oil companies to respond to the demands of the Libyan Arab Republic and also a warning to the United States to end its recklessness and hostility to the Arab nation."

It took the U.S. government a month to make up its mind how to answer the "blow on its face." It didn't exactly turn the other cheek, but neither did it protest nationalization as such or bring up the question of appropriate compensation. Instead, the State Department protested that Libya's action was "political reprisal against the United States government" and branded it as "invalid and not entitled to recognition by other states." The department gave Hunt a copy of the diplomatic note and advised other governments so that Hunt would have official backup in taking legal actions against anyone buying its nationalized oil. This didn't prevent a crowd of European and American customers from pushing and shoving one another to line up for contracts with the Libyan government at rising prices.

Six months before Hunt was nationalized, Libya had demanded he turn over 50 percent of his assets. At that time the other Libyan producers had reconfirmed their "safety net" agreement to help him withstand the pressure. However, now with outright expropriation facing them, the heat was too much. Six independent companies—Occidental, Continental, Marathon, Amerada Hess, Grace and Gelsenberg—producing about half of Libya's oil, capitulated to an immediate 51 percent nationalization. The terms were Libya's—compensation on mere net book value and repurchase of their former oil at above market prices. What that was going to mean to consumers was immediately evident in an Occidental telex notification to all its customers in Europe and the United States. It advised that nationalization had added 97 cents per barrel to its crude oil costs, which it was passing along to its customers. This was the biggest single price increase ever recorded in the history of the oil business.

The next multimillion-dollar question was the fate of the majors, which were making an unusual last-ditch stand. The last week of August, Major Jallud called them into his office one by one. He was so sure of the outcome that he did not indulge in his usual dramatic tirades. "He spoke almost more in sorrow than in anger," one company representative reported. He told them he understood their position, but a revolutionary government had to have all companies accept the same terms. He gave them a one-week deadline. On their part, each major frankly told him they would rather lose their Libyan holdings than jeopardize the participation deals with the Gulf producing states and the settlement with Iran. There was no question in the majors' minds on the date nationalization would be announced. September 1, 1973, the fourth anniversary of the revolution, would require appropriate celebration. Qaddafi also needed something sensational to bolster his fading Arab image following his abortive attempt to merge Libya with Egypt. The only question in the companies' minds was whether they would be taken over 100 percent.

The September 1 answer was 51 percent nationalization of the subsidiaries of Exxon, Mobil, Texaco, Socal and Shell. Surprisingly, the government gave them thirty days' grace to transfer their holdings. In a joint statement, the companies referred to the action as a "purported nationalization" and announced they would take it to arbitration but would be willing to resume negotiations with the government "to reach a mutually acceptable agreement."

The Libyan oil grab forced President Nixon to make his first public mention of the importance of Middle East oil to the United States. In a press conference on the day Congress returned from its summer recess he threatened that if it did not act on his energy proposals, submitted earlier in the year, the United States would be "at the mercy of the producers of oil in the Middle East." In response to a question concerning U.S. reaction to Arabs using oil as a club to change U.S. Middle East policy, he threatened Libya and other Arab countries that if they continued to expropriate and raise prices, "they will lose their markets and other sources will be developed." Neither Congress nor the Arabs were particularly intimidated. Besides, the time and season had passed for anybody to prevent what happened next. The Yom Kippur war began.

Not since the Trojan horse and the atomic bomb had a new war weapon been devised that was as devastatingly effective as the Arabs' use of its newly acquired oil power. Paradoxically, nobody had planned it that way—except the fanatic Colonel Qaddafi, and the scenario hadn't developed exactly as he had in mind. Beginning with his blockbusting tactics against the oil companies in 1970, he had led the Arab nations to economic power, but he was not their leader. Neither Egypt nor Syria consulted him before or during the October war. Qaddafi railed at his Arab brothers for being traitors to the cause when they accepted cease-fires and entered peace negotiations. Qaddafi lived up to his own bitter self-portrait: "I am a leader without a country."

Although oil power for the Arabs had suddenly become a means to achieve a devout, dedicated goal in their quarter century war against Israel and Zionism, the success with which they wielded their new weapon had a heady effect. Governments looking for more revenues have a lot in common with drunks and gamblers— they never know when to quit. The oil weapon was double-edged— political and economic. The Arabs slashed with both sides.

The Gulf producing countries called a meeting in Vienna on October 8, the day the war began, to renegotiate the Teheran agreement upward. "We are here to talk oil, not war," Saudi Minister Yamani told the oil company negotiators. The companies asked for a two-week recess to consult with the major consumer governments in regard to the Gulf countries' latest demands. Three days after the company negotiators left Vienna, they were shocked to read in the newspapers that the Gulf countries had unilaterally increased posted prices a staggering 70 percent, or about $2 a barrel. Libya waited only three days to leapfrog. It boosted prices by 93.8 percent.

The Shah of Iran was even more ambitious than the Libyans. He was not participating in the cutback or embargoes. Although Iranians are Moslems, there is no love lost between them and the Arabs. The shah plays both sides of the fence with Arabs and Israelis, shipping Iranian oil through Israel's pipeline from Eilat on the Gulf of Aqaba across Israel to an outlet on the Mediterranean. The shah welcomed the war as an opportunity to manipulate OPEC into forcing oil prices up as high as possible.

At the end of December, 1973, the ministers of OPEC's six Gulf member states—Iran, Saudi Arabia, Kuwait, Iraq, Abu Dhabi and Qatar—met in Teheran to discuss further increasing posted prices again. Just prior to the meeting, the shah had publicly announced that he thought the Arabs should end their oil embargo. "Playing with the oil weapon is extremely dangerous," he said. Behind closed doors with the ministers it was another story. The shah insisted on quadrupling the price of oil over the last massive jump. A confrontation developed between Iran and Saudi Arabia.

Sheikh Yamani maintained that a 50 to 60 percent increase would be enough and that any more would be disastrous for both the industrial and developing countries. Yamani and Algerian Energy Minister Belaid Abdessalam had just finished touring Europe, Japan and the United States, explaining the Arab viewpoint to government officials and financial leaders. Yamani had been disturbed by the far-reaching economic effects of the cutback and embargo and the violent reactions in the consuming countries. The Arabs had ridden a bull out of the chute in a new kind of international rodeo without knowing what kind of bull it was or even how to ride. The "political" use of their weapon also had a backlash. Americans don't like to be blackmailed, and American public opinion was running high against the Arabs.

The OPEC price arguments between Saudi Arabia and Iran became so heated that Yamani reportedly threatened to walk out. However, on the surface a compromise was finally reached. Although the shah didn't get all he wanted, it was much higher than King Faisal had authorized Yamani to agree to, and Yamani had difficulty in surviving the king's wrath. When the shah personally announced the price decision, it set off an economic earthquake which shook the whole world. The ministers jumped the price of oil by 130 percent over the 70 percent jump of two months before. This meant that, including both jumps, the oil-consuming nations' import bill in 1974 would rise by an astronomical $95 billion over 1973 just for the exporting governments' take in royalties and taxes. This didn't include production costs, profit margins and transportation. The Gulf producing countries celebrated New Year's Eve with the knowledge they had forced the price of oil up by a total of 470 percent in 365 days.

The shah called the new tax price rise a "minimum." In a press conference, he agreed that it would be a shattering blow to industrialized and developing countries. "The industrial world will have to realize that the era of terrific progress and even more terrific income and wealth based on cheap oil is finished," he proclaimed. "They must find alternative sources of energy. Eventually they'll have to tighten their belts." According to the shah, industrialized countries should stop using oil as fuel and restrict its use to the petrochemical industry. He said one of his country's aims in increasing the price of oil was to demonstrate that oil was "too noble" to be used in engines or for domestic heating.

The shah's rhetoric was lost on the drivers of America's 118,000,000 cars, trucks and buses who had their own ideas about the aristocracy of gasoline. As a matter of fact, few of them were aware that the higher prices they were paying for it had anything to do with the Shah of Iran, King Faisal, Colonel Qaddafi, or anybody else except the oil companies. Oil imports into the United States did not begin to dip because of the Arab embargo and cutback until December. However, the first OPEC price jump was already hitting the American consumer. Petroleum prices had been under government control since August, 1973, but regulations allowed oil companies to pass along increased costs of raw material and purchased products to their customers. Since one out of every three barrels of oil consumed in the United States came from abroad, the costly foreign oil boosted prices. OPEC government revenues rose from $1.75 to $7 on a typical barrel of Middle East crude. This meant the cost of the oil companies' share of crude oil rose by $5.25 per barrel.

OPEC was exhilarated with the look-ma-no-hands ease with which they established control of world oil prices. The next item on the agenda was to control more oil to make more money. It was a first-grade arithmetic problem: If an oil company pays a government $7 a barrel in royalty and taxes and then sells the barrel for a profit, how can the government get that profit too? Answer: The government takes the barrel away from the oil company and sells it for itself.

The late 1972 agreements which Yamani had negotiated for the Gulf countries to obtain 25 percent participation in the oil companies' share of production, rising to 51 percent by 1982, were now as out of style as the bustle. Libya had already obtained immediate 51 percent participation by nationalization and had totally nationalized Texaco, Chevron and Atlantic Richfield in order to force the remaining three majors to capitulate to 51 percent. Now it was Kuwait's turn to be the big leapfrogger. In February, 1974, Kuwait announced a 60 percent take-over of Kuwait Oil Company, jointly owned by British Petroleum and Gulf. This signaled a round of sixty-forty take-overs in the Gulf. However, the two big bulls—Iran and Saudi Arabia—made only "interim" agreements. They were circling each other warily, apparently ready to lock horns in a showdown world oil leadership battle. The consumer was due for another trampling in this fray.

The preliminary staging ground was Quito, Ecuador—OPEC's June, 1974, meeting. At this point, everybody involved had almost forgotten how the whole show got on the road. Oil embargoes had been lifted in March and cutbacks practically restored. The political side of the Arab oil weapon had slashed deep enough—Dr. Kissinger was doing his daily shuttle among Cairo, Tel Aviv and Damascus. The Arabs no longer had to worry about an "evenhanded" policy. Only the Israelis had furrowed brows. The political victory had created another war. It was not now simply a question of who had what ancient rights to the small piece of real estate known as Israel, which is the size of New Jersey. As Israeli ex-Prime Minister Golda Meir once wryly remarked, "Moses made a mistake by turning right instead of left to find the Promised Land." It was what was under the land of the Middle East that counted—not just to the people who lived on it but to the entire world. Albert Einstein said, "The third world war will be fought with stones." Who could have anticipated a preliminary economic world war with barrels of oil?

The Quito OPEC meeting had two faces—what went on behind closed doors and what was told the press. The public was led to believe that Saudi Arabia wanted to lower oil prices whereas Iran was pushing to up them and that a real battle ensued. Saudi Minister Yamani has carefully fostered the myth that Saudi Arabia is on the side of the consumers, but he is as determined as the shah to get more than the traffic can bear. Furthermore, reports of battles in OPEC meetings are part of their strategy. "OPEC is like a club," an OPEC representative told me. "Everything is always very amicable, and if one member has reasons to get a point across for public consumption, all the others help him do it." In Quito everything went according to Saudi plans to preserve the status quo—no price increases at that time. Saudi Arabia didn't want any boat rocking because it was after the biggest prize of all—a negotiated, immediate, total take-over of the American-owned Aramco without the so-called stigma of nationalization.

Saudi Arabia's public announcement of the commencement of Aramco take-over negotiations marked the end of the international oil world as it once was. It officially ushered in the new era of unparalleled world economic problems for the consuming countries. Symbolically, the occasion was commemorated by Saudi Arabia's becoming Number One in world oil production. The United States lost the crown which it had held since the turn of the century.

The breathtaking six-month rush of events from quadrupling of world oil prices to the new precedent of 100 percent take-over was of far greater importance to consumers' pocketbooks than they realized. The oil companies now had almost no leverage to keep prices down. Under the participation agreements, the governments sold some of their share back to the companies. This was known as buy-back oil. The governments also sold oil directly in the marketplace. Because of the shortage created by the cutbacks, the governments received unusually high prices. Auction prices in Nigeria were more than $20 a barrel and about $17 in the Gulf. Consequently, the producing countries raised the price of buy-back oil to the companies. They could buy it at 93 percent of posted prices. Since the governments set posted prices, this meant that buy-back oil cost more than the companies' equity oil. For example, in Saudi Arabia, Aramco's equity oil, amounting to 40 percent of production, cost them $7.12 per barrel, of which $7 were taxes and royalty to the government and 12 cents were production costs. However, Aramco had to pay $10.83, or 93 percent of posted price, for buy-back oil from the government's 60 percent share. This made Aramco's average cost $9.28 per barrel.

Consuming countries were endeavoring so intensively to persuade OPEC to lower prices that in its September, 1974, meeting OPEC didn't quite dare raise them directly. It chose an indirect rout of raising government taxes on the international oil companies' remaining equity oil by about 45 cents a barrel. They maintained the oil companies could absorb this in their "profits." Since the companies' profits on Middle East oil are between 40 and 50 cents a barrel, this was obviously unlikely. This maneuver deftly shifted any blame on increased prices to the consumer away from OPEC and to the companies. The OPEC strategy is likely to cost consumers of their crude from $4 to $5 billion yearly. Saudi Arabia did not join in this since negotiations were continuing on 100 percent take-over, but instead raised the price of buy-back oil to Aramco. This will increase cost to the consumer by about 13 cents a barrel. All OPEC countries make no secret of the fact that they will continue to raise oil prices in proportion to rising inflation rates in the industrialized countries.

There are indications that the Gulf producing countries, under the 100 percent take-over pattern, now want to eliminate entirely any lower-cost equity oil. If the companies have no access to lower-cost equity oil, this would increase world oil costs an estimated $17 billion annually, at mid-1974 production rates and prices. It would also mean that "negotiated" 100 percent take-over would be just a fancy Dior label sewn on the old Macy's basement dress of outright nationalization.

The oil companies no longer have any power to determine production levels, investments and prices. They must do as they are told by the producing governments. The companies have been reduced to the role of a contractor supplying technical services. However, they do this superbly. The national oil companies created by the producing countries cannot possibly handle the distribution of the huge volumes of oil they control. The international oil companies have developed to a high pinnacle of efficiency the art of finding oil, moving and refining it and distributing it to the consumer on the mammoth scale the world requires. The networks of private oil companies' facilities are vital to the world's energy trade. Even more important are the accumulated experience, technology and managerial and planning know-how which makes the complex system work.

Producing and consuming countries alike will need the services and expertise of the international oil companies for many years to come. However, the radical changes in the international oil scene have created problems which commercial companies cannot solve. What had originally begun as a controversy between host governments and operating oil companies over who got the biggest piece of pie had turned into a formidable conflict between the governments of producing and consuming countries with consumers caught in the middle.

Producing Countries vs. Consuming·Countries

The suddenness with which the petroleum-exporting countries repealed the law of supply and demand has placed the whole free world in the predicament of the boa constrictor that swallowed an elephant. Nobody knows how to digest it. How can the consuming countries deal with rocketing balance of payments problems for their oil costs? With no security of either supply or price, how can consuming countries or private companies raise the vast amounts of capital required for facilities to meet expanding demand? How can the poor countries cope at all? How are the producing countries going to use their fantastic new revenues and financial power? What are the international political dangers which may be created by this new topsy-turvy economic world? Can the producing and consuming countries find any way jointly to create a world economic environment in which their mutual needs will be equitably met?

In the midst of the turmoil created by oil embargoes and cutbacks, the United States took the initiative to seek answers. In a major policy speech in London, in December, 1973, Secretary of State Kissinger proclaimed, "The energy crisis of 1973 should become the economic equivalent of the Sputnik challenge of 1957. The outcome can be the same. Only this time, the giant step for mankind will be one that America and its closest partners take together for the benefit of all mankind."

Dr. Kissinger proposed that the nations of Europe, North America and Japan establish an energy action group of "senior and prestigious individuals" to develop within three months an initial action program for collaboration in all areas of the energy problem. The goal would be "the assurance of required energy supplies at reasonable cost." Plans should be made to conserve energy, develop new sources and pool research and technology. The producing nations should be invited to join from the very beginning with respect to matters of common interest. He pledged a "very major financial and intellectual contribution" from the United States to solve the energy problem on a common basis. "There is no technological problem that the great democracies do not have the capacity to solve together—if they can muster the will and the imagination," he said.

Capacity the great democracies had, but the Arab blackmail fox was loose in the biggest consumer chicken house of all. Every European chicken was frantically trying to find its own safe perch. The week following Kissinger's appeal, the heads of state of the nine member nations of the European Common Market assembled in Copenhagen to discuss the situation. One of the nine was Holland, which the Arabs had embargoed because of its pro-Israel policy. The other eight members couldn't even muster up the courage to make a show of solidarity in their own organization, much less the world. The Arabs adroitly hijacked the summit meeting. The foreign ministers of Algeria, Tunisia, the United Arab Emirates and the Sudan showed up uninvited and caused a great commotion with their unveiled threats that they didn't want to make Europe suffer, but that, as Foreign Minister Adnan Pachachi of the UAE, put it, "The world must understand that Israel must be stopped." The act was staged, apparently, with the connivance of the French and British, each of whom felt they had more clout to gain Arab amelioration of their oil woes by wrecking a common front. Kissinger's scheme was not totally rejected at the meeting. The Common Market leaders mustered up enough "agreement" to announce that they would "study the energy situation" and have a report ready by the end of February, 1974.

In the meantime, the European consuming countries began a steady stream of separate pilgrimages to the Middle East oil Meccas. It was every country for itself. Consuming country foreign ministers were practically tripping over each other in oil-producing country hotel lobbies, trying to make secret diplomacy bilateral state-to-state oil deals. Most of the producing countries were shying away from long-term deals, but the consuming countries plucked some fruit from the trees. Great Britain bartered $242,000,000 of industrial goods with Iran for 36,500,000 barrels of oil. Britain courted Saudi Arabia, as did Italy. West Germany agreed to build a $1.2 billion refinery for Iran in exchange for 182,500,000 barrels of oil annually for five years. Japan lent Iraq $1 billion in return for an agreement to buy 560,000,000 barrels of oil and 490,000,000 barrels of products over ten years. French Foreign Minister Michel Jobert was a veritable traveling salesman in his tour of oil countries. He offered fighter planes, tanks, antiaircraft missiles, petrochemical plants, road building, hotels, mineral water, Concorde planes and refineries in exchange for oil contracts. He stirred up a lot of interest but only got one firm deal—200,000,000 barrels from Saudi Arabia over three years, at a high price. However, Arab officials told

Minister Jobert they were counting on France to check efforts to establish a bloc of consuming countries to counter the producing countries.

U.S. officials vigorously protested the bilateral oil deal scramble, calling it "madness." They believed a global cooperative approach essential. President Nixon quickly invited the nine member countries of the European Common Market, Canada, Norway and Japan, plus the Secretary-General of the Organization for Economic Cooperation and Development, to which all the countries belong, to attend a February 11 meeting in Washington to work out a joint action program. He proposed that following the meeting between the thirteen nations, representing 85 percent of world imports, a meeting be held with oil-consuming countries of the developing world, and, then, in May, a conference with the oil-producing countries.

The consuming countries were in such total disarray that the European Common Market group held a meeting to decide whether or not they even wanted to come to Washington. France argued that it was nothing but an American plot to set up a new type of organization so that the United States could dominate Europe. France wanted to set up a European-Arab conference and exclude the United States. With reluctance and suspicion, all but France accepted the invitation. They made it clear in a formal statement that they would entertain no thought of a permanent organization, nor would they make any commitments on the cooperative action program Washington proposed.

When the international energy conference finally convened, it turned into the Battle of Europe. French Minister Jobert arrived at the last minute. His tactics were so obstructionist that there hadn't been so much caucusing on American soil since the last national political convention. Tempers were high, diplomatic gloves discarded and insults exchanged. German Finance Minister Helmut Schmidt strongly supported the United States and warned Jobert that a policy of "everybody trying to save his own skin" would create international economic problems. Jobert retorted, "Of course when everything is going well, approaches are friendly and completely elegant. But when everything is going badly, everyone tries to save his own hide. I see nothing against this. Except that we don't all have the same hide. Some of us have tight, shiny hides; others are skinny and worry about food for tomorrow. Let's remember this before making ethical condemnations."

Jobert came to wreck the conference, but he actually saved it.

French recalcitrance stabbed the countries which had been trying to "save their hides" with bilateral deals into awareness of the long-range consequences of such a policy. The Americans also played their cards well. They gave an implicit warning that if the Europeans would not cooperate on energy, the United States would have to rethink its military commitments to the North Atlantic Treaty Organization. However, they tempered this with a number of carrots on the end of the stick. The United States offered to share its energy technology, especially in the nuclear field where it is the world leader. It offered to share American oil and other energy supplies in times of shortage. Secretary Kissinger pledged that the United States would make a sustained effort to cut its proligate use of energy and would develop self-sufficiency to remove America's heavy drain on world oil supplies.

The tumultuous, contentious, remarkably undignified meeting was extended an extra day and produced surprising results. Everyone but the French agreed on the need to talk with the producing countries on "the problem of stabilizing energy supplies with regard to quantity and prices." They agreed "to develop a cooperative multilateral relationship with producing countries and other consuming countries that takes into account the long term interests of all." They agreed to hold a consumer-producer countries conference as soon as possible and established a coordinating group headed by senior officials. They agreed on a "comprehensive action program" to deal with "all facets of the world energy situation by cooperative measures." The French finally signed the official communique but attached a list of demurrers.

Before the Washington parley started, Algeria organized a counterattack against the consuming countries. It lobbied in the United Nations to call a special session of the General Assembly on raw materials and development. The ploy was to fix the blame for the economic plight of non-oil-producing developing nations in consuming countries rather than on the high oil price created by OPEC. Algeria had obtained endorsement by fifty-nine countries out of the sixty-eight to convene a session. The day the Washington energy conference ended, all nine Common Market countries endorsed it. The United States reluctantly agreed to join the others in "welcoming" the UN session to "deal with the larger issues of energy and primary products at a world-wide level." The European diplomats put their gloves back on and even told France they would agree to a foreign ministers' meeting to discuss holding a Europe-Arab conference.

The industrialized countries had by no means dropped an energy bomb on the producing countries, but they had demonstrated that they could finally "muster the will and imagination" to agree to a course of action.

One uninvited guest to the conference had been dramatically heard from in his own inimitable way. The day the conference opened, Libya's aggressive Colonel Qaddafi announced the total nationalization of Libyan operations of three American oil companies—Texaco, Socal and Atlantic Richfield—as a "severe blow to American interests in the Arab world" in order to coincide with the meeting.

The three-weeks United Nations session on raw materials and development was the first economic session in its history. It gave the so-called third world—the have-not developing nations—an opportunity to be heard. The fact that it was held served to focus world attention on what had long been an open secret. It was high time the developed countries and the developing ones seriously reassessed their economic relationships. Besides energy, there were other crises in the world facing the rich and poor nations, as UN Secretary General Kurt Waldheim pointed out. There were the crises of mass poverty, population explosion, food, military expenditures and the inefficient world monetary system. As was to be expected nothing concrete was achieved. The session served primarily to give the 135 member nations a platform for polemics, grandstanding and infighting. The Soviets and Red Chinese scored their points against each other and the "imperialist" countries. Since Algerian strategy had billed the occasion as developed vs. developing countries, the spotlight on OPEC oil price increases was successfully shoved into the wings. There could be no confrontation in the third world between oil producers and nonproducers if solidarity were to be maintained. The theme of Secretary Kissinger's address was interdependence and the necessity of cooperation between all nations, with a warning against commodities cartels. He won no popularity contest. Following OPEC's example, the countries producing bauxite, copper, coffee, tea and bananas were busily getting organized to see if they could pull off the same thing.

The General Assembly vowed its determination to establish "a new international economic order" and approved an emergency relief program for the countries hardest hit by skyrocketing costs of food, oil, fertilizer and other imported necessities. At the last minute, the United States proposed an eighteen-month $4 billion assistance program. It was too late. Algeria and Yugoslavia managed to block the offer, claiming it was an American trick to sabotage the meeting. The United States withdrew its proposal.

Although a dialogue had been opened, the session did not achieve OPEC's purpose. There was no way to sweep under any oratorical rug the plain fact that the massive oil price increases are a major contributing factor to the vicious spiraling of worldwide inflation which is burdening all countries. Furthermore, the great balance of payments deficits to oil-importing countries and the huge inflow of funds to oil-producing countries are just beginning. International economists, bankers, and government financial experts have been thrown into a tailspin of uncertainty and confusion by the upheaval. There is general agreement that the world economy would have been able to handle increased oil prices over a period of time. However, the financial world has been struck by lightning. Few will predict at what point the situation will become unmanageable for the industrialized countries. It is already intolerable for the non-oil-developing countries.

The biggest multibillion-dollar question in world history is what the Arabs will do with their staggering amounts of petrodollars and how the consuming countries can manage the big trade deficits created by their energy import bills. Upon how this question is answered depends on whether or not we have a "global recession" or a worldwide economic catastrophe comparable to the Great Depression of the 1930's.

"One country's surpluses are another country's deficits, and 1974 is likely to see some violent swings in current account balances all over the world," says Peter G. Peterson, former Secretary of Commerce and chairman of Lehman Brothers, one of the world's leading investment banking firms. He estimates that the developed countries, which had a $13 billion surplus in 1973, would have a $30 to $35 billion deficit in 1974. The less developed countries, which had an $11 billion deficit in 1973, would plunge to a $20 to $25 billion deficit in 1974. The "producer" countries, which had a $6 billion surplus in 1973, would have an overwhelming $50 to $60 billion surplus in 1974.

"Projected to 1980 at current levels of oil prices and production, the cumulative current account deficit of the consuming countries would aggregate $600 billion or thereabouts," Peterson points out. "To put such magnitudes in perspective, we should remember that this level of deficits is over five times existing foreign exchange reserve levels. The problems of the less developed countries will be tragically severe. The *increase* in their oil costs in one year, 1974, will be larger than the total official development flows. This does not take into account about $5 billion of increases in grain costs, fertilizers including urea, phosphate etc. on which many of these countries depend. For many countries, one year's increase in the costs of imported oil, food and fertilizer will more than wipe out their total reserves. Something like one billion people live in countries that are oil poor, food poor, fertilizer poor. To talk of new debt to finance these existing additional deficits is to overlook the fact that it is now almost impossible for many of them to meet existing debt charges.''

The United States would have about a $25 billion oil-import bill in 1974, as contrasted to 1973's $7.7 billion bill. It will increase annually over the next decade as imports rise. That money comes from consumers' pockets, paying more for gasoline, electricity, heating oil, food grown from petrochemical fertilizers, synthetic clothing, plastics and the myriad products made from oil. The more money consumers have to pay for imported oil, the less they have to spend on other goods. The price of other goods, using oil as energy to produce them, goes up. The nation's balance of trade deficit increases. To try to remedy the trade deficit, we obviously must increase exports. But who are we going to sell what to in order to balance such huge imported energy bills? All the other industrialized countries are in the same badly leaking boat. There is a real danger that it may turn over and sink if there is a mad scramble to pursue individual "beggar thy neighbor" trade policies. If the industrialized countries try to protect themselves by blocking imports, to prevent more money flowing out, then all world trade begins to contract.

If all the petrodollars flowed back into the countries from which they came to buy more goods, services and raw materials, countries could work out their problems. The disaster is that such phenomenal amounts of the world's money are being sucked up and piled up in a few countries which can't use all of it and—which is even worse—have no real ideas or plans about what to do with it.

The oil-producing countries use about 40 percent of their revenues to buy goods and services abroad. Some of them, like Indonesia, Algeria, Iraq, Nigeria and Venezuela, will have little or no surplus funds from increased revenues because they greatly need them for internal development. The ambitious Shah of Iran is rapidly accelerating his spending to buy arms and in industrial agreements such as a $4 billion accord with France to buy five nuclear reactors and build railroads and petrochemical plants. He has also bought a fourth interest in Germany's famous Krupp steelworks. The real petrodollar problem concerns the five Arab countries—Saudi Arabia, Qatar, Abu Dhabi, Kuwait and Libya. They are accumulating the bulk of the vast surplus and have a very limited capacity to spend their oil revenues domestically.

Even before the prices quadrupled, Saudi Arabia built up more than a $4 billion surplus during 1972 and 1973. It has difficulty spending between $2 and $3 billion annually. In 1974 alone, its surplus was estimated at between $20 and $25 billion. Saudi Arabia is anxious to accelerate its industrial development as rapidly as possible with new refineries, petrochemical plants, steel mills and manufacturing of various kinds. However, such things don't add up to that many billions of dollars. Furthermore, there is a time factor as to how fast a country can spend that kind of money. It takes two to three years to construct a major industrial plant. In the meantime, more billions of revenue are pouring in. The Arabs have no intention of buying gold and burying it in the sands whence the oil came. A gold bar isn't exactly risky, but neither does it earn any interest. The Arabs know they have the power to wreck the world economy if they do not "recycle" their excess money through the international monetary system. In other words, put it to work creatively. If they don't, they, too, would suffer in the wake of a global depression. But how, where and when will they invest their petrodollars?

A joke going the rounds of international financial circles is that the Arabs should be encouraged to invest all their money in American blue-chip industrial stocks and then the U.S. government should nationalize the industries—with no compensation, of course. This doesn't tickle the Arab funnybone. They are being extremely cautious about making any U.S. investments. The political side of the energy war is by no means settled. They do not want to invite the risk of petropolitics freezing petrodollars. They are maintaining such a low profile in American investments that when a group of Kuwaitis bought an island off South Carolina for a $100,000,000 resort development, the event received as much publicity as though it were the Louisiana Purchase in reverse. There is a steady stream of Western bankers, businessmen, engineering firms, brokers, promoters and government officials to Arab capitals proffering an incredible variety of investment opportunities and schemes. So far the Arabs are still window-shopping in the international bazaar. The speed with which they are moving to recycle their billions is on a par with trying to sop up the Pacific Ocean with paper towels.

Treasury Secretary William Simon estimated that in the first eight months of 1974 the Arabs invested $25 to $28 billion around the world, with more than half of this being held in European and U.S. banks. Of about $7 billion invested in the United States, roughly $4 billion was in various types of U.S.Treasury and government agency marketable securities.

In the meantime, petrodollars were swelling Arab bank accounts internationally. The commercial banks would have liked to take their deposits and lend them to borrowers from the oil-importing nations so they could pay their oil bills. But the Arabs were nervous and didn't want to tie up their funds for more than a few days or months, at the most. This didn't help the potential borrowers, who needed long-term loans. The commercial banks, of course, couldn't lend out short-term money on long-term credit. Bankers were deeply perturbed about the strain this whole upside-down situation was placing on the world banking system. At the mid-1974 International Monetary Fund meeting, Chase Manhattan Bank Chairman David Rockefeller told the gathering that, in his opinion, "the process of recycling through the banking system may already be close to the end for some countries, and in general it is doubtful this technique can bridge the payments gap for more than a year or, at the most, eighteen months."

Like the little Dutch boy trying to keep the dike from bursting by sticking in his thumb, the managing director of the 126-nation International Monetary Fund, H. Johannes Witteveen, disclosed that he had persuaded some Arab and oil-producing nations to pledge about $3 billion to help establish a special "oil facility" in the IMF to lend money to distressed oil-importing countries. Saudi Arabia offered $1.2 billion; Iran, $720,000,000 and other countries, $840,000,000. The pledges are only a tiny fraction of what would be needed to carry out such a plan. The poor countries have no leverage to finance their oil trade deficits such as the arrangement that Great Britain made with Iran for a $1.2 billion three-year line of credit.

The Arabs shy away from any proposals to set up special international funds to take long-term low-interest loans to the poor countries. They are making their own loans to oilless Arab countries. They have also offered a $200,000,000 loan to the Organization of African Unity to help some poor African states. However, the Arabs stoutly maintain that the responsibility of helping the stricken developing countries worldwide is a burden that should be borne by the industrialized countries. From the Arab view, the reasons for this and the arguments to justify the huge price increases can be summarized in the following points made by Saudi Minister Yamani at the UN Raw Materials and Development session.

1. The developed countries achieved their growth through cheap energy from the producing countries. Through their international oil companies, the developed countries kept the price of oil artificially low. These "irresponsible price policies" of the developed countries oppressed the producing countries economically.

2. The developed countries, depending on "unrealistically cheap energy," failed to search for new energy sources and used oil wastefully as though it would never be depleted. The producing countries should be compensated for this waste.

3. The producing countries do not need to produce their "nonrenewable" resource at such high rates for their own economic well-being. They must have "alternative sources of income to the oil that they are speedily depleting in response to the world's rising demands." Since they are "amassing foreign currency reserves in the process, they must be given adequate safeguards against the erosion of the value of currencies and the potential dangers of foreign investments."

4. The advanced industrial countries should bear the "greater part" of immediate assistance to developing countries because the industrial countries "receive from the developing countries prices for the manufactured goods they export to them that greatly exceed, in relative terms, the prices that oil producers realize for their oil."

Shortly after oil prices were raised so astronomically, Yamani, who was in New York, was invited by a prominent banker to lunch at the prestigious 21 Club. Yamani ordered a hamburger, commenting that he didn't often have a chance to have one. At the luncheon's end, to his host's surprise, Yamani insisted on paying the check. When he got it, he said, "You see? Why do you complain about oil at twelve dollars a barrel when a hamburger costs eight fifty?" His host refrained from commenting that both Yamani's oil and 21 hamburgers might be artificially overpriced. However, the point Yamani was trying to make highlights a serious grievance of all developing countries. Unless they receive an equitable price for their raw material exports, they cannot hope to pay the constantly inflating prices of the goods they import from the industrialized countries. However, the U.S. Treasury Department estimates that since 1970 the export dollar price of Middle East crude has increased 730 percent, whereas the average cost of imported goods and services into the producing countries has increased only about 70 percent over the same period.

The accusation that the developed countries failed to search for alternate energy sources while wasting petroleum is like blaming New England whalers for not looking for rock oil instead of harpooning whales during the 100 years whale oil was the world's major source for artificial lighting. As a matter of fact, the petroleum industry was born as a result of the world whale oil crisis of the 1850's. When the shortage of whales caused the price of sperm oil to jump from $18 a barrel to $107 a barrel, it provided an incentive to look for a substitute. Americans found it in the world's first commercial oil wells in the rocks of Pennsylvania and sparked the world's energy revolution. Today the world is by no means short of oil, but it has only recently realized that oil resources are neither limitless nor sufficient to meet rapidly accelerating energy demands. High oil prices will provide the classic incentive to develop substitute forms of energy. It will also make it economically possible to find more oil and gas. Eventually, reasonable energy prices will prevail. However, because of long lead times and technological problems, these developments will not be rapid and will require tremendous capital investments. Meanwhile, like it or not, consuming countries are married to Middle East oil and cannot hope to get a divorce before the end of the century.

Despite the current worldwide search for oil, the possibility of developing in the immediate future other oil and gas supplies in the enormous quantities the world demands is unlikely. The Middle East has two-thirds of the world's proved oil reserves for a very simple reason. It has two-thirds of the world's supergiant oil and gas fields. Technically, a supergiant oil field is defined as one containing 4 billion barrels or over. Supergiants are hard to find. Only fifty-five have been found in the industry's hundred-year history. The Middle East has 34, the Soviet Union 14, the U.S. 3, Venezuela 2, Indonesia 1 and the Netherlands 1, which is all gas. Even giant oilfields of half a billion barrels or over are hard to find. There are only 182 of those around. This doesn't mean that we've run out of supergiants or giants. "Who knows that there is *not* another 'Middle East,' for example, beneath the continental margin off the southern Atlantic Coast of the United States?" Dr. T. H. McCulloh, of the United States Geological Survey, asks in the survey's 1973 comprehensive study of U.S. mineral resources. He points out that the onshore-offshore region south of Cape Hatteras has much in common geologically with the onshore-offshore region of Saudi Arabia. Nobody knew the Middle East jackpot was there until it was drilled. This is what spurs oil seekers on, wherever they are allowed to explore. However, tomorrow's supergiants and giants will be even harder to find than in the past. They are not so much prisoners of the earth's rocks as they are of hostile political and geographical environments. Their most promising habitat lies under the world's offshore waters, in the Artic regions and the Amazon Valley jungles. The search for them is hindered by problems created by both man and nature.

A look around the world's most prospective oil areas shows why, during the lengthy transition time to alternate energy sources, the Middle East countries are so secure in their present oil monopoly.

No one yet knows how many hundreds of billions of barrels lie under the world's Arctic region. In 1968 I went on an expedition to the Canadian Arctic Islands, a few hundred miles from the North Pole, as a guest of Canada's Minister of Northern Affairs Jean Cretien. Accompanied by leading geologists, oilmen and government officials, we were making a survey of the first exploration work in the Canadian Arctic. It was being carried out by Panarctic Oils Ltd., a consortium of the Canadian government and private Canadian oil and mining companies. It was a first trip to the Canadian Arctic for everyone except a few of the geologists. The purpose was to understand the magnitude of the project, the logistical problems to be overcome, and to get an overview of the geological potential of the region. When we landed on Melville Island to observe a geophysical crew at work, we were 1,000 miles northeast of Alaska's North Slope, whose first oil had been discovered only three months before. Over the top of the world, 2,000 miles from us, was the Soviet Arctic where a supergiant gas field had just been found. It is an awesome experience to visit these vast, uninhabited polar areas. It is the closest an earthbound person can come to sharing the emotions of the astronauts landing on the moon. As we flew over the great belt of mountainous frozen desert islands, listening to the commentaries of the Arctic geologists, it was a preview of a new world in the making despite the formidable, inhospitable, but starkly beautiful, environment.

Not long afterward I was in Saudi Arabia and told Minister Yamani about the trip. I said that from what I had learned, the balance of oil power would one day shift from the Middle East to the Arctic, just as it once had from the U.S. Gulf-Caribbean area to the

Middle East. Yamani was frankly skeptical. "The Arctic can never compete with Middle East oil," he said emphatically. "It will cost too much to develop it." We both had a point. Arctic development has been slow because of the great costs and technological problems involved. However, since then Yamani has helped hasten the day when it *can* compete with the Middle East. Furthermore, since then there have been eighteen major oil and gas field discoveries in Canada's Arctic, including seven in the islands. They are not yet developed; but the time is close, and new exploration is intense. Since then the Soviets have discovered five more supergiant gas fields in their Arctic. The first one, discovered the year before Alaska's first discovery, is in commercial production. The Soviet Arctic is slated to become that nation's largest source of gas, and plans are under way to develop exports. Also, since then the American Arctic has been in its own peculiar deepfreeze with all development stopped for four years in the environmental court battle to prevent building a pipeline to the lower forty-eight.

Although Alaskan development has begun again, the exploration and development of the United States vast offshore oil potential are still politically crippled and limp along. Political problems also plague Canada's continuing development. Western Canada, which is the United States' largest foreign supplier of oil, contributes 7 percent of American consumption. Under the Canadian constitution, the provinces control their natural resources. However, since the world increase in oil prices, the provinces and the national government have each been raising taxes and fighting over who gets what, to the point that the oil industry, caught in a squeeze, has reached a point where net returns may be at an uneconomic level. Many big oil companies have suspended exploration operations. Drilling dropped by a third, and there has been a mass exodus of oil investment capital, both Canadian and American, from Canada to the United States.

South America's potential is still largely unrealized. Its development has been hindered by historically turbulent, revolutionary, back-and-forth Latin American politics and by the utter vastness of its great mountain chains, impenetrable jungles and rain forests. Venezuela, once the earliest star of foreign oil development, is holding its own as the world's third largest oil-exporting country. However, it has consistently been the unpublicized and unilateral head of OPEC's comet, always taking the biggest participation bites in taxes and royalties first. Its complete nationalization of the oil industry is scheduled soon as an announced policy. It is based on the fact that the majority of old concessions are expiring. However, as government participation has ascended, new foreign exploration investment has diminished proportionately. The undiscovered oil isn't going to move. It has been resting there quietly for hundreds of millions of years. My friend, Dr. Juan Pablo Pérez Alfonso, former Minister of Petroleum and co-architect of OPEC, thinks it is a fine idea if it continues to do so. In his retirement, he is now known as "the hermit of Los Teques"—a Caracas suburb. But he is a lively, influential and famous "hermit." On a recent trip to Venezuela, I lost the instructions to get to his villa. When I stopped in a bar to telephone him for the route, the bartender asked me with awe, "Were you talking to the *great* Dr. Pérez Alfonso?" Juan Pablo and I argued amiably for hours in his garden about the wisdom of a developing country keeping its capital in the ground and using it only sparingly or whether it should go all out, take the market gains now and put them to work in other national developments. I was for maximum diversified development now, but Juan Pablo, knowing his people, was thinking of their capacity to use their capital wisely without wasting it. In any event, his passionate espousing of complete nationalism has prevailed. Venezuela's new president, Carlos Andrés Pérez, has announced that the oil industry will be nationalized during his five-year term and that government oil policy will be one of conservation rather than development.

Finding oil in South America's huge upper Amazon Valley jungles and pipelining it over the Andes mountains ranks with Arctic oil pioneering as among the greatest technological achievements of man. This has also opened up a brand-new oil frontier. Its potential was not successfully tested until 1962 because the formidable Andes mountain range, which extends the full length of western South America, with many peaks more than 22,000 feet high, turns eastward in southern Colombia, effectively sealing off easy entrance to the basin. Spurred by world demand, Texaco and Gulf oil companies jointly spent $16,500,000 wildcatting in Colombia's Amazon area before discovering oil in their fifth test. In order to determine if there were enough oil reserves to justify solving the tremendous problems and great capital costs of moving it over the Andes to the Pacific Ocean, they made a multimillion-dollar gambling decision. Building temporary access roads through the jungle from one new drilling location to the next was not feasible. This is one of the world's greatest rainfall areas, averaging 250 inches a year. Torrential rains would wash out at night what had been built during the day. Consequently, the companies launched the most intensive helicopter operation in the world, outside the Vietnam War, to jungle-airlift men, equipment and supplies. When sufficient oil reserves were proved, Williams Brothers, the world's leading pipeline builders, began the monumental three-year job of laying the $52,000,000 194-mile pipeline, to move 100,000 barrels a day. Soon after its completion, when I followed the pipeline, by road and by helicopter, I understood why it has joined the list of man's greatest engineering feats since the building of the Pyramids and the Great Wall of China. Each awesome mile testifies to the Herculean battle of conquering nature from the jungles to the icy 11,000-foot peaks, through tortuous canyons and down to the ocean. Most of the pipeline was daringly laid by helicopter, as there were only a few mule trails in the mountains when work began. It took six years and a total expenditure of $250,000,000 for the Amazon Valley's first barrel of commercial oil to reach the Pacific in 1969. Owing to the construction of roads through the mountains for the pipeline, thousands of Colombians who had been living in comparative isolation for centuries, have been given access to towns and the incentive to produce and bring goods to market.

Texaco and Gulf expanded their exploration to the adjoining Amazon Valley jungles of Ecuador, finding even more prolific oil fields. The Williams Brothers tamed the Andes a second time, laying another almost equally difficult 250,000-barrels-a-day pipeline. Dozens of American, British, French and Japanese oil companies have joined the new Amazon exploration rush. Discoveries have been made in Peru, which expects to become an exporting country in 1976, when the state oil company finishes construction of still another trans-Andean pipeline.

As in the Arctic, only exploration and time will prove how many billions of barrels the Amazon Valley harbors. Exploration is difficult, slow and costly. The rate at which it expands depends also on how favorable the political climate is. Great sums of exploration capital will be risked only in proportion to the profit incentives provided. Ecuador, following a military revolution in 1972, the year its pipeline was completed, revised its oil laws and became a member of OPEC. It has followed OPEC policies in price and participation. Now, following Venezuela's lead, it has announced that it is in favor of more "conservative and cautious" development of Amazon Valley oil resources. Texaco and Gulf had planned to increase production to 400,000 barrels daily in 1975, but the government is restricting them to 250,000 barrels.

The world's biggest oil exploration surprise occurred in 1970, when the Phillips Petroleum Company announced it had made a major oil strike in Norway's offshore waters of the North Sea. A huge new oil province had been discovered in a 600-by-350-mile sea whose waves lapped the shores of some of the world's most oil-hungry nations—Great Britain, the Netherlands, Germany, Denmark and Norway. It has become the richest, busiest, most accessible target for big oil since the first Middle East discoveries. One giant field after another is being discovered. Probable reserves already are estimated at 40 billion barrels. Great Britain expects to achieve energy self-sufficiency by 1980 from its fields. The whole offshore region is expected to provide up to 50 percent of Western Europe's total requirements sometime between 1980 and 1985.

The North Sea exemplifies the unpredictability of oil exploration. Wells had been poked around the land fringes of the North Sea for forty years, discovering piddling little accumulations of oil or gas. It was not until 1959, when Holland's supergiant Groningen gas field was discovered, that geologists began to suspect the offshore area might be elephant-hunting country. In three years' time the industry has already turned up a third more oil than has been developed in the Gulf of Mexico in twenty-five years. North Sea drilling has been the industry's greatest technological challenge as it is the harshest offshore environment in the world, with men and equipment almost continually buffeted by 100-miles-per-hour winds and pounded with 95-foot waves.

The North Sea bonanza was welcomed as a politically safe source of supply, but it hasn't turned out that way. The governments, which protest so mightily about Middle East politics, are demonstrating that they themselves are blue-eyed Arabs. Government royalties and taxes have advanced as rapidly as the oil is found. The Dutch are demanding 40 percent participation, the Norwegians 80 percent. Prime Minister Harold Wilson's British Labor government recently announced it planned to nationalize the whole oil industry. This drew a public blast from Frank McFadzean, chairman of the Shell Transport and Trading Company, who said nationalization "would be about the most lunatic thing we could possibly do unless the Government wants to postpone production from the North Sea into the indefinite future." The government pulled in its horns a little and is now seeking higher taxes and participation in all new contracts. It has "invited" all companies operating in its North Sea to discuss participation in developed production since the oil companies have consented to it "in almost every other major oil-producing country in the world." The government also proposes to create the British National Oil Corporation to handle government investment and ultimately to go into refining and distribution. The German and Danish governments haven't tried to change their original contract agreements with the oil companies since they are still waiting for big oil to be found in their waters. The unwritten rule of the new oil exploration game is not to pluck the goose until after she starts hatching golden eggs.

The other great new prospective oil area in the non-Communist world is Southeast Asia, principally in its offshore waters. Indonesia sparked the boom by a dramatic change of political climate and the innovation of a new approach to reconciling the conflict between host governments and international oil companies. President Suharto put out the welcome mat for foreign private investment in 1966, following the overthrow of Communist power and influence of the Sukarno era. The nation was eager for new oil development to restore its ruined economy, and General Ibnu Sutowo, head of Pertamina, the state oil enterprise, had a dynamic new concept of how to achieve this. All foreign contracts had to be made with Pertamina, which General Ibnu, a medical doctor turned oilman, had built from a heap of scrap iron and a war-ravaged oil field into a rapidly expanding oil company. At his instigation Indonesia had joined OPEC in 1961, the year after it was formed. However, his studies of international oil politics and policies in the Middle East, together with the conflicts between the Sukarno government and established oil companies in Indonesia, convinced him that there was a better way for a nation to conduct its oil business than to haggle constantly over royalty percentages, taxes and posted prices. His idea was a brilliantly simple one—production-sharing contracts. Or, as he put it, "share oil, not money."

Indonesia has more than 2,000,000 square miles of unexplored, prospective oil areas, of which two-thirds are offshore. I was in Indonesia in 1967, when General Ibnu opened up this huge potential treasure chest for production-sharing contracts. A few independent oil companies leaped at the opportunity to sign, but there was no stampede of the big international majors because General Ibnu insisted that Pertamina retain management control of foreign contractors' operations. He was unruffled. "Now that I have established the principle of production sharing, they will all come," he predicted to me. "They will eventually realize that this formula establishes a genuine partnership where we can work together for mutual profit." His prediction was correct. Today 90 percent of Indonesia's prospective oil areas are under production-sharing

contracts to more than thirty foreign oil companies, including all the
international majors. The government share of oil is a minimum of
65 percent. From 1969 to mid-1974 there have been 135 major oil and
gas discoveries, and Indonesia's oil production has tripled. It is now
the world's eighth largest oil-exporting country. Oil's contribution
to government revenues has risen from 5 percent in 1966 to 60
percent in 1974, providing Indonesia with the means to become one
of the great success stories among developing countries. Furthermore, only 10 percent of its prospective oil area has been explored.
It is supergiant and giant hunting grounds.

General Ibnu has had a profound effect on shaping the new
international oil world. His production-sharing concept has been
followed by other nations in Southeast Asia which have offshore oil
potential—Malaysia, Thailand, South Vietnam and even India. It
has also become the pattern for new oil ventures in South America,
Africa and even the Middle East. He has developed Pertamina into a
unique billion-dollar, fully integrated oil company and pioneered a
successful model for other emerging national oil companies. Most of
all, he has proved that national and international oil companies can
work together creatively when there is a will to do so on both sides.

Although there are so many huge prospective oil areas in the
world, including the Middle East, which is not yet fully explored, it
will take decades to realize their potential. The risk, uncertainties
and high costs of oil finding combine with environmental and
political obstacles to produce one inescapable truth. Outside the
Middle East there is no place where there are yet sufficient proved
reserves to meet the current demands of a world depending on oil
for half its energy and expecting to double its consumption by 1985.
To meet the projected demand, Middle East governments would
have to double their current production by 1980 and triple it by 1985.
They have the capacity to do this, but it is unrealistic to expect them
to do so. They want to make their oil resources last as long as they
can stretch them out and, at the same time, receive the highest
possible prices.

Not even the Arabs are immune to the forces of supply and
demand—or cause and effect. By mid-1974 world oil production was
back to what it was prior to the embargo and cutbacks. *But* a world
surplus of almost 2,000,000 barrels a day had developed. Crude oil
was begging in the marketplace, and prices began to slip. The reason
was simple. Whopping high energy costs reduced consumption. The
consumer conserved because of his pocketbook. Industries and
governments had launched conservation programs. When OPEC

governments held auction sales of their oil, demanding at least 93 percent of their posted price, buyers stayed away in droves. The bids received were considerably below the demanded price. Algeria, Tunisia and Libya reduced their demands, but no lines formed.

The U.S. government submitted a report to the Energy Coordinating Group, formed by the thirteen consumer nations at the Washington conference, predicting that the world oil surplus would continue to grow through the first half of 1975, unless oil-producing countries cut their production to shore up weakening prices. At the same time Undersecretary of the Treasury Jack F. Bennett bluntly warned producing countries that production cutbacks would be regarded by the United States as "counterproductive." His original statement said cutbacks would be regarded as "unfriendly acts," but he changed it when the State Department pointed out that such terminology has a special diplomatic meaning, bordering on threats of war. Bennett also called for a rollback in foreign crude prices, saying that it was "the appropriate remedy" for solving current international monetary problems.

Rollback or cutback? That is the question. It is the heart of the confrontation between producing countries and consuming countries. Following the U.S. warning not to cut production, Secretary of the Treasury William E. Simon, who also heads U.S. energy policy, made a tour of Middle East countries with a dual purpose. He wanted to stimulate petrodollar investments in the United States, including buying billions of dollars of special U.S. Treasury bonds. He also was trying to persuade the governments to roll back prices. An incident occurred on his trip which dramatically showcased how little real bargaining power the consuming countries have. The day before Simon arrived in Kuwait, its government took action which meant a further increase in world oil prices. Kuwait had been infuriated by the lack of bidders for the state auction of its 60 percent participation share of oil produced by British Petroleum and Gulf. It forced the two companies to buy back half of the state participation oil for the last half of 1974 at 94.85 percent of posted price. This was an increase of almost 2 percent over the established buy-back price in the Gulf and meant that the other countries would leapfrog their prices, adding another $1 a barrel to the price of oil to consuming countries. Furthermore, Kuwait's Oil Minister announced that the auction system would be abandoned for the "safer system" of fixed selling prices. If there were no buyers for their barrels of oil, "we will keep them in the ground," he said. The Kuwait oil companies had no choice in the matter. The government told them that if they didn't do it, they might not receive any participation oil at all in the future.

As OPEC price attitudes stiffened and the world economic situation continued deteriorating, the United States once again sounded a strong alarm. In a September, 1974, speech at an international energy conference in Detroit, President Ford warned that the high oil prices set by producing nations brought "dangers of confrontation. . . . Sovereign nations cannot allow their policies to be dictated, or their fate decided, by artificial rigging and distortion of world commodity markets," he said. "No one can foresee the extent of the damage nor [*sic*] the end of the disastrous consequences if nations refuse to share nature's gifts for the benefit of all mankind." He stated further that "exorbitant prices can only distort the world economy, run the risk of worldwide depression and threaten the breakdown of world order and safety."

On the same day, Secretary of State Kissinger conveyed a similar warning to the United Nations General Assembly in a speech which received little applause. "Unlike food prices, the high cost of oil is not the result of economic factors, of an actual shortage of capacity or of the free play of supply and demand," he said. "Rather it is caused by deliberate decisions to restrict production and maintain an artificial price level." He added crisply, "What has gone up by political decision can be reduced by political decision."

The efforts of the consuming countries' governments to create a united front to persuade producing countries to be "reasonable" on prices will be a protracted war. Yet plans have been implemented since the February, 1974, hectic Washington conference in which the consuming countries decided to do something. A week following the Ford-Kissinger blast, the Energy Coordinating Group announced a draft of a proposal to create a new International Energy Agency as a long-term cooperative framework to deal with consuming countries' problems with OPEC. The countries would agree to an emergency oil-sharing system in case of cutbacks or embargos, to cut down consumption, to build up oil stockpiles for a ninety-day supply for each country, to work cooperatively with international oil companies and jointly to develop new oil sources. Unlike most international agencies, decisions would require only a majority vote, rather than a unanimous one. It is hoped, when the proposal is finally ratified by all consuming countries, that consumer solidarity and organized planning will strengthen their economic bargaining powers with producing countries and, at the same time, prove to be a deterrent for Arab use of oil again as a political weapon.

Still underlying all the economic uncertainties of the international oil scene are the dangerous petropolitical hazards which exist. The use of the oil dagger as a political weapon has been temporarily sheathed, but it can be used to stab the consuming countries at any time until the Arab-Israeli conflict is finally settled. Even the most optimistic diplomats do not foresee this occurring for another two or three years. Since the oil weapon proved so successful, consuming countries will live under the constant threat that it will be used politically at any time to achieve Arab objectives during the thorny, complicated peace negotiations that lie ahead involving emotional problems, such as the destiny of Jerusalem and the rights of the Palestinian people, which seem almost insurmountable.

The most astonishing part of Secretary of State Kissinger's extraordinary performance as Middle East peacemaker was the sudden blooming of improved Arab-American relations. However, the television lights don't reach all the dark corners. There is nothing more dangerous than a sore loser—particularly if it happens to be the Soviet Union. A year after the 1967 Arab-Israeli six-day war, I visited all the Arab countries and Israel to see what the war had done to American political and economic interests. I was appalled at what I found then and on subsequent trips. The continuing Arab-Israeli crisis enabled the Soviet Union to become an economic force in Middle East oil affairs for the first time in history. Although the Soviets have long been striving for political, economic and military influence in the strategic Middle East, the majority of the Arab world was oriented to the West. The 1967 war reversed that. The Soviets began to achieve a degree of penetration that would have aroused the envy of the czars, who tried to obtain control of the Middle East long before oil was discovered there. Economic and political advantages began falling into the Soviet lap like ripe apples. They didn't have to bother to shake the tree much. In Arab opinion, the Western world had abandoned the orchard.

The Soviets first made massive loans and barter deals with Iraq, to be repaid in oil, and supplied Iraq's state oil company with technical assistance and machinery to develop the international oil company holdings Iraq had expropriated. In rapid succession the Soviets also made exploration agreements with Egypt, Syria, Iran, Algeria and Libya. In addition to extending Soviet political influence, bartering for Arab oil freed more Soviet oil to be sold to Western European countries for greatly needed hard currencies. At the same time the Soviets were arming Arab countries—at a profit—and providing military training. Their gains on every score were tremendous, and their presence was overwhelmingly evident.

America's leading role in obtaining a cease-fire in the Yom Kippur war and its efforts to obtain a genuine settlement of the Arab-Israeli conflict are a severe setback to Soviet objectives and ambitions. The Russian bear's embraces are no longer so ardently welcomed. The Soviets have lost face throughout the Middle East because they had nothing to offer in helping the Arabs solve their problems through diplomacy. However, they still can provide the Arabs with unlimited arms for a military solution. Furthermore, since stability in the Middle East is the last thing the Soviets want to see, it is to their self-interest to use all their influence to obstruct any peace settlement and to keep the radical Arab countries as stirred up as possible. As history demonstrates, this is not a difficult task.

Also, Western diplomats have a new, major petropolitical worry. The huge accumulation of wealth in Arab countries and the dependence of the Western world on their oil resources has set a tempting stage for a Communist power play. Détente with the Soviets is still a fragile, sometime thing. Nineteenth-century political adventuring has not gone out of style as far as the Soviets are concerned and the potential to spark revolutions exists in almost all Middle East countries. If anything, the Soviets will be stimulated to make new plans to protect and expand their so recent penetration of the Middle East. The fantastic new economic stakes alone would keep the Kremlin power dreamers awake at nights.

As the Duchess told Alice, "Everything's got a moral, if only you can find it." When we look at the hard realities of the world oil situation, the moral for Americans is clear. Our economic and political security depends on having a workable national energy policy to develop energy self-sufficiency as soon as possible.

4

Profits, Politics and Policy

By the summer of 1974 the December to March gasoline lines were a blurred memory, as unreal as somebody else's nightmare. Nobody talked or thought about the energy crisis. Inflation and Watergate were the topics on everyone's tongue. When I asked a seasoned New York taxi driver if he thought we still had an energy crisis, he snorted derisively, "Who do you think you're kidding? We never did have one. The oil companies got what they wanted—high prices. That's what *that* was all about." This summed up, for the majority of Americans, the scenario of the energy crisis. They believed it from the beginning to what was seemingly the end.

Since the 1970–71 winter fuel oil crisis, oil companies had been accused by Congressmen and the media of "conspiracy" to create "artificial" shortages in order to raise prices and to eliminate independent dealers. The OPEC drama of producing countries' steadily increasing oil prices and raising their share of ownership in the companies wasn't box office for American audiences. As we squeaked through every summer gasoline and winter fuel oil crisis, and prices, along with volume of imports, continually rose, we kept putting the wrong carts before the wrong horses. The syndrome of warnings of an impending crisis, a price rise and then no shortage of supply lent itself to the simplistic diagnosis of conspiracy. However, oil company earnings remained virtually at a standstill from 1969 to 1973. In fact, they declined in 1972. But 1973 was a different story.

Mark Twain once remarked, "Few of us can stand prosperity. Another man's, I mean." There was a great outcry in July, 1973, when oil companies reported their net income for the first half of the year, and the thirty largest companies showed an average increase of 49 percent over the first half of the year before. The announcements, combined with the highly publicized prospective summer gasoline shortage, seemed to confirm oil profiteering, particularly since the industry and government managed to prevent shortages through a combined all-out effort. No sooner was this done than circumstantial evidence of "collusion" between international oil companies and Arab governments reached the height of

Mount Everest. The Arabs dropped their energy bomb at the same time oil companies announced third-quarter profit increases as high as 91 percent over the same quarter of the previous year. If there were any public doubting Thomases left, concerning oil "windfall profits," they disappeared when reports of fourth-quarter profits were again spectacular. According to the *Wall Street Journal*, oil industry earnings were up 63.1 percent over the same quarter in 1972. It was front-page news and the number one story on every television network. Actually, the earnings percentage increase of chain grocery stores, aluminum companies, and copper and other companies exceeded those of the oil companies in that quarter. But nobody was standing in line to buy food or metals, whereas every American motor vehicle driver was going through one of the most frustrating experiences in his personal history.

The oil companies were flabbergasted by the avalanche of public wrath, suspicion and demands for government action and retaliation against them which these events triggered. In trying to explain what had happened, they were as frustrated as the people waiting in gasoline lines. They held press conferences and launched newspaper, magazine and television advertising campaigns. The situation was too complicated. For the first time, people were listening, but they had little background to understand what was being said. How we had got to where we were through soaring consumption and the maze of interrelationships of national and international policies affecting the price of gasoline at the pump and oil company profits in annual reports couldn't be explained satisfactorily in a few paragraphs or a few minutes. The shorthand explanations were about as clear and understandable as if the oil companies were saying that two and five are four but five and two are six. Furthermore, by this time, the oil companies had all the credibility of a fat cat trying to persuade a colony of mice that he was a vegetarian.

The reason why the price-and-profit trauma was so severe was that up until now gasoline has been one of the most stable commodities of all those essential to our well-being. Between 1960 and the fall of 1973 the price of gasoline increased about 27 percent on average whereas all other commodities rose 53 percent, according to the Consumer Price Index put out by the U.S. government. Consequently, during the last thirteen years the price of gasoline increased only half as fast as the prices of other goods. Gasoline prices rose less than a half cent a gallon per year. Then the Arab oil embargo and the quadrupling of foreign oil prices by the

OPEC countries skyrocketed gasoline prices by 10 to 15 cents a gallon in a few months.

The confusion surrounding the sudden jump in prices at the pump was caused by the fact that the motorist had only a vague idea of who was getting what out of the price he was paying for a gallon of gasoline or where it came from. There had never before been a real reason to understand that the price of a gallon had to cover the costs of exploration, development, refining, transportation and distribution of oil both from U.S. sources and foreign countries; the royalties paid to U.S. landowners; the taxes paid to federal and state governments; and the royalties and taxes paid to foreign governments. Or that these costs also included the profit margins of the myriad different companies and individuals paid for products and services rendered in getting it from the ground to the pump—from a seismograph crew down to the independent service station owner. If it were possible to add up all the hundreds of thousands of people involved in getting a gallon of gasoline to the consumer, it would seem that it would have to command the price of Chanel Number Five—$1,600 per gallon—to do the job. In fact, consumer reaction to the price jump was much the same as if they were being charged by the ounce. Furthermore, gasoline was under government price control. So how could it jump so quickly?

Government regulations allowed oil companies to *pass along* the increased costs of raw material and purchased products to their customers, using May, 1973, prices as the base point. This is why prices jumped dramatically when the Arabs cut back world production and quadrupled the price of foreign oil. You can use as a rule of thumb that every $1 increase in the price of a barrel of crude oil translates into a 2.5-cent increase in the price of a gallon of gasoline. After OPEC price increases, a barrel of foreign crude oil landed in the United States was approximately $4 above the pre-embargo price, so that represented a 10-cent increase in the price of a gallon of gasoline refined from imported oil. Since one of every three barrels of oil consumed in the United States came from abroad, this cost was passed through to the consumer.

Domestic crude prices also increased, but not as sharply. Since 1971, U.S. production had been under government price and profit margin controls, but they applied only to oil being produced as of then. This was called old oil and represented three-fourths of our production at the time of the embargo. New discoveries and stripper production—wells producing 10 barrels daily or less—were noncontrolled. As gas lines began to form, the Cost of Living Council authorized a dollar increase in the price of old oil, making it $5.25 a barrel, to provide incentive to discover new supplies. This, of course, meant a 2.5-cent increase per gallon of gasoline. Because of the shortage of supplies, the price of uncontrolled oil increased by $4 a barrel to $10. So, in averaging U.S. production, there was about a 24 percent overall price increase. Then when you averaged in the imported oil increases, this accounted for about 7 cents of the extra 10 cents per post-embargo gallon gasoline price rise. However, service station dealers and jobbers, the majority of whom are independents, were affected by the reduction in sales volume, so the government permitted them to increase their prices 3 to 3.5 cents per gallon.

If it was difficult for the irate car owner to understand all this as he fumed, waiting for the "privilege" of buying $3 worth of gasoline, it was even more difficult to understand why gasoline prices differed so much from service station to service station and state to state. Oil companies buy different proportions of foreign and domestic crude and products. Consequently, they passed through different costs to their customers. Also, differences in prices of the same brand of gasoline at stations in the same neighborhood reflected the fact that price increases are regulated according to what a station was charging in May, 1973, when stations were in uncontrolled competition with each other.

These, then, were the facts behind the price jump. But what about the profits? They were being labeled "obscene," "indecent" and all similar words from the thesaurus. Nobody believed the major oil companies when they stoutly maintained that their profits averaged less than 2 cents on a gallon of gasoline. As a policeman friend of mine protested indignantly, "Even if the government did let them pass along price increases for the crude oil, it comes from their own wells, and they are making enormous profits at my expense! And I can't afford it!" He believed what almost everyone else did—that the money leaped from his pocket directly into the coffers of big oil companies. Those who had not been following the OPEC script did not realize that in the breakdown of a barrel of imported oil landed in the United States at a price of $11 to $12, $7 of that went to OPEC governments, 50 cents or less represented profits to the major oil companies in the country where it was produced, and the rest was the cost of handling and tanker charges. Since one-third of the gasoline sold at American pumps was made from imported oil, the major oil company profit on its foreign oil was less than half a cent a gallon.

Shell Oil Company made an analysis in March, 1974, based on its own operations, showing where each penny was going on the 11.9-cent-per-gallon gasoline price increase since August, 1973. It gives a representative picture of the "mix" for a major company. Ninety-eight percent of Shell service stations are operated by independent businessmen, and 3.5 cents was the amount the government allowed them to increase prices to compensate for reduced volume of sales. The increased cost of Shell's foreign oil, on which it made no additional profit, but was allowed to pass along, was 2.9 cents. The increased cost of the U.S. crude Shell purchased domestically, from independents and other oil companies, was passed along and amounted to 3.3 cents. The remaining 2.2 cents of the 11.9 cents-per-gallon increase was the only part involving additional profits to Shell. It produces a substantial amount of its own crude oil and was allowed to pass through, as higher cost for its refined products, the increased value allowed by the government on domestic crude oil. This 2.2 cents resulted in millions of dollars of additional revenue. However, much of it went for taxes and for the increased cost of doing business, leaving only a small fraction for greater profits. The average of 2.2-cents-per-gallon profit which the major companies made on gasoline in 1974 contrasts with the average 1.5-cents-per-gallon profit which they made in 1972.

The profits which so infuriated everyone were those reported in the quarterly and annual reports of the majors. These reports did not give an accurate picture of the whole industry. Majors buy almost a third of the oil they refine and distribute from the nation's 10,000 independent producing oil companies. This cost increase was passed through to the consumer. Independents, who find three-fourths of our oil, had been drowning in the Sargasso Sea of depressed domestic prices. The new high prices were like the arrival of a rescue squad. They began to plow back their profits in the most vigorous exploration program for new oil and gas sources the country had seen in fifteen years. In the second quarter of 1974 exploratory gas well completions were 70.5 percent higher, and exploratory oil well completions 61 percent higher, than during the same period in 1973.

The tendency to conclude that because gasoline prices were up and oil profits were up, therefore gasoline prices were responsible for profits, was a clear example of post hoc reasoning—"after this, therefore, because of this." The increased price of gasoline in a three-month period was by no means the main reason for the major companies' 1973 profit increase. There were a number of reasons why some of these profits, along with "record profits" of other American industries, were not real, but illusory.

Early in 1973 it became apparent that it would be a banner profit year for the oil industry. For the first time in a decade, oil company profits joined the parade of other American industries in showing the same average rate of growth of about 28 percent over the first quarter of 1972. The industry's poorest profit period for many years was 1972. It was now beginning to catch up. Demand for oil products throughout 1973 hit an all-time high worldwide. Production rates increased, as did world crude prices. Petrochemical operations recovered from a prolonged price recession and began contributing strongly to profits. The international majors ran their worldwide producing, transportation and refining facilities at, or near, capacity. The oil industry deals in the greatest volumes of materials of any industry in the world. Operations in nearly every phase of the business reached record highs, and increased sales at higher prices offset rising costs. The industry was congratulating itself that with profits returning to the levels achieved in former years, it could generate more capital to help meet the vast amounts of investment for expansion of energy sources and facilities so urgently needed to alleviate the American energy shortage. However, the rosebushes were full of thorns. Accusations by critics that the industry was contriving fuel shortages to drive up prices and increase profits mounted in proportion to improvement of profits.

When 1973 ended, it had lived up to the industry's expectations. A survey of 97 petroleum companies by New York's First National City Bank showed an average gain in earnings of 53 percent over the previous year. Other industries did well, too. The profits gain of 2,136 manufacturing firms surveyed by First National City Bank was 31 percent. The gain of 4,640 corporations in all industries was 23 percent. Some industries did better than oil. Lumber was up 73 percent, nonferrous metals 69 percent, paper 67 percent, metal mining 63 percent, and iron and steel 61 percent. Meat-packing had the same gain as oil. However, there was a big difference between oil industry performance and other domestic industries. The 30 largest oil companies reported that 75 percent of their increased revenues occurred outside the United States and 85 percent of the profits growth came from abroad.

There were two factors which made oil profits abroad seem higher than they really were. The devaluation of the dollar caused earnings in other currencies, when they were translated into dollars, to be much higher. For the 30 companies, an estimated 25 percent of the profit growth was due to this reason. Inflation was another factor. One-sixth of their "profits" was due to increased book value of their inventories of crude oil to reflect new higher prices.

Public reaction to what they considered exorbitant oil profits at the public expense put a brilliant spotlight on the manner in which *all* publicly owned companies—not only oil companies—present their earnings reports. They don't explain profits or their sources in a way which is easily understood by the layman. They are overanxious to prove that their profits are higher each quarter over the same quarter of the prior year in order to demonstrate what remarkable "growth" companies they are. All the dazzling and constantly increasing percentage "all-time-high," "we-broke-our-record" figures are aimed at convincing their shareholders and financial institutions how valuable their stock is or may become and what good credit risks they are to those who lend them money for expansion. This approach succeeds in companies setting themselves up as targets for public misunderstanding of their long-range economic situation and invites "knee-jerk" political action against them.

A more realistic way of understanding a company's profit picture is to look at how much each dollar of shareholders' equity, or net worth of the company, earned for the year. Shareholders' equity and net worth are the same. They represent the sum of all the company's stock (at the price at which it was issued), plus its accumulated retained earnings (meaning the profits not paid out as dividends to shareholders). To determine the amount of profit a company made on each dollar of shareholders' equity, or net worth, you divide the net income, after all taxes, for the year by the total shareholders' equity, or net worth. This gives the percentage of profit return or, as some call it, the return on equity investment. In other words, a 10 percent return on shareholders' equity, or net worth, means that for every $1 of equity employed in the business the company earned 10 cents. The return on net worth calculated by First National City Bank for the 97 petroleum companies showed that profit return on equity increased from 10.8 percent in 1972 to 15.6 percent in 1973, which was only slightly greater than the 14.8 percent average return of all manufacturing. However, over the last ten years the petroleum group averaged 11.8 percent compared with 12.4 percent for all manufacturing.

For the first time in their history, oil companies went to astonishing lengths to explain their earnings increases in annual reports and at annual meetings. In the midst of their explanations,

1974's first-quarter profits were announced. They fanned the flames of public suspicions of profiteering into a veritable holocaust. Profits of the 30 largest oil companies were up 78.4 percent over the same period of 1973. To their chagrin, the oil companies had been trapped by an inventory accounting procedure, used by most American business corporations, called "first-in, first-out." Translated, this means that when a company has merchandise in its warehouse and withdraws it to sell, it assumes that it is selling the merchandise that has been on the shelves the longest—first in, first out. When prices go up and sales are made from inventory which was acquired at a previous lower cost, then the difference is figured as a profit. However, this is nothing more than a book profit, because the additional revenues generated merely go to replace stocks at the new higher cost. Oil company inventories typically amount to twenty to forty-five days of a company's deliveries. Consequently, when OPEC jumped crude oil prices as of January 1, 1974, all the inventory oil, which had been acquired at a lower price, which was sold after Janary 1 was accounted for as being sold at the new prices, which produced an abnormal profit. It was a one-shot situation, as new inventories had to be acquired at the new higher prices for oil. Many financial analysts have long deplored this first-in, first-out accounting procedure as distorting the profit performance of American business to its disadvantage in the eyes of the public and the government during sharply rising inflation. At this point, nobody deplored the practice more than the oil companies. Wall Street and the investing public well understood what had happened. They understood that although the seemingly spectacular earning performance of oil companies was not realistic, the threat of punitive legislation which would affect future profitability was indeed real. They reacted accordingly in oil stock trading. Since the end of the third quarter of 1973, the price of oil company stocks declined sharply, much below the average overall stock market decline.

When I mentioned to my policeman friend that the oil industry had money problems, he exclaimed incredulously, "With all those profits? Impossible!" In these days, when the word "profits" is generally prefaced with the adjective "unconscionable" and has become symbolic of corporate greed and exploitation of the consumer, the role profits play in keeping our economy going doesn't command much attention. The word "profit" originally comes from the Latin *profectus,* meaning "progress." Without profits there is little progress and growth in the nation's standard of living. In 1973, more than 60 percent of the after-tax profits of American corporations was reinvested in business expansion and improvements. Of the remaining 40 percent, which was paid out in stockholder dividends, a great part was also reinvested in business. Large as oil industry profits seemed to the public, they did not seem nearly enough to oil company executives, who were looking at the staggering sums which had to be invested to supply future energy needs. They are actually worried about where the money's coming from.

At the same time sensational first-quarter oil company profits were making headlines the U.S. Treasury sent a paradoxical report to the House Ways and Means Committee, which was considering new tax legislation to boost oil taxes by $16.1 billion over the next six years. Even with such a major prospective increase in taxes, the Treasury Department expected domestic profits of U.S. oil companies to climb steadily above the 1973 level of $3.7 billion, with a cumulative increase of $31.1 billion by 1978. High as these profit figures might seem, the Treasury said they weren't high enough to meet the investment needs of the oil industry for the next decade. In order to achieve 83 percent self-sufficiency in oil by 1985, the Treasury estimated that the oil industry should be spending $26 billion a year, more than three times the 1972 level of $8 billion. According to Treasury calculations, even if all domestic oil goes to world prices of $10 a barrel, the industry will still have a cash-flow deficit of $4 billion annually relative to its capital requirements. Some of the required $26 billion annual expenditures could be borrowed, but the majority of the funds would have to be generated internally, in the opinion of the study. Crude oil price and profits would be the critical factors in the companies' capability of doing this. The Treasury's rule of thumb on price and profits is that every dollar of increased crude price will yield about 50 cents of after-tax profits to the corporate producer of existing oil. An independent producer, depending on his tax, would receive about 37 cents on the dollar. This doesn't take into account future increases in operating costs.

During 1973 the domestic oil industry plowed back $15 billion of profits in its first big expansion program in years. Industry capital spending budgets for 1974 were a record $19.5 billion, or nearly a 30 percent gain over 1973, according to the *Oil and Gas Journal*'s annual survey. The greatest part of this, $12.13 billion, will be spent to find and produce more oil. Refinery and petrochemical plant spending of $2.69 billion will be a record, more than in 1972 and 1973 combined. Another $2 billion will be spent on transportation, principally crude oil, products and natural gas pipelines. Capital projects for alternate fuels, such as shale, coal, nuclear and a variety of diversification efforts, show the largest gain of any sector, an 89 percent increase to $1.68 billion. The budgets were based on anticipated continued high earnings. Any price rollbacks and/or excess-profits taxes would, of course, reduce such spending.

Other factors which might limit oil company investments from profits were spotlighted in mid-1974, when Mobil announced plans to pay $800,000,000 in cash to acquire Marcor, Inc., the parent company of Montgomery Ward & Company and Container Corp. of America. This precipitated sharp governmental, Congressional and editorial criticism, accusing Mobil of diverting funds from oil and gas exploration to diversify its operations. Mobil had previously announced plans to spend a record $1.5 billion on oil expansion, more than half of which was slated to be spent in the United States, primarily in exploration for gas, oil and other energy sources. Herbert Schmertz, Mobil public affairs vice-president, explained that acquiring Marcor did not affect the company's oil plans. He said the decision was based "on a real concern over potential future restraints" on investment in U.S. oil and gas activities, in view of environmental opposition to offshore drilling, impending tax legislation and other legislative controls proposals. "We wonder whether we'll be permitted to invest as much as we'd like to in the U.S. oil business," he commented. "We felt we should make investments elsewhere to cover ourselves."

American international major oil companies are investing more profits in the United States than they are abroad, according to New York's Chase Manhattan Bank, which since 1945 has made an annual study of the financial performance of the world's thirty largest oil companies, twenty-six of which are U.S.-based. The group produces four-fifths of all the oil produced throughout the non-Communist world. In 1973 the thirty companies reinvested about $14.4 billions of profits worldwide, of which $7.6 billion, or more than half, was spent in the United States. This domestic spending was 12 percent higher than in 1972, while overseas spending rose 6 percent. During the past five years the thirty companies invested nearly two-thirds more money than they generated in profits. And in the United States they spent nearly twice as much as they earned. They were able to do this through net cash flow and borrowing.

In the furor over the abnormal 1974 first-quarter oil profits, it was not generally pointed out that the oil industry's capital expenditures were on a par with retained earnings, total profits or cash flow. The Chase group's total capital expenditures were nearly twice as large as a year earlier. But there was an extraordinary difference. In the first quarter of 1973 the group invested $1.3 billion in the United States and $1.4 billion in the rest of the world. However, in the same period in 1974 it spent $3.2 billion in the United States and $1.6 billion elsewhere. The group earned only 31 percent of its worldwide profits in the United States but allocated 66 percent of its overall capital spending to the United States. Consequently, its capital expenditures in the United States were two and a quarter times as large as its profits.

Achieving near self-sufficiency in energy in the United States depends on greatly increased new investments in the oil industry during the critical transition period while alternate energy sources are being developed to come into play by the end of the century. This is the real significance of the historical relationship between profits and capital expenditures and the importance of generating profits. Domestically, as well as worldwide, there is a tremendous gap between the capital needs of the oil industry to meet energy demand and its ability to generate the necessary funds. Chase estimates that capital investment and other financial requirements of the industry worldwide during the 1970–1985 period will total $1.35 trillion. The bank estimates that the industry can raise $695 billion of this through loans, sales of securities, depreciation and depletion allowance. Profits must supply the remaining $655 billion. However, this means profits will have to grow at an 18 percent average annual rate, more than double the 8 percent growth rate over the 1955–70 period. "In the light of political realities, it may be impossible to achieve," the bank study reports. "Within the ranks of government in many nations of the world, there is an extensive failure to recognize that profits must necessarily be the major source of the funds needed for capital investment. And, for that reason, there is the likelihood that political actions may restrain the growth of profits."

If the oil industry can't generate the necessary capital, investments will not be made, and the world will be progressively short of oil. The study pointed out that alternate sources of energy would not be available since they also depend on adequate capital investment made from profits.

No one reflected soberly on such matters during the turbulent confusion of the gas lines. There was a mass hysteria surrounding the anguished disruption of America's love affair with its automobiles. Cars almost became more important than people, and a gallon of gasoline more precious than blood plasma. The crisis began to peak when Congressmen were at home during Christmas vacation for their seasonal voter pulse taking. The message was loud and clear. Their enraged constituents were convinced that the whole mess was a gigantic hoax and were clamoring for the perpetrators of the plot to be drawn and quartered.

When Congress convened in January, 1974, it was in a punitive mood. It was also running a higher political fever than any Congress in history. The Watergate crisis was rapidly moving from investigation to impeachment hearings.

A blizzard of energy and energy-related bills in the Senate and the House quickly totaled more than 3,000. They were concerned with emergency and long-range problems. They covered every phase of the energy problem and represented a bewildering variety of contrary and opposing political solutions to everything.

However, what made the news were the immediate investigations launched on whether or not there really was an energy crisis, who was to blame and why. Presidential aspirant Senator Henry M. Jackson, Democrat of Washington, had the front seat on the bandwagon. As chairman of the Senate Interior Committee he had already grabbed energy-policy leadership in Congress through his two-year national fuels and energy study and the previous year's investigations into fuel and gasoline shortages. He wore another spectacular hat as chairman of the Senate Permanent Subcommittee on Investigations. In this capacity, he launched the first hearings in January to get what he called "a full and honest account of the shortage situation."

For a second time, using the new Watergate-style television theatrics, Senator Jackson staged an extraordinary spectacle which did more to confirm public suspicions than it did to get at the facts. He summoned executives of the nation's seven largest oil companies, representing half the U.S. oil industry's sales, to the same big marble Senate Caucus Room where Watergate witnesses had been grilled. The seven oil officials, representing Exxon, Texaco, Mobil, Standard of California, Shell, Standard of Indiana and Gulf, were lined up under television lights, behind a long witness table confronting the Senators. They were asked to rise and jointly to take an oath to tell the truth. After this the Senate panel took up the first hour in alleging that the energy crisis was contrived, the shortage exaggerated and inventory figures demonstrated that there was no shortage at all. When questioning of witnesses began, the atmosphere was hostile. The oilmen denounced the charges as completely erroneous. Interchanges between them and the Senators became acrimonious. The Senators were openly skeptical and dissatisfied with answers.

The oilmen had been told to be prepared to answer questions primarily concerned with supply, transportation and inventories and had been selected for their expertise in these fields. But the Senators quickly broadened the field of inquiry. They bombarded them with questions about pricing, profits, marketing, foreign tax credits, and the role of U.S. companies' negotiations with OPEC. None of the witnesses was prepared for such an onslaught.

An angry Senator Jackson demanded they produce documents to show whether Saudi Arabia forced the owner companies of Aramco to stop selling oil to the U.S. military when forces were put on alert. He termed such an act a "flagrant case of corporate disloyalty." Senator Abraham Ribicoff, Democrat of Connecticut, accused the companies of cheating and "reaping the whirlwind of 30 years of arrogance" in taxes and other matters. He charged they "misled the American people" and deliberately "created a panic situation" to freeze out small independent companies. Both he and Jackson claimed industry and company data reporting was confusing and unreliable.

When Senator Jackson asked Roy A. Baze, senior vice-president of Exxon, how much of Exxon's 1973 profit per share had been paid in dividends, he could not remember or find the figure among his papers but said the amount was public information. "That's a childish response to tell us it's public information," Senator Jackson exclaimed. He accused Baze of coming to the hearings poorly prepared and said, "I can get the information in five minutes." Grandstanding for the television cameras, he went to a staff telephone in the chamber and called a local stockbroker for the figure.

At the end of the three-day hearings, oilmen were bitter about their treatment. David Bonner, president of the Gulf Oil Company, U.S., held a press conference in which he angrily stated that the hearings were run like a "criminal trial" and "went beyond the ethics of fair play." In addition to being chastised, the oil executives were made to appear evasive and unknowledgeable. Committee hopscotch tactics from subject to subject prevented any logical, credible development of facts. Senatorial rhetoric simply confirmed public belief that there was no real shortage, despite the fact that

Senator Jackson conceded that the hearings failed to show a conspiracy to create one.

Oil company credibility was already nonexistent before the nationally televised hearings. We had been exposed to a barrage of sensational circumstantial evidence accusing the oil industry of creating the shortage. On television we saw all those tankers lined up off the East Coast and were told that "supposedly" they were waiting for prices to rise. Nobody believed oil company explanations that it was normal tanker traffic waiting for berths. Subsequently, when Coast Guard, U.S. Naval Intelligence and CIA investigations confirmed this truth, it was no longer a newsworthy item. When the Shah of Iran asserted, in a Mike Wallace CBS television program, that the oil companies had engineered the gasoline shortage to increase their profits, few people realized that the shah was doing a public relations whitewash on his own role in being the chief architect in raising world oil prices.

Among other reasons, the public didn't believe the oil industry was telling the truth because of its secrecy in withholding information concerning supply, distribution and price statistics. In California a joint committee of the state legislature voted contempt citations against Standard of California, Union, Exxon, Mobil and Texaco for refusing to comply with subpoenas demanding information on how they set oil prices in California. State officials in New York, New Jersey and Connecticut served subpoenas on oil companies and distributors seeking data to determine if the shortage was real. New York State Attorney General Louis J. Lefkowitz called a grand jury which held extended hearings. Ultimately, the jury did not explicitly charge the oil companies with conspiring to create fuel shortages but charged that the companies had access to each other's inventories and knew in advance there would be a shortage and did not produce sufficient products for consumers "even though the industry at that time possessed the over-all capability" to do so.

The oil companies initially maintained that supply, distribution and price statistics were confidential trade secrets, the disclosure of which would be highly prejudicial to any company forced to provide them. Congress was vociferous in its criticism of such secrecy. Obviously, in a competitive society there must be some degree of confidentiality, but public opinion now took precedence in these particular matters. Texaco was the first company to make public its supply statistics. Other companies followed suit. Major companies in California voluntarily provided information to the legislature.

Subsequently, the Federal Energy Office audited refinery inventories and announced, several months later, that there was no evidence that the major oil companies had lied. However, by that time few people were listening.

All industry data became suspect, and the information problem was the subject of hearings by the House Select Committee on Small Business. Government petroleum data are based primarily on industry-gathered material, all of it voluntary. Oil industry witnesses testified that the companies would welcome a government-sponsored data-collection system, as long as there were adequate safeguards for proprietary information. Congress had already given the Federal Energy Office authority to require mandatory data from the industry, but the agency wants legislation for specific requirements and to expand its authority to all other energy sources.

Congressional investigations proliferated at such a rate that the Senate Democratic Conference even named a committee to determine whether one committee should be named to conduct all the probes. Senator Daniel K. Inouye, Democrat of Hawaii, said, "It's become quite clear to all of us that we have become totally confused. We have to convince the people of the United States that we haven't lost our heads and to bring some semblance of order."

Nowhere was Congressional confusion more evident than in the prolonged efforts of the Senate and House to pass an Emergency Energy Act to give the administration authority it requested in November, 1973, for rationing, mandatory conversion and switching electric utilities from oil to coal and other conservation powers. It was easy to agree quickly on separate emergency legislation to reduce national speed limits to 55 miles an hour and make Daylight Saving Time year-round, but the issues of how broad or narrow the administration's full emergency powers should be bogged down in partisan political squabbling. Congress adjourned for Christmas with no action. When it reconvened, OPEC had zoomed oil prices, a quarter of U.S. oil supply, not under price control, had almost doubled from $5.25 a barrel to $10.35, 1973's final-quarter oil company profits were released, and the gas lines had formed. It was a new political ball game with the bill being tossed back and forth between the House and the Senate. Congressmen vied with each other to see how many different types of amendments could be added from slicing profits to giving federal help to people needing storm doors.

Senator Jackson was the chief sponsor of an amendment to roll back the price of all domestic crude oil to the $5.25 controlled base for "old oil." This became the heart of the controversy. "The American people are having their pockets emptied while oil company profits are going up and up," he proclaimed. "These enormous excess profits being raked in by the oil giants who so much influence our lives have to be controlled—because the money is being gouged right out of the American workingman."

The viewpoint of those opposing a rollback was summed up by Senator John Tower, Republican of Texas. "The government should not be permitted to control excess profits when it hasn't the foggiest notion of what it is trying to control," he said. "Neither I nor any other legislator knows what 'excess profit' means in the context of the oil industry." He pointed out that passing such legislation without the details of oil industry profit being studied by an appropriate Congressional committee "would constitute the most intolerable irresponsibility." Since the answer to the energy crisis is to increase domestic fuel supplies, he strongly believed increased profits would stimulate investment to do so.

The administration was opposed to the mandatory rollback, which it considered inflexible. Despite a Presidential veto threat, the "emergency" bill passed the Senate, 67–32, on February 19, after the Senate rejected three attempts to send it back to the Senate–House conference committee to be rewritten for the second time in three weeks. On February 27, the House approved the bill, 258–151, but was fifteen votes short of a two-thirds majority needed to override a veto. On March 6 President Nixon vetoed the bill, announcing at a press conference that although the nation's fuel shortage was still a serious problem, "the crisis has passed." Two hours after the veto, the Senate sustained it, 58–40, eight votes short of the required two-thirds majority to override it.

Senator Jackson was not about to give up the rollback fight. He said he would discuss a new "bare bones" energy bill with House members and Federal Energy Office officials, to cover the "emergency" provisions. But, he added, "We'll put a little of our own meat on those bare bones." The meat on the jointly introduced Senate–House bill turned out not to be a mandatory price rollback, but a price-control system to be imposed on all domestic and imported crude oil and refined products, without specifying the prices. It also limited the "pass-through" costs on imported crude only to increases in foreign taxes and royalties. Members of the House decided the meat wasn't fleshy enough, and amendments were added which would have rolled back crude prices to November

1, 1973, levels. After much debate in the House, the bill did not even receive a simple majority when it finally came to a vote on May 21. Even if the Senate eventually passed the bill, it would be sent back to the House for burial. Members of Congress no longer considered the shortage and high prices a major political issue. Nor did the bill's "emergency" authorities for rationing and conservation, originally requested six months previously, seem so urgent.

No group was more apprehensive or concerned about the possibility of a price rollback, or lobbied more vigorously against it, than the country's 10,000 independent oil producers. Public and Congressional wrath against profits and prices was aimed primarily at the big oil companies. But the independents, who find three-fourths of our oil, and produce a third, were having their first boom in fifteen years owing to higher prices which began to rise in 1973. Like the majors, they were pouring their money back into expansion, and practically all of it was going into exploration for new oil and gas. The success rate for new-field wildcats in the United States climbed to an all-time high in 1973, and the percentage of discoveries among all exploratory holes was the highest in almost twenty years, according to the American Association of Petroleum Geologists' annual review. Success rate for all exploratory holes hit 20.53 percent in 1973, as compared to 1968's low of 14.56 percent. The association stated the high rate of completions among exploratory holes was due to the new higher prices of oil and gas. Wildcats which once would have been uneconomical to complete were now profitable. Independents found more than 80 percent of the new oil in 1973.

During the first six months of 1974, total drilling completions were 21 percent higher than the same period the previous year. It was the highest second quarter for drilling since 1966.

If Senator Jackson had his way in rolling back domestic crude oil prices, "he could prove to be the worst enemy the American oil consumer and the small business man has in Congress," C. John Miller, Michigan oilman and president of the Independent Petroleum Association of America, charged. "A rollback would curtail already inadequate petroleum supplies and impose disastrous supply restrictions and unnecessary suffering on the consuming public."

Independents were reworking shut-in and abandoned wells and bringing them back to life, including old wells in Pennsylvania, where America's first oil was discovered more than a century ago. They were poking down holes in old, supposedly worn-out areas and finding new oil and gas. Texas Independent Producers & Royalty Owners Association estimated that if there were a price rollback, 3,000 to 5,000 additional wells that would have been started in the United States in 1974 would not be drilled. The 275,000 000 barrels of oil that could be developed from discoveries from these wells would not be produced. Secondary-recovery projects feasible at new prices would not be worthwhile under a rollback. As independents pointed out, the consumer-oriented vote-getting politics of trying to associate price rollback with the consumer's best interest would soon backlash. Any reduction in domestic crude oil supplies would have to be replaced by higher-priced foreign oil. This would accelerate our overdependence on foreign oil. We would head in the opposite direction of self-sufficiency.

The aroused independents also spearheaded the drive to fight proposed tax legislation, which, like a price rollback, would greatly reduce the amount of risk capital available to them for expansion of their efforts. If Benjamin Franklin were still with us, he would undoubtedly expand his famous statement "Nothing is certain but death and taxes" to include "and the battles *over* taxes in the American Congress." The Ninety-third Congress, mindful of November elections, engaged in one of the most strenuous battles yet over politically acceptable new tax measures to satisfy the voters that Congressional watchdogs would never permit the oil companies to profit unwarrantedly at their expense. This time the battle was not *whether* to tax the oil industry, but how much and by what means.

The opposing forces were generally drawn up along traditional lines—liberal tax reformers vs. conservatives, East Coast "consumer" Congressmen vs. oil-producing states' Congressmen, Republicans vs. Democrats. However, the battle was complicated by party politics, power struggles and much political posturing. Senator Jackson stated the attitude of many Congressmen when , in a speech to the Manufacturing Chemists Association, he said, "Personally, I am opposed to an excess profits tax, but it's a good platform to run on."

There were three major issues: taxing excess, or "windfall," profits; eliminating or reducing the percentage depletion tax allowance which permits oil producers to deduct 22 percent of their gross income from their taxable income, up to a limit of half their net taxable income, in order to provide exploration risk capital funds; and eliminating or changing the foreign tax credit, under which the international oil companies subtract directly from their

U.S. tax bill the taxes they pay foreign governments in order to avoid double taxation. Both these tax provisions have been consistently attacked over the years as "bonanzas" and "loopholes."

Trying to put an energy tax package together, encompassing these issues, precipitated bitter struggles in both the House and the Senate. There was intensive lobbying by oil and gas associations, consumer groups and labor unions. The focal point of the controversy was the fate of the percentage depletion tax allowance. After months of party fights, the powerful House Ways and Means Committee, chaired by Representative Wilbur Mills, Democrat of Arkansas, completed action in April on a bill to raise oil industry taxes by more than $16 billion over six years, primarily by phasing out the depletion allowance tax provision and imposing an excess profits tax. However, the oil producers would have the option of plowing the money back into new exploration and development instead of paying it in taxes to the government. On foreign oil, beginning when the bill passed, companies would be prohibited from crediting more than 52.8 percent of foreign income, if paid to foreign governments as taxes, against their U.S. taxes, even if the foreign tax rates are higher.

Like all compromises, the bill pleased very few in government and industry. However, the fact that for the first time in fifty years the death knell of depletion allowance had been sounded encouraged zealous liberal tax reformers to make an all-out try to eliminate it immediately and even make the elimination retroactive to January 1, 1974. Their strategy offended Chairman Mills, who promptly persuaded House leaders to postpone any action at all on the legislation.

Major oil companies and independents were united in opposition to phasing out or repeal of the percentage depletion allowance, which would prevent industry expansion and dry up sources of risk capital. The Independent Petroleum Association obtained data in a confidential survey of 123 of its members, with gross income from oil and gas operations of $625,460,367, to determine the impact of legislation to repeal percentage depletion. The survey was reported to Treasury Secretary William E. Simon and showed that repeal would reduce cash flow by 35 percent, but the impact would be even greater than the figure indicated. Tax returns, filed by the 123 operators showed they had plowed back 99.4 percent of the depletion allowance deduction into exploration and drilling. If depletion were repealed, they would have no internally generated funds left, after equipping new wells, for acquiring leases, geological and geophysical expenses, repayment of debt or payment of dividends. Substantial borrowing or reduction in drilling would be required merely to equip new producing wells. "Hence," the report concluded, "the only logical alternative for most oil and gas operators would be to curtail drilling, pay tax on the funds available because of reduced drilling, and use the net funds for other capital expenditures in their oil and gas business or make alternative investments outside the oil and gas industry."

As one independent oilman friend of mine pointed out, "Nobody in his right mind is going to borrow money to risk in wildcatting, and nobody in his right mind, outside the oil industry, is going to invest risk capital if he doesn't have the lure of a tax break. If the nation wants to increase its oil supply, let's at least leave the incentives alone until we get the supply we need."

Independent oil producers, with the exception of a few large ones, had no interest in tax proposals reducing the foreign tax credits for oil companies operating abroad. The arguments of the international majors that such a cut would weaken their competitiveness in the world market, increase the outflow of dollars for oil imports, cut foreign earnings, dangerously reduce import sources and depress U.S. refining construction owing to lack of secure access to foreign oil fell on deaf and unsympathetic ears. It was difficult enough to get a hearing on tax consequences for domestic oil operations. There were no Congressional tears shed over the problems of the international majors, whose profits had prompted the universal voter outcries. From the viewpoint of Congress and consumers, the interdependence of the international and national oil situation was still unexplored territory. The feverish Washington political atmosphere was not yet conducive to looking at the energy problem in all its interrelated aspects.

While politicians in the House were maneuvering themselves into a Mexican standoff on energy tax legislation, on the Senate side liberal tax reformers were staging their own drama. The tax reformers, led by Senator Hubert H. Humphrey, Democrat of Minnesota, Senator Edward M. Kennedy, Democrat of Massachussetts, and Senator Walter F. Mondale, Democrat of Minnesota, launched a bold maneuver to bypass Senator Russell Long's Finance Committee and get the Senate to vote on eliminating the depletion allowance. They put the elimination in a tax package which would have made a $6 billion cut in individual income taxes and tried to get the package attached as an amendment to a critically needed bill increasing the federal debt ceiling. Even some of the greatest foes of depletion allowance were opposed to this tactic, and the liberal forces were soundly trounced.

Although all of us have been well educated about what goes on in the White House's Oval Office, we have less opportunity to know about the wheeling and dealing, maneuvering and trade-offs of our elected representatives in Congress. When we read that a bill passes Congress, we have little idea of how or at what political expense. In the midst of public concern about the energy crisis, when the Senate voted 82–0 for Senator Jackson's bill to provide $20 billion of federal funds for energy research and development to increase energy supplies in the next ten years, it reads like a big step forward in doing something to solve our problems. Few people realized how such a unanimous vote was achieved or that it had any connection with the Senate's *not* acting on decontrolling the price of new natural gas contracts at the wellhead to encourage new exploration.

Interior Secretary Rogers C. B. Morton had sent a letter to every Senate member urging decontrol of new gas sales as "the quickest, most efficient, and most effective solution to the natural gas shortage." Senator James Buckley, Republican of New York, lobbied among his colleagues to obtain support of an amendment to this effect to be attached to Jackson's upcoming pet project—the research and development bill. Buckley lined up 42 votes for the natural gas amendment. When Jackson learned this, he went into action. He advised Buckley that he could try to test Senate reaction to decontrol, but that if he did, Jackson would retaliate by introducing amendments to put the Tennessee Valley Authority in the oil and gas business worldwide with tax money competing with private firms, extend federal control to intrastate gas sales, bar electric utilities from using natural gas, impose an excess profits tax of 50 percent of the earnings above the 1963–73 average return and, finally, disallow foreign depletion and foreign tax credits to any company subject to the excess profits tax. The conservative Senator Buckley was appalled at this barrage of threats, which, if carried out, would have opened up an incredible can of political worms squirming in every direction. To prove he meant business, Senator Jackson and members of his staff called officials of the American Petroleum Institute and the American Gas Association to tell them what he was going to do and recommended that they discourage Senator Buckley from insisting on a vote on decontrolling new natural gas sales. When Buckley started counting his Senate supporters again, he found ten of them had disappeared and his amendment would be a lost cause. Consequently, Jackson's research and development bill serenely passed 82–0, with no amendments proposed. Proponents of decontrol lost their best opportunity, as from then on, Congressional sentiment mounted for more controls rather than less.

However, decontrol advocates managed to win a negative victory. They stopped a drive to extend federal regulation of natural gas wellhead prices, which is confined to interstate sales, to include intrastate sales, to regulate the oil industry as a public utility and to put the government in competition with the oil industry. These proposals were part of a package bill appealingly titled "The Consumer Energy Act of 1974." Its principal backers were the Democratic majority of the Senate Commerce Committee, led by Senator Adlai E. Stevenson III, Democrat of Illinois, freshman member of the committee, and Senator Warren G. Magnuson, Democrat of Washington, the chairman. As Magnuson allowed Stevenson to preside over hearings on the bill, it became known as "the Stevenson bill."

The essence of the bill was to regulate all prices of crude oil, natural gas and refined products of major oil companies. Independents would be exempt in order to encourage them in their historical role of finding three-fourths of the nation's oil. However, as a yardstick to measure the private sector's results, it would set up the Federal Oil and Gas Corporation, known as FOGCO, to compete with private firms.

Every aspect of this plan to restructure totally the nation's oil and gas business was met with tremendous opposition from the administration, industry, producing states, bankers and economists. The most indignant protesters were the very people whom the bill was supposed to benefit—the independents. C. John Miller, Independent Petroleum Association president, called it "a hoax that attempts to mislead both producer and consumers." He said that the bill would reduce drilling and "decimate what is left of the independent" segment of the industry.

The idea of FOGCO's providing a "yardstick" for performance, prices and profits of private industry when prices would be controlled was a contradiction in itself. Nor would FOGCO stimulate new enterprise. It would be financed by unlimited interest-free government funds, would not need to show a profit, would get the best leases from the nation's 50 percent of prospective oil lands which are federally owned and would have advance access to geological and geophysical information for which private firms spend millions. Private companies could not compete against such a "yardstick." Furthermore, as Treasury Secretary Simon pointed out wryly, in commenting on the chances of success of a federal oil company, "Can't you imagine a fellow going to the appropriations committee asking for more money after drilling his thirty-first dry hole?"

Radical as the Stevenson bill proposals were, they were taken seriously enough in the hostile mood of Congress toward the oil industry, that one-fourth of the 100 Senators said they were willing to cosponsor the legislation when it eventually came out of the committee.

Beginning immediately after the embargo and throughout the Ninety-third Congressional session, intermittent hearings of the Senate Foreign Relations subcommittee on multinational corporations provided a series of intermezzo performances to the national energy drama. The subcommittee chairman, Senator Frank Church, Democrat of Idaho, another Presidential aspirant, billed the subcommittee's probe as lifting the "curtain of secrecy" which "enveloped the government-industry relationship concerning international oil," leading to the "most far-reaching suspicions" in the public mind.

The secrets turned out to be not all that secret. But the hearings developed a great deal of significant information concerning the need for government to formulate a new foreign policy concerning international oil supply and prices and what the respective roles of the U.S. government and international oil companies should be in the future.

Throughout the hearings Church made no secret of his purpose in holding them. He was, he said, establishing "a record that will demonstrate that, in the future, government cannot be indifferent to the business consequences of negotiations so important as those that entail the supply of oil to the Western world and must play not only an informed role but a much more direct role; that this is not a matter that can be left to business, to the oil companies themselves to negotiate."

The hearings, much to the subcommittee's own surprise, laid to rest a number of myths surrounding the energy crisis. Church had invited Dr. Robert B. Stobaugh, Harvard University professor of business administration, to analyze the costs and benefits to the United States of the foreign operations of U.S. oil companies, especially the big five—Exxon, Mobil, Texaco, Standard Oil of California and Gulf. He was asked to focus specifically on their role during the crisis period from October, 1973, through March, 1974. Dr. Stobaugh's study revealed that the crisis was worldwide and the United States lost a slightly greater proportion of its total oil supply and of its total energy supply than the average for the rest of the world; that, in the absence of any accord between consuming governments, the oil industry allocated oil to all markets as a percentage of demand; that there was no evidence that the United States was systematically charged more or less than other countries; that in some cases, but not always, crude oil was supplied to nations, including the United States, at a lower price than could have been obtained elsewhere and the oil companies made shipments into the United States that they might have more profitably sold elsewhere; and that the Arab boycotts were effective—more than 98 percent of the Arab oil the U.S. had been receiving was lost, but the oil companies managed to reshuffle supply patterns worldwide to provide as much oil as possible, on a proportionate basis, to the consuming countries.

"In spite of obeying the producing nation's orders," Dr. Stobaugh said, "the companies still managed to negate the apparent interest of the orders—which was to punish some nations and reward others. For in the end, there is no evidence that the nations deemed to be 'friendly' by the Arabs got a larger share of available oil than the 'unfriendly' ones." He attributed the ability of the top managements of the oil companies "to cope with the constraints and pressures" to the use of their giant computer facilities, which in normal times enable them to allocate the flow of international oil to maximize profits, but during the crisis were put to work to handle the emergency.

Dr. Stobaugh pointed out that despite pressures brought on the companies by individual consuming countries, the companies resisted them. "The oil companies have some leverage in negotiating with the consuming nations," he said. "For example, during the embargo the companies told the Dutch and Italian governments and others that crude oil would be shipped elsewhere if product exports to the United States were blocked."

Contrary to what Senator Church was trying to prove, Dr. Stobaugh considered the role of the U.S. international oil companies a beneficial one. "During normal times they are efficient in the operation of their worldwide networks," he said. "During a time of severe shortages, the United States could have a more assured supply of oil than if it were depending solely on oil companies headquartered abroad." He also pointed out that "the fact that U.S.

companies control an important share of the world's oil could give the United States more power in attempting to arrange an international sharing agreement for use in an emergency. The issues are complex and the supply of oil important. Thus, we should ensure that if legislation reduces the foreign activities of the U.S. oil companies, including the majors, then something is available in their place to meet U.S. needs."

Senator Church's big "secret" was to force the State Department to declassify the full text of the Libyan Producers Agreement of 1971. This so-called safety net agreement, which had been approved by both the State and Justice departments, was the insurance policy for the independent oil companies operating in Libya that participated in joint negotiations with the majors in the 1971 Teheran price agreement. Its purpose was to enable them to withstand the Libyan government's thumbscrew tactics since if any independent's production was cut back, the majors agreed to share their Libyan crude pro rata, supply Gulf crude or pay the victim 10 to 25 cents a barrel, depending on the circumstances. The existence of such an agreement had been generally known since it was made, but its details had been kept secret primarily in order not to jeopardize the companies operating in Libya by exposing them to the unpredictable Colonel Qaddafi's reprisal instincts.

The Church committee probed deeply into all the past history and circumstances surrounding oil company joint negotiations in Teheran, which led to the five-year price agreement, lasting two and a half years until OPEC tossed it out and acted on prices unilaterally; into the Libyan negotiations, which led to expropriations and nationalizations; into the part the State Department played in both helping and hindering events; and into the antitrust clearances given by the Justice Department to the companies to enable them to present a solid front. Almost all the testimony presented had been public knowledge from the day it happened. There was nothing of substance that had not been reported in press reports at the time, oil industry trade journals or such publications as *Foreign Affairs*. I, of course, had followed all these events closely both on the scene and through my association with the principal participants. I learned little that was new from following the Church hearings in detail except some gossipy tidbits of who said what to whom when, which Libyans threw what papers in whose face and lengthy, tedious details of how the negotiations proceeded. Business "secrets" as a whole are terribly boring in retrospect. Confidentiality is generally important only at the time. The Church hearings generated headlines in 1974, which the events did not command when they happened, simply because the negotiations, relationships, and reasons for them were plucked out of the context of the past and showcased in the present as "news" because of the energy crisis. They supposedly substantiated devious dealings, not in the public interest, in support of the conclusion the public had already jumped to—that there had to be a plot and a conspiracy, or else something as mysterious as the energy crisis couldn't possibly have happened.

Of all the Congressional hearings, the testimony of government and industry witnesses at the Church hearings had the most important and realistic bearing on why and how oil prices rose domestically and worldwide so quickly and dramatically. Anyone who was there or who had patience to read them had the opportunity to learn that this was so. However, few people spend their leisure reading time curled up with copies of the green-bound U.S. government volumes of full texts of Congressional hearings as a substitute for the works of Agatha Christie or Jacqueline Susann.

Technically, economically and logistically the operations of the international oil industry are extremely complicated. To understand a part, you must necessarily understand the whole. The Senators—and the media—found it hard going despite the plethora of charts and explanations. The subcommittee's staff had prepared a "Glossary of Terms Relating to the Petroleum Industry" to guide them. In addition to marketing and transportation terminology, it was replete with sketches of how oil is trapped in the rocks and is produced, providing, it was hoped, a crash course in geology and petroleum engineering. Senatorial frustration was summed up at one point by Senator Clifford P. Case, Republican of New Jersey. After questioning one witness he commented, "You have answered the questions I have sense enough to ask now."

There was a real communications problem between the Senators and the witnesses, but an even greater one as far as public understanding of what was being discussed. The lack of continuity and the spacing of the hearings prevented any logical presentation of what had happened in the past or why. Furthermore, the television and newspaper media excerpted and abbreviated only that material which had headline value. There was seldom any interpretative background or follow-up. Senator Church gave his own summaries of what took place in examining witnesses in executive session. When he released full texts later, the whole story was no longer news. A good example was the testimony of George C. McGhee, originally a geologist and independent oilman, who in 1949 became a State Department career diplomat for twenty years, including serving as Undersecretary of State and holding ambassadorships to Turkey and Germany.

Although the Church subcommittee is not involved in tax legislation, the Senators were investigating the question of how tax policy had been and should be used to pursue foreign policy objectives of the United States. On January 30, 1974, when Senator Church opened public hearings, he announced that they would show that a particular tax decision "that had such a tremendous impact upon the Middle East was never made by the Congress; it was never deliberated or debated, and though Congress, under the Constitution, has some right to assume that tax decisions belong to the Congress to make, this decision was made in the National Security Council by the Executive for reasons that seemed sufficient to that National Security meeting—of course, in secret session." He said that in 1950 the Treasury Department decided to grant tax credit status to increased payments to the Saudi Arabian government made by Aramco, which reduced their U.S. tax payments from $50,000,000 in 1950 to $6,000,000 in 1951. He related that Ambassador George McGhee, who from 1951 to 1953 was Assistant Secretary of State for Middle Eastern affairs, had testified in the subcommittee's executive session, two days before, that this shift in tax policy was, according to Senator Church, "the brainchild of the National Security Council." "The State Department argued that increased payments to the Middle Eastern governments would assure the continued viability of pro-U.S. governments in the Middle East," Senator Church said. "For the last 23 years the American people have been reaping the results of this tax decision, which was made within the executive branch, and which never met the light of public discussions or received Congressional approval, and it is now time for a thorough Congressional assessment of that tax decision." He then called witnesses to discuss taxation of foreign oil companies in detail.

However, the statements by Senator Church were what made the front-page news story of the day, such as the one in the New York *Times* with the headline OIL PROFITS, TREASURY LINKED TO SECRET DECISION. The subheadline was "Senators and Witnesses at Inquiry Tell of Dealings That Gave Big Companies Vast Petroleum Interest Return."

The testimony of the expert witnesses on the pros and cons of foreign tax credits, applying to the oil industry, which have been the subject of open debate in Congress for many years, was too lengthy and complicated to report. Furthermore, the nineteen pages of sworn testimony of Ambassador McGhee in executive session were not made public until a month later and were no longer "news." Those people waiting in gas lines who had been led to believe that a government-industry conspiracy, dating from 1950, contributed to current high profits, did not have the benefit of knowing what Ambassador McGhee had really said or what the circumstances of the Treasury decision were.

Ambassador McGhee testified, in response to Senator Church's question if Congress had been consulted on the tax ruling, "There was, to the best of my knowledge, consultation between the Treasury Department and the appropriate congressional committee. This ruling was widely known at the time, and I don't recall any objection being raised. It wasn't done secretly. It is a difficult concept to understand. Perhaps everyone didn't understand it. But there was no particular secrecy attached to it." The media's "secret decision" story, implying that not until January 20, 1974, had this matter seen the light of day, was based entirely on Senator Church's introduction in which he said the decision had been made by the National Security Council"—of course, in secret session." Technically, he was correct, as the National Security Council does not hold public sessions.

Nor were the reasons for the council's decision a secret. Ambassador McGhee reminded the subcommittee of world conditions in 1950. "The Middle East was perhaps the most critical area in the world in the contest between ourselves and the Soviets," he said. "The principal threat to the Middle East lay in the possibility of nationalist leaders moving to upset regimes which were relatively inept and corrupt, and not attuned to the modern world." He pointed out that there were strikes in Saudi Arabia and its Finance Minister had threatened to shut down the oil fields unless the Saudis got more money. He pointed out that there was a world oil surplus at the time, with the United States being a net exporter, and that the State Department concluded that "some greater sharing of profits with Saudi Arabia must take place, otherwise there would be an increasing threat to the regime and to Aramco's ability to maintain its concession." The Saudi government was pressing Aramco for a fifth-fifty profit-sharing agreement such as the oil companies had made in Venezuela. Based on the State Department's political assessment, "in the Council the U.S. policy was put together which led the Treasury Department to making the tax credit concession."

This enabled Aramco to treat the increased Saudi fifty-fifty profit-sharing payments, above their royalty payments, as foreign income tax to be credited against U.S. income tax payments. The company profits remained the same. By this ruling the company received the same tax treatment to prevent double taxation, as all other U.S. companies operating abroad receive. The political stability which was sought then was achieved.

In public discussions, much of the controversy over the application of the foreign tax credit is due to a lack of understanding as to how it works and its limitations. U.S. oil companies cannot offset increases in foreign tax liabilities by a corresponding lowering of tax payments to the U.S. Treasury through the foreign tax credit. It is available only up to the point where foreign tax rates equal U.S. rates. Since the mid-1960's foreign tax rates have exceeded U.S. tax rates, by and large, and have had very little effect on tax payments to the Treasury since the companies have had nothing to write off against all the foreign tax increases. They have built up large amounts of unusable excess foreign tax credits.

Senator Church again created front-page headlines when he charged that the international oil companies had benefited from the high posted prices set by Middle East oil countries and had no incentive to resist them. Oil company witnesses were incensed by this. George Piercy, Exxon senior vice-president, who had been a leader of negotiations continually since 1970, said, "I can assure you that we had the will and incentive to keep prices down and I think we did a good job until the oil-producing nations said we have had enough of you and we are going to go our own way." J. D. Bonney, Socal vice-president, who had led his company's negotiations in Libya which resulted in nationalization, challenged the Senator's accusations. He gave a graphic, detailed description of how hard the company had fought and the personal abuse he had taken in the process. Senator Church backed down, saying he knew the companies had tried to keep prices down and he was trying to find out if they had any real negotiating leverage any more. However, at this point, Senator Church was not on national television.

Senator Church also charged that the oil companies conspired over the years to restrict Middle East oil production to maintain high prices. The companies maintained the record proves otherwise. "It is hard to see how they arrive at that conclusion," Piercy said. "During the 1960's we had full, ample supplies and prices fell. If there was a cartel operating or an agreement, it was certainly one of the most inefficient in the world. The oil shortage since October is not the result of poor planning, and certainly not a creature born of oil company conspiracy or monopoly, but rather the result of political events that the oil industry could neither prevent nor insure against with alternative supplies."

While the Church hearings were in progress, the importance of American overseas oil ownership to the United States was dramatically underscored. The Treasury Department announced that the entire decline in the "real" gross national product—the output of goods and services after adjusting for higher prices—in the second quarter of 1974 was due to the announcement of the Saudi government that it was increasing its ownership in Aramco from 25 to 60 percent, retroactive to January 1. The drop in overseas oil income, which, like other remitted overseas profits, is included in the GNP, was $2.5 billion in the second quarter of 1974. This reduced the net exports of goods and services in GNP calculations to the extent that it accounted for that quarter's entire decline.

The main thrust of the Church subcommittee was to demonstrate that, as Senator Church said initially, the international oil business was too important to leave to oil companies to handle and that the government must play a stronger role. The oil companies also favor a stronger government role, but the crucial question for government, industry and consumers is: What kind of role?

The testimony and questioning of two key experienced witnesses shed the most light on the problem. They suggested the course which, in their opinion, would be most beneficial for the nation to follow.

The first was James E. Akins, now ambassador to Saudi Arabia, who is the most astute and knowledgeable government official on international oil affairs and had, far in advance, consistently warned the government that the Arabs would use the oil weapon. As head of the State Department's Office of Fuels and Energy he participated indirectly in, and followed for the government, all the critical negotiations with OPEC and Libya. After testifying at length about the negotiations, he was asked by Jack Blum, the subcommittee's associate counsel, "what the U.S. stake in the issue of government-to-government direct deals in petroleum is. Would such deals be adverse to the U.S. national interest?" Ambassador Akins replied:

. . . we certainly don't want to get in the position of our going in and taking over negotiations for the companies. I don't think that we really could have considered this unless we were going to take over control of the oil companies.

The danger that I saw and still see to a certain extent is if a government is negotiating rather than a company, you can have political confrontation much more easily—that is, if our companies are negotiating with OPEC, that is one thing, and governmental prestige is not involved. You do not have hardened positions and you can talk with the companies and ask them to do things or request them or suggest they do things, but if the Government is involved then you can have a government-to-government confrontation.

Another danger that still exists is that we could get in a position of outbidding each other for the available oil—that is, we would go in and say we bid something and the Japanese would go in and bid something more and have a skyrocketing of prices soon. The companies were able to handle the negotiations in the past very easily. . . And the companies in the past had various strengths. They had first of all their own diversity. They had interests throughout the world, and second, we have the demand of oil producing governments to increase production, everybody wanted more production because they want the resources as fast as possible. Well, the companies are still represented around the world, but we do not, anymore, have any pressure from producing governments to increase production. Quite the opposite, every country in OPEC is now talking about production limitations, even Saudi Arabia. That being the case, and it is the case, the companies have lost their flexibility. They are not in the strong position that they were 10 to 15 years ago. . . Well, if the companies have no more flexibility, if they are much weaker than they were before, should we be looking at the much greater role of governments?

Ambassador Akins told the subcommittee that there should be "a joint consumer approach to the problems" among the consuming nations and that he had proposed a joint consumer organization three years earlier. He has long been on record as sponsoring this approach to back up operations of the companies, but as he says, "in the long run, the only satisfactory position for the United States must be the development of alternative energy sources."

The second important witness to discuss the key problem was John J. McCloy, the seventy-nine-year-old distinguished New York lawyer who, like the late Bernard Baruch, is a member of that rare and dwindling breed, known as "elder statesmen." During World War II he was the Assistant Secretary of War. He has served as president of the World Bank, U.S. military governor and high commissioner for Germany, and chairman of the government's General Advisory Committee on Disarmament for the past ten years. McCloy was the legal counsel for the international oil companies in their OPEC and Libyan negotiations. Owing to his great experience with both government and industry, the Senators were particularly anxious to learn his thinking on whether the government should play a more direct role in future negotiations. He told them:

> This is almost the $64 question, in my mind. I don't know that I have come to rest yet. I can see the disadvantages of having the Government in here with confrontations, particularly in a sensitive, strategic area such as this. The concern that President Kennedy had way back, that you might have confrontations here, particularly with the oil reserves being as big as they are in this part of the world. I have the feeling that it is dangerous to have the political aspect so completely predominant in your dealings with these people. It is just as in the case of BP, British Petroleum. You are familiar with that. Because the Libyans didn't like the way the British acted in regard to those islands in the Gulf, immediately they cut them off. They nationalized them. It didn't have anything to do with the Arab-Israeli war. It was something they didn't like.
>
> This is a dangerous, sensitive area. If I may just speak from the top of my head from here on, I think, in looking at this, we have to bear in mind that over all these years in which the free world has had the advantage of a steady flow of relatively cheap oil from this area on the basis of which our security has been helped and our economy has been helped, not only ours but those of our allies—there has been a long period of a stable flow of this very important commodity.
>
> To be sure, we are running into a shortage situation here and maybe there were some miscalculations about it. But to jump from the type of negotiating that we have been doing for these years, which has kept this flow moving, to the thought that the Government must come into it is a pretty big jump.
>
> I think I would compromise it. I think I would have a more knowledgeable, more in-depth organization than the Government dealing with this problem of energy, as important as it now seems to be. I have the thought of perhaps the formula of the individual company plus the backup in the event that it seems to be necessary on the basis of real knowledgeability, and maybe it ought not reside in one department of the Government alone; maybe it ought to be an interdepartmental approach. I am rather inclined to think that the State Department should be very importantly involved in it. I see somebody has criticized the Government for not having an oil policy.

I don't agree, at least in certain periods of time, that we haven't had an oil policy.

We had a very good and aggressive oil policy . . . where we really did move into a point where the U.S. influence on the energy situation was very important. I think it goes back to President Wilson's days. It certainly was in Franklin Roosevelt's days, when Harold Ickes and Jim Forrestal were so concerned about the fact that we were drawing down our oil reserves. We had oiled the war. We wanted non-domestic sources of supply. The whole Government put a thrust in that direction and we did get a presence in this area.

With all the bold talk about self-sufficiency by 1980 I think we need to have a continued presence in what is, after all, perhaps the most productive oil reserves in the world. So if there was a combination of private oil companies that had the knowledgeability, the good bargaining ability, together with the strength of the governments, that may be the best formula. I think the British probably come as close to this as you can, but I don't believe we have that organization now.

I would certainly strongly urge that this Government reequip itself, as I think it once was, with a much more in-depth knowledge of the whole energy oil situation. . . .In the first place, I would say whatever you do, think it through. Don't rush your jumps because you might very well throw the baby out with the bath, to mix my metaphors a bit. We need that presence in that part of the world. Second, I think you ought to look closely at this relationship between the private companies and the Government, and examine it a little more thoroughly and keep a little more continuity of interest flowing than has been the case in the past.

Senator Church agreed with McCloy on the importance of an active and informed government concerning oil. He said he hoped the hearings would contribute to this happening. However, Church is pressing for immediate legislation which would require Federal Energy Administration approval of all oil contracts between oil companies and the OPEC nations that would last more than six months or involve 1,000,000 barrels of oil daily. Treasury Secretary Simon, appearing before the subcommittee, agreed on the necessity of a stronger government role in oil company negotiations with foreign countries but declined to endorse Church's proposed bill. "I would like to see the government out front," Simon said, but added that the bill might "put us in the back seat. . . . In my judgment," he said, "it is proper for our government to provide advice to U.S. companies, but I don't believe the decision-making responsibility on the operation of their foreign trading activities and their foreign investment should be assumed by the U.S. Government." Simon said he and Secretary of State Kissinger were meeting daily, "working on what our oil policy should be."

John C. Sawhill, Federal Energy Administrator, told the subcommittee that his agency was conducting a study to determine the kinds of company-foreign-government deals over which the U.S. government should have veto power. Also, the FEA is making a study of how to measure proper costs for intracompany transfers of imported crude oil. If the FEA decides that any international oil companies paid their overseas affiliates too much for imported oil and passed these profits along to U.S. consumers as costs, the FEA may require rollbacks in product prices, as well as refunds.

Government intervention in international oil negotiations is also a primary issue in a study being made for the FEA, under a $300,000 consulting contract with a Los Angeles law firm. Questionnaires have been sent to all international oil companies for their views on this and related matters. The study which will make policy recommendations by the end of 1974, will also consider a variety of national petroleum objectives, such as a government oil and gas company for domestic and international business, establishment of an international organization to allocate global petroleum supplies, another to reduce petroleum demand, an organization to coordinate national policy with other importing countries and public utility regulation of the oil industry.

As the first anniversary of the Yom Kippur war approached, the nation had taken only a few steps forward on the long journey to energy self-sufficiency. Congress had spent most of its time publicly castigating the oil industry for high prices and profits, but it had done very little either in the way of punitive legislation or in getting its priorities straight to evolve a national oil policy and encourage development of domestic energy supplies.

Congress passed only two bills designed to increase energy supplies. In November, 1973, the five-year court battle over the environmental impact of the Alaska pipeline was ended when Congress authorized its construction. However, the $6 billion pipeline will not be completed until mid-1977, when 600,000 barrels of oil daily will flow to the lower forty-eight states. The amount will be doubled a year later in a second construction phase. The second bill was to decrease the demand for oil and natural gas by relaxing Clean Air Act standards to permit power plants to convert to coal on the condition that primary air standards are met. One other bill was passed with an eye to the future. Congress speeded up energy research and development by approving a $2.2 billion 1974–1975 appropriations bill for research projects in seven different agencies on atomic energy, oil, gas, coal, geothermal, solar energy, pollution and conservation. This was a 64 percent increase over the previous year's appropriations.

The majority of Congressmen encouraged increased oil and gas exploration by resisting all efforts to roll back prices. But the other hand took away incentives in proposed tax reform measures. Every effort to spur exploration for natural gas by deregulating price control was met by overwhelming Congressional opposition, thus assuring continuing natural gas shortages. The nation had not yet recognized the economic facts of life of the cause-and-effect relationship among price, profits and supply.

Nor had government and Congress really come to grips with the problem of accelerating development of offshore oil, siting the refineries and nuclear plants and coal resources' development. Opposition of environmentalists was a powerful political issue. There was no question that the quickest route to self-sufficiency lay in developing our offshore oil and gas potential whose undiscovered recoverable resources are estimated by the U.S. Geological Survey at 200 to 400 billion barrels of crude oil and natural gas liquids and 1,000 to 2,000 trillion cubic feet of natural gas. When the energy bomb dropped, only 3 percent of U.S. offshore acreage had been leased, and offshore production was declining. Interior Secretary Morton announced that his department would increase leasing from 1,000,000 acres a year to 3,000,000 acres in 1974 and increase it to 10,000,000 acres a year in the next few years. Over strenuous opposition, he extended leasing to the coastal waters of three new states—Florida, Alabama and Mississippi. He also approved a controversial plan to develop already-discovered oil reserves in the Santa Barbara Channel, which had been in a deepfreeze since the 1969 oil slick.

The Council on Environmental Quality made a cautious endorsement of exploring new offshore areas, but the real offshore battle lies ahead. Secretary Morton announced proposed lease sales for mid-1975 of offshore acreage in Southern California and the Gulf of Alaska, proposals bound to encounter stiff environmental and Congressional opposition, as will any proposal to develop offshore Atlantic acreage, which is the biggest political "hot potato" of all. Senator Jackson introduced a bill, which his Interior Committee approved, which would open all available offshore lands for development by 1985, but he attached such stringent environmental requirements that his proposed legislation would slow down and delay offshore development during the next ten years. When exploration of new offshore areas does begin, it will still take five to ten years to develop new reserves.

Congress at least decided to organize to get organized about handling energy problems. A Federal Energy Administration was created in mid-1974 to run until June, 1976, when Congressional leaders hope that it will become incorporated in a new Department of Energy and Natural Resources to pull together the sixty-odd federal agencies and departments dealing with energy matters. Although the FEA's daily task is handling allocation programs and price controls, its most important responsibility is to develop a plan for Project Independence, which Nixon so confidently announced would achieve energy self-sufficiency by 1980. No one in government or industry takes such a date seriously. The most optimistic forecasters speak hesitatingly of "near" self-sufficiency by the late 1980's. So many ifs are involved, depending on political decisions, that there is general agreement that the 1990's may be the earliest the United States can expect to be in a position to handle the greater part of its energy needs.

The unfinished business of a national oil policy would await the decisions of a new President and a new Congress, together with the influence of the public which did not yet fully understand the meaning of all the issues involved. In the final analysis, the checks and balances of our system had, as usual, served our country well. We hadn't done much, but at least we hadn't done anything overly foolish. Our options were still open to learn what the real issues were and to make judgments about them in a calmer atmosphere based on a more accurate appraisal of facts.

Our greatest danger still remained that we were lapsing back into the comfortable feeling that the temporary absence of a shortage meant that the energy crisis had gone away.

5

Environment vs. Energy

A Gallup national opinion poll in January, 1974, at the height of the gasoline shortage, indicated that while 25 percent of the public blamed the oil industry for the energy crisis and 23 percent blamed the federal government, only 2 percent blamed environmentalists. Few Americans yet saw any connection between energy supplies and the underdevelopment of energy resources resulting from the highly organized political activities of environmentalist groups.

When Congress passed the 1969 National Environmental Protection Act in response to public alarm, it did not anticipate that the government would be smothered, buried and hamstrung in the avalanche of paperwork and lawsuits which the act propagated. The requirement for all federal agencies to prepare Environmental Impact Statements, or EIS's, justifying "major federal actions significantly affecting the quality of the human environment" resulted in 3,600 EIS's being prepared and filed in the first three years of the act, together with thousands of days of public hearings. One federal agency found it necessary to allocate sixty analysts, on a full-time basis, to do nothing but screen, review and comment on EIS's of other federal agencies. Under the NEPA, any private group opposed to any project or environmental control could bring suit to delay action by compelling agencies to prepare or improve EIS's. Consequently, the fairy godmother of all little old ladies in tennis shoes changed them overnight into ambitious young men with law degrees. They kept the courts, agencies and industry hopping. Although they were concerned about everything relating to the environment from pollution to wildlife, their chief targets were the Alaska pipeline, offshore oil and gas development, building of oil refineries and nuclear power plants and strip mining.

Political lobbying has been one of the nation's major industries ever since George Washington spent almost as much time lobbying in the Continental Congress for Army funds as he did fighting the Revolutionary War. The environmentalists added a new fillip to the time-honored practices and purposes of lobbying which, although Americans profess to hold it in disrepute, has always been a necessary part of the preservation of self-government. Almost all lobbying groups are, by their nature, "self-interest" groups whether they are associations of oil, coal, power or manufacturing companies, labor unions, veterans, doctors or farmers. As Senator James Reed of Missouri once remarked, "a lobbyist is anyone who opposes legislation I want." However, environmental groups, like consumer groups, added a new philosophy. They lobbied as "selfless" groups—concerned with the good of all citizens.

"Big Oil" has always reputedly had one of the most powerful lobbies in Washington, although its inability to deregulate natural gas since 1954 would raise a question about that. Whatever clout the oil industry may have had, it met its match when the environmentalists climbed in the ring. No Congressman could ignore the grass-roots influence of the League of Conservation Voters, for instance, whose directors include officials of the Sierra Club, Friends of the Earth and Environmental Action. The nonpartisan league devised a system of point-rating Congressmen and state legislators on their voting records on selected environmental issues. Charts are prepared to use in environmental campaigning. In 1972, environmentalists chalked up sixty House, Senate and gubernatorial victories as the result of their political activities. Another Washington group, Environmental Action, concentrates in each election on defeating twelve House members whom it brands "the dirty dozen." In the last two national elections, half their choices for this honor were defeated.

Environmental political action literally stopped energy development dead in its tracks, since half our potential energy resources lie in public lands, and all the activities of energy industries are affected by state and federal legislation, either current or contemplated. Environmentalists put political roadblocks in the way of all action and planning for energy growth. The success of environmental political action was due to the national mood. Emotionally we all were new converts to the religion of saving the environment. When the "prophets of doom" exhorted us, we started pushing each other out of the way to hurry down the aisle, confess and be saved. We weren't asking questions, demanding proof, counting costs or ascertaining just what the conflicts between energy and environment really are, what is being done about them and what should realistically be done about them in the future. Nobody had thought any problem through or had any real fix on the complicated interrelationship of all energy activities, which, like a balloon, if you punch on one side, bulges out on the other. The confrontation between environmentalists and the energy industries is such a new national problem that the public hasn't yet had a chance to separate emotion from facts or balance idealistic goals with practical actions. Since you and I foot the bills and pay the consequences, we need to know exactly what decisions we are being asked to make and why.

The most important and immediate decision involves the very problem which triggered the whole issue of environmental concern—offshore oil. The 10,000 barrels of oil which spilled into the Santa Barbara Channel, following an offshore well blowout in 1969, did more than pollute the beaches. They created a contagious mental malady—petrophobia. The fear of oil spills is an astonishing national phenomenon and a peculiarly American state of mind. It has been magnified out of all proportion to the facts. On my college lecture tours, I found that the most emotional environmental subject was the obsession with the necessity to prevent oil spills by not drilling oil wells. Students had reached this conclusion, although few of them had any exact knowledge of what oil pollution is, what it does, how much there is and what can be done to prevent or counteract it. Nor did they have any concept of whether or not the disadvantages of not producing oil outweighed whatever risks might be involved. At the same time, I discovered that once we got into details, the majority of students quickly understood the importance of looking at the whole problem. In general, their attitude was, as one student commented, "I don't want to be sold a bill of goods either by the oil companies or the environmentalists. I want to know the facts and make up my own mind."

What happens when people have an opportunity to do just this was demonstrated in a mini-research project conducted at Boston College by Dr. Jerome B. Carr, an outstanding environmental specialist who is a geologist and oceanographer. In mid-1972 the Boston *Globe* made an environmental public opinion survey of its readers. One question was: "Should oil exploration and drilling be permitted off the Massachusetts Coast?" Of those responding, 60 percent said no, 21 percent said yes, and 19 percent were undecided. Dr. Carr decided to verify these results and to perform an experiment on public attitudes about oil and oil pollution with a group of 21 students enrolled in his evening course on Environmental Science and Water Pollution. The group was a representative cross section of the general public as the students' ages ranged from nineteen to about fifty-five. One-third were women. Their backgrounds included housewives, secretaries, police officers, foreign students, day school students and graduate students. It was an elective course, and the majority had little or no scientific or technical backgrounds.

When the course began, he polled their attitudes on offshore New England drilling and found 67 percent were against, 14 percent in favor and 19 percent undecided. The material he presented to the class included basic facts of pollution, the U.S. import situation, the economics of rising costs of imported oil, economics of domestic oil and the petropolitics of dependence on Middle East oil. The material was presented as one lecture during the whole course. The topic of oil pollution was dropped, and other forms of water pollution and water resource development were covered. Two months later, at exam time, among the questions was: "How do you feel about oil exploration off the east coast of the U.S.?" Dr. Carr asked for an essay explaining their position, and since it was an opinion question, there would be no wrong answer. The new survey revealed that 85 percent of the students were in favor of offshore drilling, 5 percent were against it with 10 percent undecided. This experiment was conducted a year before the Arabs dropped the energy bomb and quadrupled oil prices. Consequently, the students' reasons for their complete reversal of opinion are significant. In listing the importance of the factors influencing them, 58 percent cited the rising cost of oil for the consumer; 37 percent, a "wartime situation;" 37 percent balance of payments; 32 percent, political instability of supplier; 16 percent, new jobs for New England (not discussed in the lecture); 10 percent, new awareness of potential oil shortages from local news sources; 10 percent, national emergency (of unspecified nature); and 5 percent, increased federal income from oil-bred taxes. The importance of pollution as a governing opinion factor had disappeared once the facts were explained and put into perspective.

Nature was polluting the oceans, beaches and land with oil from seeps long before man ever appeared on earth. It still continues to do so. Ironically, the biggest natural oil seep in the world today is in the Santa Barbara Channel, where on an average day from 50 to 70 barrels of oil seeps into the ocean off Coal Oil Point. This, of course, is what led oil explorers to drill in the area when offshore drilling technology was developed. The first search for California oil was stimulated by Benjamin Silliman, the Yale University chemistry and geology professor whose report on Pennsylvania's rock oil had inspired investors to drill America's first commercial oil discovery in 1859. Five years later Thomas A. Scott, Lincoln's Assistant Secretary of War and vice-president of the Pennsylvania Railroad, sent Silliman on a private mission to investigate stories about oil seeps in Southern California. "California will be found to have more oil in its soil than all the whales in the Pacific Ocean," Professor Silliman reported enthusiastically. "The oil is struggling to the surface at every available point and is running down the rivers for miles and miles." His description of the Santa Barbara seeps, written on shipboard, would send a 1970's environmentalist into instant shock:

> Often for hundreds of acres square at one view, there is no part of the sea but was thus covered. The sea boils like effervescing soda water, with the escaping gas which accompanies the oil, and great globules of pure oil rising with the gas flash out on the surface of the water, tossing it up in jets, and then breaking into films of rainbow hues like the tints of a dying dolphin. The effect is wonderfully beautiful and exciting, every fantastic form of animal, plant and fish is reproduced on this marbled surface in thin films of fine oil.

How much oil the oceans worldwide have absorbed from natural seeps over the millennia, without deleterious effects, will never be determined. However, we now know that man is outstripping nature as an oil polluter simply because he is mining it in such volumes and moving it all over the planet. Up until now, he hasn't thought it was especially important when some of it has accidentally, or purposefully, been spilled. During World War II, U.S. Coast Guard records show that ninety-five U.S. flag oil tankers were sunk during four years of war by the Nazi U-boat wolf pack along the East Coast, in the Gulf of Mexico and in the Caribbean. They carried more than 5,500,000 barrels of oil and products. Whatever happened to the oil? It left no permanent damage on American beaches. How seriously did it affect marine life? We don't know. It is only since the Santa Barbara blowout that we have seriously started to try to find out about such things.

A two-year research study directed by Dr. Dale Straughan, of the University of Southern California, on the biological effects of that particular oil pollution, failed to show any lasting effects to the flora and fauna and substantiated that the Santa Barbara Channel had recovered. She found that birds, fish, whales, seals, plankton and the multitude of sea organisms were thriving as they always had. This doesn't mean that a scientific question has, by any means, been answered. The inquiry into how toxic oil is to marine ecology in the long run has really just begun. What it does mean is that on the basis of historical evidence and immediate investigations, we don't need to panic. In the meantime, while we are waiting for science to give us the final word, it is essential that we do everything practical to avoid pollution and be able to counteract accidental spills. It so happens that our newly awakened concern has prodded industry and the scientific community to devise new ways to make this possible to a remarkable degree.

The U.S. Coast Guard is in charge of marine pollution prevention, cleanup and enforcement. Since it began keeping statistical track of oil spills in 1970, we know that there are about 10,000 oil spill incidents annually in and around U.S. waters. The majority of these are small—between 1 and 100 gallons each. The amount of oil spilled compared to the amount handled and consumed is an infinitesimal fraction. During 1972 we consumed 5.7 billion barrels of petroleum products. Only 45,000 barrels of oil and products were spilled in our coastal and inland waters, or 0.0008 of 1 percent of consumption. One out of every three barrels we used was brought in tankers from abroad. One out of every six barrels we used came from offshore. Spillage from ships amounted to 34.5 percent of the total volume, whereas spillage from all offshore facilities amounted to only 1.3 percent, or approximately 5,600 barrels, an amount which nature seeps into the Santa Barbara Channel in less than three months' time. More than two-thirds of the total spillage was on the Atlantic Coast in port and harbor areas owing to huge imports and the great number of onshore facilities required to handle them.

Two years before the Santa Barbara oil spill the American Petroleum Institute initiated a nationwide program to develop cooperative oil spill cleanup organizations, operating like a volunteer fire department. Oil companies initially pooled funds and equipment and trained personnel. Municipalities, state and federal agencies and public organizations have joined these cooperatives. Today there are almost 100 operational groups on the East, West and Gulf coasts and on inland rivers and lakes. The largest cooperative is Clean Seas, Inc., a Santa Barbara-based nonprofit firm founded by fifteen major oil companies after the spill. It is responsible for monitoring and being a reaction force along 250 miles of Suthern California coastline. It is armed with an arsenal of oil booms, skimming boats, scrubbers, foams, dispersants and equipment of all kinds to contain and combat spills. Oil spill technology is developing into a major art.

It is paradoxical that public concern over oil spills and fears about further offshore development were prompted by an accident in the type of marine oil operation which historically is one of the safest.

There are approximately 16,000 U.S. offshore producing oil and gas wells, most of them in the Gulf of Mexico. Including Santa Barbara, there have been only four major oil spills, in excess of 5,000 barrels of oil, in twenty-seven years of offshore operations. One of these spills resulted from a blowout, two from fires, and one from a storm. Since Santa Barbara, safety is a priority concern of industry and government. New technology to improve safety and efficiency has advanced enormously. Safety factors and regulations have been stringently increased. In the Gulf of Mexico, the U.S. Geological Survey now has a field force of twenty-eight technicians and twelve engineers for intensive inspections. Helicopter flyovers, covering 100,000 square miles of leased areas, are conducted seven days a week. Also, helicopters take engineers on inspection trips on board the nearly 2,000 offshore platforms and drilling rigs to check compliance with federal safety and pollution control rules.

When offshore development began in the Gulf, fishermen and environmentalists were alarmed that it would endanger and destroy marine life. Oil installations have actually contributed to increasing the abundance of fish of all kinds. The real testing ground has been Louisiana, where Gulf offshore and coastal water oil operations first began twenty-seven years ago and which is the nation's leading commercial fishing state. Louisiana produces more than a billion pounds of fish and shellfish every year, a quarter of the nation's total. The state's fisheries make 98 percent of their catch in the 5,000,000 to 7,000,000 acres of marshland between the Intracoastal Canal and the Gulf shoreline, the world's largest estuarine area. There are 24,000 oil and gas wells producing in the coastal marsh and 14,000 outside the 3-mile limit. More than 100,000 miles of pipeline thread through the marshlands. In all other U.S. fishing grounds except Hawaii, fishing has declined over the last twenty-five years, but the Gulf has doubled fish production in the last decade, along with the expansion of oil operations. Louisiana had no offshore natural reefs, which are a natural home for an abundance of marine life, creating a food chain from algae to the biggest fish. But the 2,000 drilling platforms created artificial reefs, which over the years have attracted and sponsored the growth of a tremendous fish population. They have revolutionized commercial and sports fishing. Fish, formerly unknown in the area, including tropical fish, are migrating to them.

As Gulf exploration intensified, fishermen protested that the explosion of dynamite charges underwater in seismograph exploration was frightening the fish away from their normal feeding grounds to quieter waters farther away. Exxon research scientists invented a substitute for dynamite. A mixture of propane and oxygen, ignited by a spark plug inside a rubber sleeve, inflates the sleeve like an instant balloon. The sudden expansion is fast enough to give a seismic echo and makes only a small popping sound which doesn't scare the fish. The invention was a boon to both fishermen and the oil industry. The popper costs only a penny a pop and gives better seismic results than dynamite, which costs $15 a shot.

Louisiana has always held first place in U.S. oyster production. In the 1940's the oyster catch began to decline as coastal oil production increased. Oystermen immediately blamed oilmen. State university and oil company research scientists went to work and found that oil had no effect on oysters. The real villain was a fungus which exists in salt water. The oysters were saved by preventing saltwater intrusion into the estuaries. The world's largest oyster bed lies in the middle of a Louisiana oil field at Marsh Island. Shrimp fishermen were even more apprehensive about oil than oystermen. Morgan City had become the shrimp capital of the world when jumbo shrimp were discovered in 1933. The city was the first staging area for the Gulf offshore oil industry. Shrimpers considered the Gulf their private domain and were openly antagonistic to the oil invasion. However, as shrimp production increased as rapidly as oil, they paid the oil industry their greatest tribute. Every Labor Day weekend one of the most colorful festivals and pageants in the country was held to celebrate and bless the shrimp harvest and the fleet. Beginning in 1967, Morgan City changed the name of the annual affair to "The Louisiana Shrimp and Petroleum Festival." Priests now bless the oil harvest as well as shrimps.

In mid-1974 Louisiana's Governor Edwin W. Edwards, arrived in Glen Cove, Long Island, with state officials, four chefs and thirty crates of fresh oysters, shrimp, crabs, pompano and other seafood. At a luncheon, hosted by a Long Island businessman and attended by government officials and business leaders, Governor Edwards said he was there to reassure environmentalists who were fighting offshore drilling. "The production of oil and gas in coastal waters is compatible with the theory of environmental excellence," he said. "There is no need for fear."

Few of the people in the fourteen Eastern Seaboard states, which are totally dependent for their energy supply on oil from other states or imports, have ever seen an oil well except on television. Nor will they have an opportunity to see them whenever oil exploration and development begins in the Atlantic offshore, as the prospective oil and gas areas lie on the outer continental shelf some 30 to 120 miles from the shoreline.

I have been visiting offshore exploration wells and development platforms in oceans and seas all over the world for the past ten years. What has impressed me most is the rapid advance of technology and the remarkable research and engineering with which the oil industry has pioneered the way to developing ocean resources. The complex mechanical man-made islands are now as highly safety-engineered as spaceships, and far more comfortable for their crews. The challenge of taming the North Sea has been the springboard for tremendous advances in the past few years in the science and equipment of offshore drilling.

Fifteen years ago we knew less about the oceans which cover three-fourths of the globe than we did about Mars. Since then, owing in great part to petroleum industry research, we have been making one impressive technological breakthrough after another. We now have the technical capability to utilize extensively the underwater resources of offshore lands to a water depth of 6,000 feet, which is equivalent to adding approximately 1,370,000 square miles to the nation's lands, or more than five states the size of Texas.

Before the first self-contained offshore drilling platform was built, the industry spent $5,000,000 researching currents, wave profiles, wave forces and other nonexistent sea data to determine the engineering and materials required. This research led to the ability to detect development of hurricanes. These studies enlarged the understanding that sea, air and land are a single complex system. Ocean currents and the roughness of the sea's surface result from lower atmosphere winds and the shape of the ocean floor and its coastlines.

Until 1974 most offshore drilling has been in waters of less than 1,000 feet. Now, offshore wells are being drilled in even deeper waters. Shell Oil Company drilled a well in 2,150 feet of water in the South Atlantic, off the coast of Gabon. Technical capability has grown to the extent that industry is already planning complete ocean-floor operations applicable to 6,000 feet of water where fixed platforms would be impractical or too expensive. Using the same total-systems analysis approach which enabled men to be landed on the moon, Mobil Oil and North American Rockwell developed a deepwater production system. Automated sea-bottom installations will operate a whole oil field. Life-support systems were devised so that technical men, who are nondivers, can work in a shirt-sleeve environment. The structures will be serviced by a small submarine to transport men to and from work. The submarine is equipped with articulated arms to enable the submarine operator to perform essential duties on the outside of the sea-bottom structures. To a ship traveling on the surface there will be no indication that men and machines are working far below with as great ease as on land. This systems approach could be the forerunner to deep-ocean mining operations, as well as the establishment of underwater industrial colonies.

In the Arabian Gulf, off the coast of the Trucial sheikhdom of Dubai, I watched the remarkable launching, by Continental Oil Company, of the largest underwater oil storage tank in the world. The 500,000-barrel tank, looking like a giant inverted champagne glass, is as tall as a twenty-story building and is anchored underwater 65 miles from shore. This is a major step toward the establishment of all offshore petroleum development on the ocean floor, at increasingly greater depths, operating independently of dry-land facilities.

From an environmental protection viewpoint, development of Atlantic offshore oil and gas fields would be a major step forward. Dr. K. O. Emery, of the Woods Hole Oceanographic Institute, Cape Cod, Massachusetts, who is one of the world's leading marine geologists, says, "The most effective environmental control is to produce oil and gas off this coast, right here, close to East Coast markets, rather than shipping it long distances in giant tankers. When we ship oil long distances, the danger of spillage is greater." Marine pipelines from offshore production are the safest form of oil transportation. Dr. Emery points out other environmental advantages to the East Coast. "Much of the oil from abroad has a high sulfur content, and this causes environmental problems too," he says. "It costs fifty cents a barrel to take the sulfur out. If we find natural gas off the East Coast, this could have an important effect on air pollution control in our cities. Natural gas is a clean-burning fuel."

The problems of sea pollution are really associated with tanker transportation, not offshore production. Oil is the single largest commodity in international trade, accounting for half of all world shipping. In the past, the worst polluters were tanker operators, who polluted the ocean in order to avoid polluting harbors and ports. Immediately after discharging its cargo, a tanker must load ballast water into its cargo tanks. But the ship must arrive at the loading port with clean ballast so that it will be able to discharge this water without polluting the harbor just before taking on new cargo. Standard practice was to clean oil tanks at sea by pumping in seawater, sloshing it around in the dirty ballast and dumping the oily mixture overboard. Then clean seawater ballast would be pumped in. International law permitted this operation 50 miles from shore. In the early 1960's an estimated 14,000,000 barrels of oil were annually being dumped into the world's seas as part of normal tanker operations. The international oil companies organized in 1962 to stop this alarming pollution by devising a new tanker-loading technique known as load on top. When tanks are cleaned at sea, all dirty ballast water is pumped into a special tank on board. Oil rises to the surface, leaving relatively clean water under a mixture of oil and water. This clean water is drained out until only a thin layer of seawater remains with the oily residue. New crude is then loaded on top of this. Refineries can easily handle the small saltwater content of the cargo. Marine authorities estimate that this practice has reduced sea pollution by 80 percent. Unfortunately, of the world's more than 4,000 tankers, about one-fifth, operated mainly by independent tanker owners, do not use this method. Pollution will continue until international controls are agreed upon.

It was not until April, 1967, that world attention focused sharply on the potential dangers of massive tanker oil spills caused by accidents at sea. The 100,000-deadweight-ton tanker *Torrey Canyon* grounded off the southwest coast of England, and English and French beaches were polluted with 700,000 barrels of oil. This record disaster was a turning point in galvanizing industry and governments into the realization of the urgency of developing sophisticated oil spill technology, international pollution laws, strict international marine traffic regulations and international agreements on legal liability for pollution damage. The *Torrey Canyon* was a supertanker of its time, but shipyards were already tooling up to produce today's mammoth supertankers and super-supertankers, ranging from 200,000 to almost 500,000 tons, to meet expanding needs and reduce transportation costs.

If problems had to wait on international agreements, they would never be solved. Seven years have passed since the *Torrey Canyon,* and only in late 1973 did it appear that any progress was being made to tackle ocean pollution on a world basis. Under the auspices of the Intergovernmental Maritime Consultative Organization, a United Nations agency, representatives of seventy-nine nations signed a convention to control sea pollution. After 1975 all new tankers over a stipulated size will have to be built to nonpollution standards and will be equipped with monitoring devices. Fifteen countries must ratify the pact before it becomes effective.

Fortunately, the oil industry and individual governments moved swiftly to do what has to be done. Under the sponsorship of seven major oil companies—Exxon, Texaco, Socal, Gulf, Mobil, BP and Shell—tanker owners and oil companies organized two voluntary agreements concerning liability for oil pollution, to ensure that governments and people, anywhere in the world, who suffered damage from oil pollution, caused by tankers, are reimbursed or compensated equitably and promptly. By 1971 owners of more than 95 percent of world tanker tonnage and owners of from 80 to 90 percent of total crude and fuel oil moved at sea worldwide had signed these agreements, which are a public acknowledgment of responsibility for pollution. They ensure that when an accident happens, cleanup operations start immediately since compensation will be paid. Also, tanker and oil owners, having assumed this responsibility, have intensified precautions against pollution. They have campaigned vigorously for international conventions which will force the remaining minority, which have not signed the agreements, to come under controls.

Individual governments have passed strict regulations and standards concerning oil traffic in their waters and inspections of equipment at transfer points. Industry and government research scientists have discovered how to track down sea polluters who do not report accidental spills or who deliberately pollute. Crude oils, like people, are similar, but also like people's fingerprints, no two are alike. Several methods to measure the physical and chemical properties of an oil are almost perfected so that it will be possible to identify the source oil field, no matter where in the world, of an unknown oil spill and thereby locate the offending tanker which loaded and spilled it. The U.S. Coast Guard and Aerojet Electro Systems Company are flight-testing an airborne surveillance system, including sensors operating from ultraviolet to microwave lengths, which will locate oil spills.

The great progress being made in new oil spill prevention and cleanup technology is only now coming into operation. Intensive research did not begin until after the *Torrey Canyon* and Santa Barbara spills. A scientific research rule of thumb is that it takes from five to seven years from the time a laboratory discovery is made before the process or product becomes generally available. This is due to all the testing and perfecting required. A prime example is the outstanding achievement of the U.S. Coast Guard to develop equipment to combat a major oil pollution disaster on the high seas. Research was begun in 1969 and became operational in 1974. If there is a tanker collision or storm damage to a tanker on the open ocean, the Coast Guard has an effective, fully engineered system and equipment to have airlifted to the scene within four hours an oil-containment barrier which will prevent any spilled oil from spreading in seas with even 10-foot waves. Helicopters also bring equipment to remove the oil from the surface of the water and offload and temporarily store any oil remaining in the ship before it breaks up.

Environmentalists' fear of oil spills has not only prevented offshore oil and gas development, but has prevented building superports in deep offshore waters to handle increasing U.S. imports in supertankers. There is a basic inconsistency in this attitude because the use of superports and supertankers would reduce the potential number of oil spills by reducing the volume of tanker traffic and putting oil transfer operations far offshore rather than increase it in crowded ports and harbors. Oil would come to shore in marine pipelines. Supertankers of 200,000 tons and up are the most economical way to move oil because the more oil carried in one trip, the less it costs per ton to carry. If Middle East oil could be brought to the United States in supertankers, it would reduce transportation costs by $5 to $6 a ton, or around $1 a barrel. That would be a saving of about 2.5 cents on every gallon of gasoline made from imported oil and could save the American public an estimated $1.5 billion annually by 1985. Supertankers have routinely been carrying Middle East oil to Europe and Japan for years. However, the United States is the only major industrial nation without a deepwater port, either natural or man-made, that can accommodate them. The average supertanker is three times the size of the largest ship that can berth in any harbor on the U.S. East and Gulf coasts. Consequently the average size tanker serving U.S. ports is only 47,000 tons. It takes nine of these to deliver the same 3,000,000 barrels of oil that a single 400,000-ton supertanker could.

The very words "superports" and "supertankers" conjure up visions of colossal oil spills. Just how safe or how dangerous are they? Since we have no basis to judge such things in the United States, last year I made an editorial research trip around the world to find out what the experience of other countries has been and the feelings of the people who cohabit with such phenomena. I visited some of the world's largest superports in Japan and Europe. I traveled on a supertanker in one of the busiest and most potentially dangerous maritime areas in the world—the English Channel. In Saudi Arabia I visited the new supertanker offshore loading terminal which is the same kind of installation proposed for U.S. deepwater offloading terminals. The trip was a revelation. I entered a world I never knew existed. It is a world where safety regulations carry more authority than the Ten Commandments. Modern technology reigns so supreme that when I saw it operating, I experienced the same kind of amazement as did some South American Indians of a primitive Stone Age tribe when they visited me in New York on their first trip out of the jungle. To my great surprise, I discovered that in this special world of superports and supertankers, people have already balanced out their desire to keep the world beautiful and at the same time utilize it to their advantage without destroying it. I learned one other remarkable thing. All those I talked to outside the United States, whether they were technical people, government officials or laymen, could not understand why Americans, who are primarily responsible for today's advanced technology, are in such a state of paralyzing political paranoia about using it themselves.

Kiire Terminal, the world's largest crude oil transshipment facility, lies in the center of one of Japan's most famous national parks in Kyushu, the southernmost island. Kiire is built in Kagoshima Bay, a spectacularly beautiful deepwater harbor. In the center of the bay is a national tourist attraction—Sakurajima, a live volcano, which constantly belches plumes of ash and smoke, rising up to 3,000 feet in the air. Sakurajima remains the area's only polluter, but its rival tourist attraction is now Kiire Terminal, built in 1969 by the Nippon Oil Staging Company, a joint venture of Japanese oil companies and U.S.-based Caltex. The impressive installation occupies a 460-acre square of reclaimed land jutting into the bay. Its orderly rows of huge 740,000-barrel storage tanks, painted sea green and landscaped with palm trees, are like a giant abstract painting blending into the blue-green of the harbor waters and the lush, verdant mountainous backdrop of the land. "It is a very important thing for us to have the terminal fit in with the beauty of the land and water," its general manager, Hirosuke Isomura, told me. "In selecting the color for the tanks we had a color consultation group with government and city officials."

Some 6,000,000 Japanese tourists annually come to the national park to enjoy its beautiful beaches, hot springs, crater lakes and mountain resorts. Kiire Terminal is now featured on Japanese tours because it is an absorbing sight to see the giant supertankers of up to 500,000 tons arriving from the Middle East, easing delicately in to the offloading docks, and watch the smaller tankers loading oil to take to Japanese refineries in ports which cannot accommodate supertankers. Kiire is also a new Mecca for port authority and maritime officials from all over the world, studying the efficiency and safety of its operations. In leafing through the visitors' book, I saw that I had recently been preceded by officials from the Soviet Union, Korea, Indonesia, Iran, Iraq, Spain, Sweden, France and the United States.

When Captain Rokuro Saito, Japan's most famous supertanker captain, who is now in charge of Kiire's tanker traffic, took me on an inspection trip, he handed me a hard hat and a pair of white gloves. The gloves were symbolic in an operation importing 12,000,000 barrels of oil monthly and with 18,900,000 barrels of crude in storage. By 1975, when the terminal is completed, its capacities will be doubled. After I inspected all the facilities, the gloves were as spotless as when I first put them on.

The heart of the terminal is the small computerized marine tower control room, where loading and unloading of crude oil are directed by push-button control. To the company's chagrin the only oil spill of any size—520 barrels—happened when the terminal first opened. An operator pushed the wrong button. The system was promptly mistake-proofed. The great ships are brought in by experienced pilots and docked in by a radio operator watching a sonar-meter count the approaching speed and the distance to the docks and communicating to the pilot. "We have the safest docking system in the world," Captain Saito said. "There has never been an accident." The terminal is closed about seven days out of each year owing to typhoons. Supertankers simply wait in calm waters until the storms blow out. The oil storage tanks are typhoon- and earthquake-proof.

When a tanker makes its first trip to Kiire, the captain is met, and presented with flowers, by the Kiire Friendship Promotion Association, representing the town, the fishermen's union, the agricultural union, ship suppliers and the terminal company. He is also given the standard foot-and-a-half long document, listing safety regulations, which every tanker captain must sign and agree to abide by.

On the other side of the world from Kagoshima Bay is Milford Haven, another extraordinarily beautiful deepwater port in one of England's national parks, Pembrokeshire, on the south coast of Wales. This famous tourist area has some of the most impressive and beautiful coastal scenery in Europe, and Milford Haven's superport has led Europe since 1961 in the size of supertankers calling there and the size of cargo delivered in them. Milford Haven is the port of first call for many of the supertankers from the Middle East to discharge part of their cargoes and then go on to other ports in the United Kingdom and Europe, which can receive them only at a lightened draft. Milford Haven is an arm of the Celtic Sea enclosing over 70 miles of coastline within an entrance less than 1¼ miles wide. The natural deepwater channel has been dredged to permit 300,000-ton tankers to berth on every tide. Although Kiire is the world's biggest transshipment superport, Milford Haven handles more oil and a greater number of tankers since it also has four big refineries, totaling 672,000 barrels-a-day capacity. About three supertankers a week arrive in Milford Haven, and in 1972 the port handled 319,000,000 barrels of oil, three times as much as Kiire.

Shakespeare, in *Cymbeline*, asks "how Wales was made so happy to inherit such a haven." Everyone who goes to this lovely area is moved to ask the same question. The haven's waters are unusually pure. Craggy, steep cliffs plunge down to miles of long beaches. There are charming villages and picturesque castles. It is a hikers' and bird lovers' paradise. What impressed me most was the environmental concern, skill and care with which the oil companies have blended their refining and tanker operations into the environment. Three of the big refineries—Texaco, Exxon and Gulf—are directly on the haven, but anyone aboard the multitude of small pleasure yachts and sailboats can scarcely see them. The refinery towers are obvious, but most of the oil storage tanks have been built below the skyline level, and a 30-foot-high embankment that the Welsh call their Chinese Wall surrounds the tank farms. The wall was topped with 4 feet of topsoil, and grass, shrubs and thousands of trees were planted. Around their properties the refineries have built public footpaths leading to the high bluffs with their stupendous views of the sea, and hikers, making the traditional long hike around the coasts of the sea arm, scarcely know the refineries are there. The new Amoco refinery, which is 1½ miles inland, is also professionally landscaped with natural stone walls, hedges and trees, carried out with the approval of county-planning authorities. In addition, great care was taken to see that it was not a noise polluter. Noise guarantees were required of all equipment suppliers. No noise at the outside property line is permitted that is above the noise level of an average birdcall. In all the refineries there is strict water and air pollution prevention with the most modern systems and devices.

As in Kiire, many of the tourists come to see the supertankers. Seldom, if ever, do they see any oil pollution. The Milford Haven Conservancy Board, which runs the port and monitors traffic, has stringent safety regulations. Harbormaster Captain G. Dudley told me that "99 percent of our pollution is very minor, each spill being no more than a half a bottle of oil, which is cleaned up immediately."

In Milford Haven, I rendezvoused with the *Esso Dalriada,* a 250,000-ton Swedish-built supertanker, making her maiden voyage from Ras Tanura, Saudi Arabia, to England. She offloaded 1,000,000 barrels of oil, and I sailed with her on the night tide for the journey around the tip of England and up the Channel to the port of Fawley, near Southampton, to unload another 750,000 barrels. I had a sense of high drama as I stood on the darkened navigation bridge with Captain Ian Smith while the tiny tugs maneuvered the giant *Dalriada,* the length of three football fields, up the haven to the turn-around basin. The atmosphere was calm, hushed and concentrated as the mammoth was precisely swung around and headed out toward the open sea. Like all modern supertankers, the *Dalriada* is a miracle of sophisticated electronic navigational equipment. Every operation possible is computerized and automated from constant checking on the functioning of all equipment to unloading the oil. The layman such as myself can only look, marvel and scarcely comprehend what each "box of tricks," as Chief Engineer Charles Henderson called them in showing me around, performs. There is so much equipment that he has more than 200 instruction manuals.

Safety and antipollution are the supertanker's twin gods. The *Dalriada* has 300 alarm systems to cover every contingency. Everything that goes over the side of the ship is clean, including sewage water, which is purified first. In the cargo control room there was a large sign over the computer panel which controls the cargo pumps and numerous valves on the cargo pipelines. It read: "Any oil spill when it occurs is to be regarded in the same way as a fire, because of the potential hazard involved and the possible danger to life on board as well as the pollution of the environment. We hope we never have to deal with one and we should do everything to prevent it, but we must be prepared to deal with it."

The most eventful thing about the trip was that it was so uneventful. The maritime traffic in the English Channel is controlled to go in north- and southbound lanes, and although we did not see them, we could follow the passing of other ships on the radar. In the port when we passed a "small" 70,000-ton tanker, Captain Smith said nostalgically, "I have a yen for that ship." When I asked why, he said, "On that I am the master—on this, the ship is my master."

Like a majority of today's supertanker captains, he trained at special schools to learn the skills required to handle and berth the mammoth tankers. The first of these was on a lake at Grenoble, France, where captains maneuver model ships. Now there is an advanced indoor simulator training school at the University of Delft in Holland. I visited this unique school and watched a group of supertanker captains being trained. In a small room there is a mock-up of a navigating bridge with all its instruments. There is only enough illumination inside the bridge to be able to read charts and instruments. Outside the mock wheelhouse windows is a projection screen. On this appears, in daylight conditions, the forward part of the "ship" and the scenery of whatever situation the exercise is about—open seas, distant or nearby coast or a harbor with navigational marks and piers. All the instruments are connected to an analog computer. The computer has a mathematical model of the ship to reflect all the forces that affect it—wind, waves, currents, propeller thrust, rudder angle and the actions of the shiphandler. As the captain maneuvers the ship, the computer changes the projected scenery accordingly. The exercise I watched was so much like the real thing, that I felt I was back on the *Dalriada*'s navigation bridge with Captain Smith. Almost any situation a supertanker will encounter in every kind of weather can be simulated, including man-overboard maneuvers. The computer also keeps a record of the captain's actions so that he can analyze them in discussion sessions. A Swedish captain taking the course told me, "A few weeks in Delft is worth more than four years at sea."

The most impressive sight in the world of supertankers and superports is a visit to Rotterdam-Europoort in Holland, which handles more oil and other cargo than any port in the world. Rotterdam, at the mouth of the Rhine, lies in the delta of most of the major European rivers. It is the center of one of the most heavily industrialized areas on earth with 160,000,000 people living within a radius of 300 miles. In 1972, 33,422 ships arrived in the port, of which 433 were 200,000- to 250,000-ton supertankers. In 1973 the number of supertankers increased to 600. The Dutch have been enlarging the port, and berths have already been planned to accommodate the 500,000-ton supertankers. From this busiest port in the world, crude oil is shipped by smaller tankers and pipelines throughout Europe. The fantastic traffic is handled with the efficiency and cleanliness of the proverbial Dutch housewife. There has never been a collision of a big ship in Europort. "That's why we have such strict rules," Captain C. Most, the harbormaster, told me. "Furthermore, we have very little pollution. We only have a few small spills, nothing over thirty-five to seventy barrels, which the oil companies clean up immediately. The biggest oil spill we have ever had in Rotterdam was a thousand barrels."

All the technology, precautions and care which prevail at superports where oil is offloaded are duplicated at ports in which it is loaded aboard supertankers. The world's biggest, busiest port devoted exclusively to shipping petroleum is Aramco's marine terminal at Ras Tanura, Saudi Arabia. In 1972, 3,734 ships were loaded with almost 2 billion barrels of crude oil and refined products destined for markets in sixty-five different countries. I have visited Ras Tanura many times, but on this investigative round-the-world trip, I was especially interested in seeing the new deepwater oil-loading facilities 40 miles offshore in the Persian Gulf which Aramco inaugurated in early 1973. These facilities are the forerunners of what we will call superports in the United States. Our superports will have nothing in common with such places as Kiire, Milford Haven or Rotterdam. They should be called offshore oil terminals, which is exactly what they are. Unfortunately, the word "superport" is lodged in political and press language and will probably stick. American superports will be man-made installations where supertankers can discharge their cargoes far out at sea.

The most economical and environmentally safe type of offshore terminal is what is called a single-buoy mooring, or SBM. It is a simple concept. A large buoy is anchored in deep water and connected to a submarine crude oil line. A supertanker moors at the buoy, and floating hoses carry the oil to or from the tanker, depending on whether it is a loading or receiving terminal. SBM's have the advantage of being operable without any sacrifice of safety in weather which would put other types of terminals out of service. The tanker is free to rotate around the buoy in response to changes in wind, wave and current. Saudi Arabia has two SBM offshore terminals. One loads crude oil from the offshore Zuluf field directly into tankers without first bringing the oil to shore for storage. The crude oil flows from the wells to an offshore gas-oil separator plant, where volatile gases are removed. Then the oil is pumped into a 1,800,000-barrel supertanker which is permanently moored to an SBM and used as a floating storage vessel. The offtaker tanker moors to a second SBM a mile away, and the oil is pumped from the storage vessel into the tanker. The other SBM offshore terminal, Ju'aymah, has two SBM berths and an offshore loading control platform linked by underwater pipelines to crude oil storage tanks onshore.

Despite the tremendous volume of oil handled at Aramco's onshore and offshore terminals, there have never been any oil spills in tanker-loading operations amounting to more than a few barrels. However, a record spill occurred in 1970, when, during a storm, a pipeline broke on land and spilled 100,000 barrels into a nearby shallow bay. The slicks were dispersed before they escaped into the open gulf.

More than 100 SBM berths have been installed and operated worldwide since the system was first devised in 1959. Together with their platforms and undersea pipelines, they have a remarkable pollution-free record. The average spill rate for these installations has been less than 1 barrel for every 1,000,000 barrels handled. The President's Council on Environmental Quality, in its East Coast study, concluded that SBM deepwater terminals using supertankers would cut spills to about one-tenth of what they would be if small ships were used in direct service or transshipment. Most large oil spill accidents occur from collisions and groundings where harbor congestion is great and where ships have to maneuver in narrow channels. Nearly 70 percent of the collisions and groundings during 1969 and 1970 were in harbors or their entrances. A prime advantage of SBM terminals is that they are in the open sea, where collisions are extremely rare.

By 1980 imports to the U.S. East Coast are expected to average 8,500,000 barrels daily. If no changes are made in port facilities or the size of tankers which the United States can accommodate, this volume of imports would require more than 2,000 ships, of the average size making deliveries today, making forty calls a day, or 14,600 arrivals per year. This is more than three times the amount of tanker traffic we have in our ports and harbors today. However, if deepwater offshore terminals were available and the average tanker size were increased to 250,000 tons, only about 250 ships would be needed to handle the same volume of oil. With fewer tankers at sea, hauling just as much oil, the risks would be dramatically less.

Government and industry studies show that the probability of an accident that might cause an oil spill is more than fifteen times greater in the smaller vessels than the mammoth ones. The supersafety features and supersafety precautions of their operators minimize accident potential. Up until 1968 the largest tankers were of the 100,000-ton *Torrey Canyon* class. The new supertankers of 200,000 tons and up now constitute 41 percent of the tonnage of the world's tanker fleet. When supertankers first came into use, three of them had tank explosions while they were cleaning their empty oil tanks at sea. Subsequent research showed that an explosive condition from vapors existed in empty tanks which could be prevented. Now, as a supertanker is being unloaded, noncombustible, inert flue gases from the ship's engines are drawn from the ship's funnel, cooled and purified, and pumped into the tanks as they are emptied, thereby eliminating any explosive condition. Only one supertanker over 200,000 tons has ever been involved in a major oil spill. In 1974 a 206,000-ton tanker ran aground in a violent storm in the virtually uninhabited Strait of Magellan at the tip of South America. It leaked some 300,000 barrels of oil before rescue tankers could offload the balance of the cargo. The only other supertanker oil spill of any size occurred in 1970, when a British 240,000-ton tanker, fully loaded, ran onto a sandbar in the Persian Gulf as the result of faulty navigation. Two tanks were broken, and 10,000 barrels of oil spilled. If there ever is a *Torrey Canyon* type of oil spill of one of today's supertankers, it would, indeed, be a whopper, particularly if it involved a super-supertanker of more than 500,000 tons or the 1,000,000-ton tanker of the future which is being planned. However, the *Torrey Canyon* accident, which was the result of negligence and a wrong navigational decision on the part of the ship's master, marked the beginning of a new maritime era with total emphasis on safety technology and operating standards. There can never be a guarantee against accidents as long as human beings, the machines they make and weather continue to exist. But the fear of supertanker spills obviously has to be balanced with their safety record, advanced safety equipment, the safety-consciousness of today's maritime operators and the rapid development of oil spill cleanup and containment technology.

The feasibility of a number of potential sites for offshore oil terminals on the U.S. East and West coasts and in the Gulf of Mexico has already been determined. Engineering plans, Environmental Impact Statements and approval of the U.S. Corps of Engineers, Council on Environmental Quality and the Environmental Protection Administration have been completed on some, and studies on others are under way. As yet, Congress has not been able to agree on and pass any legislation to permit licensing and construction of offshore terminals. It will take from eighteen months to two years for an offshore terminal, with all its subsidiary facilities onshore, to be put into operation once construction begins. How long it will be before we have such terminals will depend on when Congress passes enabling legislation and what the role of state governments' approvals will be under it. Two projects which are ready to go are: the Louisiana Offshore Oil Port, or LOOP, 19 miles offshore near Grand Isle, Louisiana, with three, and eventually five SBM's with sixteen oil companies participating in its engineering and financing; and Seadock, 25 to 30 miles off Freeport, Texas, with several SBM's and thirteen oil companies participating. These will feed crude oil to existing coastal and inland Midwest refineries and would be able to handle up to 7,000,000 barrels of crude oil daily by 1985. The state governments of Alabama and Mississippi have formed Ameraport, to study and promote the construction of an oil terminal, 26 miles offshore, and three to five new refineries onshore, in the Mobile-Pascagoula area.

All proposals for offshore terminals and new refineries for the East Coast consuming states have met fierce environmental opposition, just as offshore drilling has done. For several years, the Delaware Bay Feasibility Study, an organization formed by thirteen oil companies, has been seeking permission to build an offshore terminal to supply existing East Coast refineries. This is considered by industry and federal government agencies the best East Coast location for an offshore terminal to handle rapidly increasing imports. However, in 1971 Delaware's legislature passed a law banning heavy industry in a 2-mile strip along its 100 miles of coast, which precludes any offshore terminal since onshore installations are necessary. Repeal of the law is currently an embattled state political issue.

East Coast environmentalists want to eat the energy cake somebody else has prepared. During the early 1974 gasoline crisis the State of Maryland sued the Federal Energy Office to get increased gasoline allocations. At the same time the state passed laws to ban planned refinery construction in Chesapeake Bay. In mid-1974 at Project Independence hearings conducted in Boston by John C. Sawhill, Federal Energy Administrator, he said bluntly, "New England must join with the rest of the nation in energy development. There can be no national sacrifice areas that supply energy—at great social costs and physical costs—to areas of the country unwilling to assume their fair share of the responsibility."

The nation is already three to five years behind in the refinery expansion program needed to supply capacity for its increasing consumption. The refinery capacity crunch started back in 1959, when mandatory controls on imported crude oil went into effect. East Coast imports of fuel oil were exempted, and consumers were babied with cheap foreign imports. Those dear days are dead beyond recall, but in the meantime, as the volume of East Coast refined products increased each year, the volume of refining capacity that was "exported" increased accordingly. Instead of being built in the United States, refineries to supply freely imported products were built in Canada, in the Bahamas, in the Virgin Islands or elsewhere in the Caribbean. Now that there is no more "cheap" foreign oil, the cost advantages for the consumer lie in building U.S. refining capacity. However, builders of new refining capacity still don't know which way to jump. One 250,000-barrels-daily refinery costs somewhere between $375,000,000 and $750,000,000. No refiner is going to invest that amount of money unless he knows that he has a reliable source of crude oil supply for it, as well as a place to build it. As of now, he has neither. He knows how politically unreliable and restricted foreign sources of crude oil are. Furthermore, since deepwater offshore terminals are not yet permitted, he can't count on increased foreign supplies, leaving petropolitics aside. Since there is no acceleration of U.S. outer continental shelf exploration and development yet in sight, he can't count on that either. Even if he were prepared to discount these risks, as a number of independent and major refiners are willing to do, and go ahead with a new East Coast refinery, where could he build it? Refining capacity in the United States is now only being increased by the expansion of existing plants. This is by no means enough to do the job.

Environmental objectors to refineries are way behind the times, not only in regard to their understanding of cost economics for the energy consumer, but in their knowledge of modern refineries, which are the kind environmentalists and ecologists can live with. A meaningful example is Standard Oil Company of Kentucky's 240,000-barrels-daily capacity refinery in Pascagoula, Mississippi, which was built in 1962, long before environmental protection was a legal concern. More than $3,500,000 was allocated for pollution control facilities when it was built, and since then $7,000,000 more has been added. It costs the company $500,000 a year to maintain its program. There is no water or air pollution of any kind. Ducks and fish live happily in the refinery's canals, and the shrimp fishermen consider it a good neighbor. Newer refineries carry this concern even further with installation of all the latest developments of noise and odor control and by hiring architectural landscaping firms.

The records of the National Audubon Society's annual Christmas Bird Count are significant in regard to the effect of oil refining on ecology. Every year there is an ardent national competition among Audubon society bird-counting teams, which set up stations all over the country to see who can count the greatest number of bird species in the same daylight period. The purpose is to learn if any bird species are under dangerous stress. In 1972, with 1,018 teams competing nationwide, the Freeport, Texas, team tied with Cocoa, Florida, for first place in North America with 209 species sighted. This might not sound remarkable if you have never been to Freeport. However, if you have, you will know that it appears to be an environmentalist's nightmare industrial complex of chemical and petroleum plants. The birds obviously don't believe what they see, because for twelve years, Freeport has been among the top ten North American stations in the annual census. For the last six years it has been among the top five. In 1972 it set the all-time North American record with 226 species sighted. What makes it even more interesting is that John James Audubon, the famed naturalist, first went to Galveston Bay, where Freeport is located, in 1837 to explore and record its bird population because he had heard of its large bird concentrations.

Everybody needs a burr under his tail to keep him moving. The environmentalist burr under the energy industry tail has produced a great many beneficial results. It has accelerated environmental research, which has prompted new technology and a greater scientific understanding of the complex interrelationship of man and his environment. The Alaska pipeline is a prime example. The delivery of greatly needed oil supplies from our greatest oil strike has been delayed five years by the court battle, following the environmentalists' suit filed under the National Environmental Protection Act in 1970, which stopped pipeline construction as it was about to begin. However, because of the delay, the pipeline will be a far superior engineering job than originally conceived and will have a much less deleterious effect on Alaska's environment. Amazing new equipment and techniques for Arctic operations have been invented and designed which will benefit the growth and development of the entire region. Furthermore, as the result of oil industry studies, we now have a more detailed knowledge of the ecology of Alaska than we do about most of the lower forty-eight states.

During the past five years Alyeska Pipeline Service Company, a consortium of oil companies exploring and developing oil on the

North Slope, bordering the Arctic Ocean, have spent some $400,000,000 and 1,500 man-years to engineer and study the environmental impact of the 800-mile pipeline to transport oil to Valdez, an ice-free port on Alaska's southern coast, from which it will move by tanker to the U.S. West Coast. In addition, a special interagency task force for the Federal Task Force on Alaskan Oil Development prepared an Environmental Impact Statement for the Secretary of the Interior, which took two years to research and whose six volumes, with supplements, weighs 40 pounds. When finished in mid-1977, the pipeline, which began preliminary construction phases in mid-1974, will be the most heavily researched, safest and best-engineered pipeline ever constructed.

Environmentalists objected passionately to the pipeline's construction on the grounds that it "would destroy America's last great wilderness." They feared the effects of construction activities, pipeline operation and potential oil spills on Alaskan wildlife and tundra. When I visited the North Slope oil fields and flew over the proposed pipeline route, I was deeply impressed with the rugged beauty of our last frontier and the magnitude of the problems involved in the engineering feat now beginning. I was also impressed that the controversy involved such a small amount of land. Although the pipeline runs from the top of Alaska to the bottom, the permanent right-of-way will occupy only 8.2 square miles out of Alaska's 586,412 square miles. The use of the land is comparable to building a highway to transport oil. As a matter of fact, the citizens of Valdez, the terminal point, were so incensed against environmentalists for stopping Alaskan development that they filed a suit in California to try to prevent the building of any more freeways on the grounds that they would have an adverse effect on California's environment.

I have seen many oil geological maps in my travels, but at Prudhoe Bay on the North Slope, I saw my first oil ecological maps. Angus Gavin, a Scottish ecologist for the Alaskan operations of the Atlantic Richfield Company, has spent more than forty years in Canada studying the wildlife and its environment. He is considered one of the foremost ecological naturalists with particular expertise in the Arctic and Subarctic areas of North America. He showed me maps he had compiled in his two-year study, by helicopter and on foot, and evaluation of the effects of petroleum development and other related activities on the North Slope on the wildlife of the area and its environment. First he spread out a map of the area showing the migration routes of caribou herds from the south to their summer calving range on the North Slope. On top of this he placed an overlay map showing waterfowl use of the area, detailing breeding pairs per square mile. The next overlay showed the types of fish using the rivers. The final overlay showed where grizzly bears had been sighted.

"We are collecting data on the activities and habitats of these species and others, such as moose, wolves, wolverines, foxes, ground squirrels, lemmings and Arctic shrews, so that we can understand the overall makeup of the ecological and biological systems," Gavin explained. "We also keep a constant check on oil field activities and their relation to the total environment so that the oil companies will know best how to conduct their operations without disturbing them. With relatively few types of creatures, food chains may be broken if just one species is lost."

In environmentalists' opposition, caribou became the symbolic victim of the pipeline to Americans who have never visited Alaska. However, caribou outnumber people two to one, and open season to hunt them is 365 days a year. Nevertheless, oil companies will not permit a gun on the North Slope. Any employee or contractor who violates this rule is immediately fired. Caribou have been a major part of oil company research. We now know that there are 440,000 of them, and their migratory patterns are such that only 6 percent of them will normally cross the right-of-way of the pipeline en route to calving grounds. "On one summer day some six thousand caribou passed through the Atlantic Richfield oil field," Gavin told me, "and grazed around the rigs for several days. On another day a herd of fifteen hundred to two thousand caribou passed through the middle of the base camps, and we had to herd them off the main runway in order to allow planes to land. They seem very blasé about all our activities and pay little attention to aircraft. They only become disturbed if an attempt is made to harass them."

Caribou can migrate 40 miles a day, grazing along the way. The pipeline will alternately be above- and belowground. The above-ground portions, a total of half the length, are designed to have ample overpasses and underpasses. Aleyeska and the U.S. Bureau of Sport Fisheries and Wildlife sponsored a test of caribou reactions to the pipeline, under the direction of the cooperative wildlife research unit of the University of Alaska. A 2-mile pipeline, containing overpasses and underpasses, was simulated with a snow fence covered with burlap. It was the same height and appearance of the 48-inch diameter line which will be installed. Scientists made motion pictures at the test site in the two-season study. Some of the caribou used underpasses, others used overpasses, and some just wandered down to the end of the line, as they could to places where the pipeline will be buried. Their relative indifference can be accounted for by the fact that for centuries their migrations have been interfered with by more formidable natural barriers, such as ice-choked rivers and mile-high mountains.

Environmentalists were also extremely concerned about the danger to certain rare species in the Arctic, particularly peregrine falcons and Dall sheep. Aleyeskan ecologists, together with experts from the U.S. Bureau of Sport Fisheries and Wildlife, traversed the length of the pipeline, counting birds of prey, noting nesting habits and studying the sheep. They found that peregrine falcons which nest in regions near the pipeline will be far enough away from activity so they won't be bothered. Although Dall sheep lamb and graze in one pipeline area, construction will be timed to minimize disturbance to the sheep.

Alaska may look rugged, but the Arctic tundra bruises easily. Almost 85 percent of Alaska is underlain by permafrost, which is permanently frozen material, anything from solid rock to muddy ice, extending from a few feet to hundreds of feet below the surface. In the coldest regions, permafrost is close to the surface, topped by a layer of soil and vegetation which is subject to seasonal thawing and freezing. This is called tundra. In winter, when it is frozen, it can be traversed easily. However, when it is traversed during the short summer thaw, the ruts created by man's activities become permanent when the tundra freezes again. I flew over the north side of the Brooks Range and saw the permanent scars left by the U.S. Navy many years ago when they made tests in the naval oil reserve. Today the tundra will not be scarred as roads built in the oil fields and along the pipeline right-of-way are built on an insulating mat of gravel five feet thick. At Prudhoe Bay, I saw Atlantic Richfield's experimental farm testing new grasses and plants which can form quick new vegetation wherever construction temporarily disrupts ground cover. These have been successfully used to cover scars left by early-day explorers.

There has been much concern about hot oil melting the permafrost as it goes through the pipeline. Oil companies originally planned to bury only 10 percent of the pipeline, but after taking 3,000 soil core samples, they discovered they can bury 50 percent of the line, using specially insulated pipe, without affecting permafrost. In several places where, because of animal migration or approaches to rivers, it is not practical to have aboveground pipe laying, yet where the permafrost is unstable, they are actually going to have a special refrigerated system of burial which will keep the soil below freezing all the time. The pipeline, which will cross earthquake areas, has been designed to remain safe under the severest earthquake ever recorded in Alaska's history. The line will be safety monitored by computers, as well as by air surveillance. It is compartmentalized so that in case of a break it can be shut off to minimize spills.

Not only the present and future of Alaska have concerned researchers. So has the past. The most excited person in Alaska about the pipeline construction is Dr. John P. Cook, head of the University of Alaska's anthropology department. Financed by Alyeska grants, he and a fifteen-man team made a preconstruction survey of the right-of-way along with the oil companies and pipeliners. An archaeological study complies with the Federal Antiquities Act. Supported by helicopters, the scientists walked the 800-mile route and found 200 archaeological sites to investigate for evidence of early man in Alaska. "In two summers we accomplished what normally would require five full years, maybe ten," Dr. Cook says. Until now interior Alaska has been too remote and too expensive for such research which may provide evidence of man's migration to the New World across the Bering Strait 50,000 years ago. "It's an archaeologist's dream," Dr. Cook enthuses. "We've been given an eight-hundred-mile transsection through unexamined territory, and when construction begins, most of the digging will be done free."

It is not surprising that the five years' research and new engineering has increased the cost of building the pipeline. Since it was stopped in 1970, costs have more than tripled, from $1.5 billion to $6 billion. But then, the price of oil has also more than tripled.

Every energy pot must stand on its own legs in accommodating its development to achieving the nation's environmental goals. The oil and gas industry, which supplies three-fourths of our energy, from both domestic and foreign sources, is proving that we don't have to choose between energy or environment. We do not yet fully appreciate that we have already begun a new environmental-conscious industrial revolution which will change our lives for the better. The sooner we realize this, the sooner we will stop stepping on our own feet and creating more energy problems rather than solving the one we have now. There is one inescapable reality. During the next two decades we must continue to depend upon oil and gas to satisfy the majority of our energy needs, while alternate sources are being developed. Consequently, we have to make commonsense decisions on developing our oil and gas resources based on the facts of technological progress rather than on the fictions of unwarranted fears.

The development of our other energy resources involve different environmental, as well as technological problems. Coal is our most abundant energy resource. America has an estimated 3.2 trillion tons, one-fifth of estimated total world coal resources, according to the U.S. Geological Survey. About 150 billion tons of recoverable coal are presently known in formations of comparable thickness and depth to those being mined by present technology. Projected coal production for the next fifteen years would use less than 10 percent of this amount. Despite its abundance, coal has taken a back seat as an energy supplier. In 1973 it supplied only 18 percent of our energy, and we are mining no more coal than we were twenty-five years ago. Its use has declined because of the past low prices of oil and gas and, compared to coal, the ease and cleanliness with which they are produced and consumed. Coal is a tremendous future energy asset, but for the short term it is beset with environmental, technological and social problems.

The electric power industry uses about two-thirds of all coal consumed domestically. Now that we are short of oil, the power industry cannot turn to coal to meet its increased needs because of the provisions of the Clean Air Act of 1970 which set standards for sulfur emissions. The standards scheduled to go into effect in 1975 would make it illegal to use almost half the coal now burned to make electricity. In mid-1974 Congress temporarily relaxed the Clean Air Act to permit oil-short power plants to convert to coal, but only if primary air standards are met. The coal industry's problem of meeting air standards is that two-thirds of the nation's coal is mined in the eastern Appalachian region, where industry is concentrated. This is also where our coal resources with the highest sulfur content are concentrated. It is possible to remove some of the sulfur by various washing and cleaning methods when the coal is mined, but not enough can be removed to meet air standards. When coal is burned by power companies, sulfur dioxide can be removed from stack gases, before going into the atmosphere, but present technology is not yet advanced enough to make this universally economic. There is a sacrifice in generator utilization efficiency and reliability. In the next two or three years the coal industry is optimistic that improved stack gas cleanup systems will be perfected and available for use.

We have an abundance of undeveloped low-sulfur coal resources, but unfortunately they are in the wrong part of the country and involve one of the most controversial of all environmental problems—strip mining. About one third—45 billion tons—of our best currently recoverable coal deposits lie within 100 feet of the surface. More than 70 percent of these deposits are very low sulfur—less than 1 percent. But the majority of them lie in the Western states, principally North Dakota, Montana and Wyoming, under federal and state lands. This is cattleman's and environmentalist's territory. Until we became concerned about air quality, and because of low oil and gas prices and transportation costs to the East Coast, these known, easily recoverable resources slumbered. Strip mining in the East and Midwest was also largely ignored, because the big capital investment were in traditional underground coal mines. However, in the 1960's the picture began to change. Underground mines, which are labor-intensive, were plagued with strikes and labor union demands concerning mine health and safety regulations. New investment money went into strip mining, where machines remove the overburden of dirt and rocks from the coal-bearing rocks. It is safer, open-air work. People don't mind doing it. Production per man-hour is three times higher than underground mining, and surface mining recovers 80 to 90 percent of the coal, contrasted with half the coal which is left in underground mines to prevent cave-ins. Strip mining grew from 31 percent of coal production in 1960 to 50 percent in 1973, with most of this growth occurring in Eastern and Midwestern areas.

When strip mining began many years ago in the hills of Appalachia, mining companies blasted the overburden from the steep hillsides, ripped the coal from its seams and went on to the next site, leaving great ugly scars and thousands of miles of high man-made walls of overburden. The land was rendered useless and no effort was made to reclaim it. These horrors still exist and have created the image of strip mining. However, in recent years most coal-mining states have passed stiff reclamation laws. Modern strip mining plans land reclamation before operations begin. Topsoil is either placed in another area which has been mined and graded or is stored until a suitable area is available. After the coal is removed, bulldozers level the high wall and overburden left by the mining process. Then the land is restored to its original contour and revegetated. In some cases, it is put to new uses, such as lakes, parks and pastureland. Land reclamation follows mining by only a few months. Reclamation needs good soil and adequate rainfall to be successful. Only about 60 percent of the potential low-sulfur coal areas in the West have such favorable conditions.

For four years Congress has been wrestling over the highly controversial issue of formulating federal nationwide standards for strip-mining reclamation. Many environmental groups wanted to ban strip mining outright. However, by mid-1974 both the House and the Senate, after heated battles and debates, had passed stiff strip-mining reclamation legislation. The cost of reclamation to the consumer, at the highest estimates, would add 2 to 3 percent to the average residential electric bill.

One of the reasons the coal industry fell so far behind as an energy source is that it lived in the past rather than thought in terms of the future. As a whole the coal industry did little research to develop new technology. However, there was a drastic change in the 1960's. Major oil companies, considering energy as an overall problem, began acquiring coal properties and investing heavily in coal technology research. A primary objective was to develop new techniques to convert coal into a wide range of clean liquid fuels to replace petroleum and to convert coal to synthetic gas. Coal gasification has been used in Europe for many years, but American joint government-industry research has concentrated on developing improved lower-cost gasification methods with enough energy content to substitute for conventional natural gas uses. Several methods are now in the pilot demonstration phase. The technology for producing coal liquids is not as fully developed, but a number of pilot plants, using various methods, are operating. Research has been intensified, and the companies involved optimistically predict that during the early 1980's, the new technology will enable us to begin making use of coal gas and liquids. Today's energy economics would make this development of our tremendous coal resources commercially feasible.

Technology is already available for an exciting new product from coal—synthetic methanol, an easily stored and transported clear liquid which has a heating value about one-half that of kerosene. It is clean-burning and can be used today primarily as a petrochemical feedstock. A group of utilities in New Orleans recently conducted successful tests involving burning methanol in a boiler. Methanol could replace gasoline as a fuel for cars and replace liquified petroleum gas or heating oil for farms and trailer homes. Synthetic methanol could be the first major new use of coal.

There is one potential drawback in the prospects for synthetic fuels. Development of the synthetic industry is based primarily on the availability of Western coal reserves because the much lower cost of these reserves would more than offset the great cost of transporting synthetic fuels by pipeline to the centers of demand. Consequently, the success of the synthetic fuels industry is, in large part, tied to the resolution of strip-mining environmental problems.

We have enormous oil resources locked up in oil shales in the Western United States. To depths of 20,000 feet they contain 27.3 trillion barrels of oil, or almost five times the world's proved producible oil reserves. Formidable environmental, technological and cost problems have prevented tapping this great energy source. Nevertheless, during the past decade, the necessary technology to extract the oil has been developed. Now the increase in oil prices makes oil shale production economically feasible in some areas. The richest concentration of oil shale, yielding 30 or more gallons of oil per ton, underlies about 17,000 square miles of the Rocky Mountains in Colorado, Utah and Wyoming. It contains an estimated 418 billion barrels of recoverable oil.

About 80 percent of all oil shale deposits are owned by the federal government. In 1970 Interior Secretary Morton, who was among the first to appreciate the extent of the nation's energy problem, initiated a program to hold an auction for leases on six federal oil-shale tracts on which demonstration plants of about 50,000-bar-rels-a-day capacity would be built. These prototype plants would provide answers to technological, economic and environmental questions and lay the foundation for a large-scale commercial shale oil industry. Detailed Environmental Impact Statements were prepared to justify the plan, but it was not until January, 1974, following the embargo and increase in oil prices, that lease auctions were held. Major oil companies bid on four tracts in Colorado and Utah, which involved both strip and underground mining, but two tracts in Wyoming went begging. They were to be developed by *in situ* processing. This involves fragmenting the shale inside the mine by explosives, introducing gas from the surface through an air vent and igniting it to superheat the fractured shale. This releases the oil, which is then pumped out. The shale residue remains in the ground. This method is highly experimental and controversial. Occidental Oil Company has been experimenting with it on private oil shale land and claims success. It would be more environmentally acceptable than underground or strip mining, but other shale developers are skeptical of its successful use on a large scale. Only about 10 percent of oil shale deposits can be strip-mined. In both strip and underground mining, after the shale is extracted, the oil is "cooked" out of it in a processing plant.

A major environmental problem is disposing of the processed shale, particularly since the shale expands when heated, and the processed shale occupies 15 percent more volume than the original rock. The Oil Shale Corporation, or TOSCO, whose partners are Atlantic Richfield, Shell and Ashland, believes oil shale operations can be handled with a minimum degradation to the existing ecology and environment. TOSCO, which started an oil shale pilot plant in 1969 in Colorado on private land, has spent $3,000,000 in environmental studies and tests. Its planned commercial plant would process more than 60,000 tons of raw shale per day to obtain 50,000 barrels of oil. Eventually, some of the spent shale will be replaced in the mines, but a lead time of five years is necessary for this. Most of the material will be placed in valleys or depressions on the property. Much of TOSCO's research has been on revegetation. It has proved that grasses and shrubs will grow as well on processed shale as on native earth. After a period of maintenance, a processed shale pile can be as self-sustaining and as productive to wildlife and other elements of the ecosystem as the area's natural soils.

TOSCO had hoped to have its plant in operation by 1977, but in September, 1974, the company announced suspension of its plans to start construction in 1975. The company blamed "current double-digit inflation, tight money, and the absence of a national energy policy, which establishes clearly the role of oil from shale in the national energy picture."

An interagency federal Oil Shale Task Force is making a study of oil shale potential, as one of nine studies being drawn up for Project Independence, assessing the potential of all energy resources. The oil shale draft report concludes that under the most optimistic conditions total oil shale production could reach 2.5 million barrels a day by 1990, which is less than 17 percent of current U.S. consumption. To achieve this would require leasing 155,000 more acres of public lands by 1985, and the sales would have to begin in 1976, four years before the results of the current prototype program are available. The task force considers it most likely that 1,600,000 barrels daily will be reached by leasing 100,000 additional acres, with lease sales beginning in 1977. The group concludes that water resources are adequate at present to support accelerated mining and plant development, but the construction of new dams and regional water planning will be a determining factor in the rate of development of large-scale production. The greatest risk to the oil shale industry, according to the task force, is the fluctuation in the price of oil. No shale oil would be produced at a world oil price of $4 a barrel. But shale oil could be competitive with world oil prices between $7 and $11 a barrel. Our vast shale oil resources are an insurance policy for energy needs of the next century, but it takes time, research and tremendous capital investment to overcome the environmental and technological problems surrounding them.

The greatest controversy over the conflicts between energy and the quality of our environment rages around the role which nuclear fission power is planned and projected to play in our immediate future. Currently it supplies less than 5 percent of our electric energy. The U.S. Atomic Energy Commission expects nuclear power generating capacity to increase twelve to fifteen times in 1985 and three to four times more between 1985 and 2000. In the early 1960's the dream of limitless nuclear power was enthusiastically acclaimed as the ultimate energy answer. It was oversold. Technology has developed slowly. Construction of nuclear plants has been hampered by environmental protests and actions. Everybody wants the power, but nobody wants the plant. By mid-1974 there were 51 plants operating and 47 being built. There were firm orders for 101 more and letters of intent for 14. By the early 1980's these plants would provide nearly one-quarter of the nation's electricity. However, recently the scientific community has become sharply divided on the issue of total commitment to nuclear power as our major energy source, as well as how rapidly current technology should be put into use.

How safe is safe? This is the heart of the matter. In August, 1974, the Atomic Energy Commission released a fourteen-volume study on nuclear power plant safety, which took sixty nuclear power specialists, ten of whom were SEC employees, two years to prepare under the direction of Dr. Norman C. Rasmussen, professor of nuclear engineering at the Massachusetts Institute of Technology. The study compared the chance of mass destruction from an atomic reactor accident to that of a meteor striking an urban area—once in a million years. The study estimated that in any year there was only one chance in a billion that a nuclear power plant would fail accidentally and that the release of radiation would cause as many as several thousand deaths. "From the viewpoint of a person living in the general vicinity of a reactor, the likelihood of being killed in any one year in a reactor accident is one chance in 300 million," the study stated, "and the likelihood of being injured in any one year in a reactor accident is one chance in 150 million. From a broader societal viewpoint, one individual of the 15 million people living in the vicinity of 100 reactors might be killed and 2 individuals might be injured every 25 years."

As AEC Commissioner Dixy Lee Ray says, "There is no such thing as zero risk." However, she points out that much of the hostility to the nuclear power program is based on the fear of the unknown. A nuclear plant cannot explode, but public fears have been primarily based on associating nuclear power with the atom bomb. According to Sigvard Eklund, director-general of the UN's International Atomic Energy Agency, after more than 1,000 years of cumulative nuclear reactor experience in sixteen countries there have been no fatalities or uncontrolled radioactive emissions. The AEC safety report will by no means end the scientific controversy, but it gives a better perspective on potential risks to human safety.

A problem of even greater concern than accidents is how to dispose of the highly radioactive waste products from normal operations of nuclear plants. They are small in quantity, but deadly poisonous in quality. They will remain radioactive for centuries. No long-term solution to this problem has been found yet. For the present, the lethal material is being safely stored at AEC installations at Hanford, Washington, and Savannah River, South Carolina. However, as nuclear power plants proliferate so does the amount of radioactive waste. The AEC has learned how to solidify these wastes and is considering storing them in underground salt domes and mines, but no satisfactory permanent disposal system has yet been devised. It is also vital that some international understanding be reached concerning dumping nuclear wastes as nuclear plants increase worldwide.

A nuclear power by-product problem that is currently deeply troubling the industry is only beginning to be called to public attention. Even to talk about it has been considered almost as explosively dangerous as the atom bomb itself. Nuclear scientists speak of it in guarded tones in reports and studies because it concerns the possibilities of international war and political terrorism. A nuclear power plant by-product is plutonium, which can be reused in the power plant after it is extracted from the spent fuel at a reprocessing plant. However, plutonium is the stuff atomic bombs are made out of. What happens if a nonnuclear power nation, for whom we or other countries have built nuclear power plants and provided with nuclear fuel, decides to take the plutonium and make atom bombs and then gets trigger-happy? Also, what happens if terrorists or revolutionaries organize a *Mission Impossible* type of raid on a nuclear power plant, steal plutonium for homemade atom bombs and blackmail a whole nation? Given the state of human behavior today and the advanced scientific knowledge freely available, these possibilities are not improbable. The greatest precautions and security measures are being taken against civilian thefts from a nuclear power plant. But who can control the government of a potentially troublemaking nation?

As far as environmental air or water pollution from nuclear plants is concerned, there is no air pollution, and water pollution problems are the same that face all power plants, whether they use fossil or nuclear fuels. They all have to use large quantities of water to cool the heat-generating operations of their equipment. That water gets hot, so what do you do with hot water? We didn't use to think much about the effect of what is called thermal pollution when we dumped it back into the streams, rivers and oceans. However, with the growth of concern of the impact of man's activities on the ecology of his environment, thermal pollution has become a major problem-solving area. Most states now require that power plant water be returned to the ecosystem at temperatures with upper limits of between 90 to 95 degrees, depending on the temperatures of the receiving waters, so that it will not endanger marine biological systems and growth. One of the great dangers to marine life is any quick change in temperatures. Power plants have devised elaborate and expensive systems for cooling the waters they use. All cooling is done by evaporation of some sort, whether it is in cooling retaining ponds, cooling canals or cooling towers, the method which has the greatest acceptance by the Environmental Protection Agency. This method involves drawing the water up in towers and letting it cascade down to cool.

We are just beginning to learn that man-made warm water can be a new resource. The prospect of the increasing amounts of heated waste water from all the new power plants being built has opened up a new field of research. "If it were possible to use only 10 percent of the heat rejected from the generating stations to be built over the next 30 years," according to an AEC report, "the net effect would be to use more rejected energy than the equivalent in electrical energy generated today."

Initial research is concentrating on agriculture and aquaculture. The University of Arizona's Environmental Research Lab has experimental air-inflated plastic greenhouses humidified and heated with power plant waste water. It is growing tomatoes twice the size of the same field-grown variety and cucumbers ripen in half the time. Its researchers envision a new form of urban agriculture under plastic domes located near power plants. Oregon State University researchers have determined that heated water distributed through the subsoil or sprinkler systems can prevent frost damage, extend the growing season, promote crop growth and improve crop quality. Fruit and nut trees sprayed with warm water were undamaged by frost, while unsprayed trees were damaged. Cauliflower and corn yields were increased more than 50 percent by raising root and soil temperatures. Researchers are also experimenting with cultivating algae in large open-air basins as a future source of protein. These plants produce protein at rates ten or twenty times greater than soybeans per unit area and grow fastest in waters with temperatures of 80 to 90 degrees. The University of Miami has experimented with shrimp breeding utilizing power plant thermal discharge waters. Catfish, which thrive in warm water, are being raised commercially in similar waters in Texas and Tennessee. The most successful commercial venture to date is the Long Island Oyster Farms hatchery in a power plant discharge lagoon. Oysters can now be grown year-round and grow five times their natural rate. Natural oyster fishing had almost died out on Long Island, but now it is expected to become a major industry again.

Planning for siting a nuclear power plant may consume up to five years. An additional one to two years of this time is devoted to preparing Environmental Impact Statements, safety analysis reports and holding public hearings to overcome local objections to the plant site. Actual construction takes about eight years. Consequently, from plan to power is now about fifteen years. Sometimes environmental objections are almost, if not entirely, impossible to overcome. Projects encounter further delays, or the site is abandoned. The most serious environmental objections have primarily involved safety factors. However, in the nation's first purely environmental vs. nuclear energy conflict, a $1.3 billion nuclear power project has been blocked by the California Coastal Zone Conservation Commission on the grounds that it would deface scenic cliffs, obstruct public access to a beach and harm marine life. The project had been approved by the AEC and the California Public Utilities Commission after three years of public hearings, beginning in 1970. The 1972 state law which created the Conservation Commission, a citizens' board, is the strictest in the country. It gives the commission authority over all future developments within 1,000 yards of high tide along California's

1,000-mile coastline. The case has been appealed in the courts, as provided by law, but a lengthy battle is expected.

Environmental opposition to land-based nuclear plants has prompted the industry to prepare to go offshore. From the viewpoint of less costly electricity for the consumer, power plants need to be close to the consuming area. But this is exactly where the people are who don't want the power plants. Consequently, locating plants offshore will solve a number of problems. There is no problem of land acquisition. Floating power plants can be moored offshore where they are close to the consumer but have less visual impact. Cooling water, always a problem on land, is readily available and thermal wastes will have a negligible effect on a small area of the ocean. The first offshore nuclear plant is being built in Florida by Offshore Power Systems, a joint venture of the Westinghouse Electric Corporation and Tenneco. A contract has been signed with the Public Service Electric and Gas Company of New Jersey to deliver a $1 billion floating plant by 1979. The plants' two units will be towed from Florida and moored in a horseshoe-shaped breakwater about 3 miles off Little Egg Inlet on the New Jersey coast. Intensive environmental studies are being prepared, including an oceanographic survey, meteorlogical program, environmental radiation survey and geologic survey program. Needless to say, when public hearings are held, there will be tremendous opposition. However, it may well pioneer the best way to resolve the environmental and nuclear power plant siting conflict.

Uranium, the metal which is the source of nuclear fuel, is in short supply in the United States as a natural resource. Domestic resources, recoverable at present prices, totaled about 273,000 tons at the end of 1971, and the total of all countries is about 1,600,000 tons. These supplies will last into the 1980's, but after that uranium needs will be so great that there must be intense exploration for new deposits. However, from the very beginning of our nuclear power program, the AEC has pinned its hopes on developing technology for a different kind of nuclear fission reactor from that being used now. It is called a breeder reactor because it literally breeds more usable nuclear fuel than it consumes in the process of producing heat to make electricity. Existing reactors waste 99.3 percent of the energy in uranium, but the breeder utilizes almost all of it by converting it into plutonium, which serves as a fuel to generate electricity. It produces more plutonium than the uranium it consumed. Another advantage of the breeder reactor is that it could convert the metal thorium into a nuclear fuel. Thorium is about three times more abundant in the earth's crust than uranium. Breeder reactors could provide an almost limitless source of low-cost energy.

The Soviet Union started the world's first commercial nuclear breeder reactor in 1972. Both Britain and France now have breeder reactors. However, U.S. development of breeder technology has been deliberately cautious and is now bogged down in environmental disputes. In 1971 the government announced a priority commitment to complete a $700,000,000 demonstration reactor by 1980 near Oak Ridge, Tennessee. The AEC forecast forty-nine such reactors in use in the 1980's with breeders generating one-fourth of all U.S. electric power by 2000.

Scientific and environmental groups protested that too little was known about them to warrant such rapid development. The Scientists' Institute for Public Information in New York sued in federal district court to force the AEC to comply with the National Environmental Policy Act of 1970 and provide an Environmental Impact Statement assessing the long-term effects of breeder reactor use. The AEC had issued an EIS only on building the Oak Ridge plant. The environmentalist suit was dismissed, but when they appealed it, the U.S. Court of Appeals reversed the lower court decision in June, 1973, saying that the "program presents unique and unprecedented environmental hazards to human health for hundreds of years." The decision added that in addition to the AEC's providing a full Environmental Impact Statement, it should make a detailed statement about alternatives. In response to the court order, the AEC issued a five-volume draft statement in March, 1974. It drew immediate fire from the Environmental Protection Agency as being "inadequate" on all scores. AEC officials agreed that some of the missing information could not be given until more research is done. The statement failed to make explicit comparisons of the breeder reactor power program with alternatives, such as solar power. The AEC took the position that it was unreasonable to ask for such a comparison since so little is known about the potential of solar energy and that using the sun for electric power is so far in the future that it cannot be considered as an alternative to breeder reactors. When the final AEC Environmental Impact Statement is prepared, the blanket criticisms of the EPA will undoubtedly be used as a basis for further court challenges by the environmentalists. In the meantime, the cost estimate for the demonstration breeder reactor project has more than doubled—from $700,000,000 to $1.74 billion. The prospects of the AEC's achieving its goal of breeder reactor generation of electricity commercially by 1987 grow dimmer rather than brighter.

Perhaps the greatest difficulty in reconciling environmental problems with the development of all sources of energy is for consumers and Congressmen to try to understand which "experts" are right and which are wrong. Whatever we do or don't do depends on the political actions we take. Congressmen vote according to what they think the people want. The people may know what they think they want, but they don't always know the best way to achieve it. Nor do they have all the facts. You and I generally react emotionally to situations. Too many environmentalists, consumer advocates and academicians appeal almost entirely to our emotions and cater to our fears. When we hear sweeping generalities uttered by a professor or scientist from a prestigious university, we are impressed and think he must know what he's talking about. It seldom occurs to us that it is important to know how well versed he is in all aspects of a problem.

Environmental specialists, in particular, are woefully short in their understanding and knowledge of technology and economics. This is why, by following them, we have made a great many unwise decisions too quickly and have postponed making so many others. We haven't had time to understand environmental economics, what trade-offs we are being asked to make and what our options are. Without this knowledge we can't get our priorities straight. However, one thing is exceedingly clear: No matter what decision is made, you and I pay for it in cash.

Our primary immediate concern about the environment is to avoid polluting our air and our water. Technology created pollution. It can also prevent it. But there is a price tag attached. Pollution control equipment and processes increase the cost of energy. Research and development of new technology are costly. Environmental impact statements add to construction costs—as much as 20 percent of the cost of a new power plant. Reclaiming land after strip mining is expensive. New health and safety measures add to the cost of coal mining. All these costs increase the price of the energy we use, whether we use it directly as electricity, heating and cooking fuels, gasoline and oil for our cars, or indirectly as part of the cost of producing almost everything we buy, including food.

Our concern for air quality has produced one of the most tangled, complicated group of interrelated problems the nation has had to cope with, involving auto emissions, gasoline quality, fuel, economy and energy conservation. Cars account for nearly half our air pollution, and in the haste to tackle this major source we have created waste. Also there is mounting controversy over the wisdom and necessity of measures taken to date.

The emission-control devices, which came out in 1973, compounded our fuel shortage. The Federal Office of Emergency Preparedness stated that gasoline consumption increased 300,000 barrels a day because of them. That figure amounts to about 4.5 percent of U.S. gasoline demand. We face an even greater drain in our fuel resources with the requirement of the availability of no-lead gasoline, beginning in July, 1974, and for lead phasedown in leaded gasoline beginning on January 1, 1975. It takes 6 percent more oil to produce lead-free gasoline and increases refining costs. The reason lead is added to gasoline is to raise its octane rating, which is simply a number indicating how much compression the fuel can take without making the engine knock. Upgrading octane rating by adding lead eliminates superrefining costs to obtain the same desirable efficiency. Refiners estimate that the requirements for nonleaded gasoline will cut the U.S. gasoline supply by a minimum of almost 800,000,000 barrels between 1974 and 1980, or an average annual loss of about 5 percent of the present annual gasoline consumption.

The controversy over lead in gasoline has little to do with health. According to the United Nation's World Health Organization and the American Medical Association, lead from auto exhaust does not constitute a danger to people. The automobile companies, government agencies and environmentalists have been adamant about getting lead out of gasoline because it destroys all the devices anyone has come up with yet to make other pollutants in auto exhaust harmless. Automobile manufacturers made the decision that a catalytic converter for 1975 cars, whch cleans the exhaust after combustion, was the best way to meet the stiff clean-air standards required by 1975. Leaded gasoline destroys the effectiveness of the converter. The oil industry is spending several billions of dollars for necessary manufacturing changes to make unleaded gasoline available. Yet at the very time when 1975 automobiles with catalytic converters went on the market, Environmental Protection Agency experts expressed concern that traces of sulfur in gasoline will cause autos equipped with catalytic converters to emit sulfuric acid mists from their tail pipes. These could create serious health problems when large numbers of 1975 and later models are on the road. All 1975 General Motors models have them. About 70 percent of Ford and Chrysler models and 35 percent of American Motors cars are so equipped. To complicate the situation further, Ford and Chrysler engineers have indicated that they can control pollution emissions by the late 1970's without using catalytic converters. Lead removal may prove to be one of the most costly environmental mistakes made, from the view point of the consumer, who has to pay the added costs of automobile equipment and unleaded gasoline, even though enough time has not been permitted by Congress and the federal government for research to determine if the requirements are actually necessary.

In 1970, when an environmentally emotional Congress passed the National Environmental Protection Act and the Clean Air and Clean Water Acts nobody in Congress, industry or the public had any idea of what such legislation would cost the consumer and industry. Standards were set arbitrarily and without adequate research. Now that enough research has been done to analyze and evaluate problems, the question of relaxing or extending standards is once again a highly political matter. Environmentalists are greatly perturbed that the gains we have made in cleaning up and protecting the environment will be lost because of energy shortages and mounting consumer costs which will make the public begin to evaluate costs and benefits.

The Clean Air Act decrees that there should be a primary air-quality standard to protect human health, which must be met by 1977. A stricter secondary standard to protect human welfare concerns plants, livestock and property but has no fixed date. To prevent further deterioration of air quality, Congress only said that its purpose was "to protect and enhance the quality of the nation's air resources." The Environmental Protection Agency, as well as other government agencies, did not interpret this as meaning that nondeterioration should be enforced by preventing industrial development in areas where air quality is already cleaner than primary and secondary standards. However, the Sierra Club and other environmental groups took a different viewpoint. They argued that such air must not be polluted at all, sued the EPA and carried the case to the Supreme Court. The Court ruled that Congress meant to forbid any "significant deterioration" of existing clean air but didn't define "significant." The EPA, forced to issue regulations on "nondeterioration," in August, 1974, passed the buck to the individual states. The regulations allow the states to make their own choices between pollution and industrial and economic growth. The Sierra Club planned to go to court again. This underscores the necessity of making some practical sense out of a confused situation. Congress has asked the National Academy of Sciences to review the Ambient Air Quality Standards, as set by the Environmental Protection Agency, to determine—for the first time—if the standards, which must be met by 1977, are more severe than necessary to protect public health and welfare. It would be as foolish unnecessarily to hamper industrial growth and force economic waste and social dislocations as it would be to abandon our environmental goals.

Now that we see all the problems we have created by trying to solve problems, it is obvious that we cannot do simultaneously all the things we would like to do as quickly as we would like. We have made tremendous progress, but there is much more we must do in the years ahead. We are evolving dynamic new concepts and approaches. We are giving ourselves new tools to work with. However, just as the Lilliputians managed to immobilize Gulliver by tying him up with myriad tiny strings, so have our multitude of haphazard, uncoordinated, conflicting laws, regulations and legal actions managed to place a giant nation in an astonishing predicament. Our highest priority now should be to set realistic standards and policies, with a rational timetable for the orderly development of our technology so that we may achieve our goals efficiently, safely and economically.

6

Zero Growth vs. Building America Twice

In early 1972 a thought bomb exploded which sent shock waves around the world. A group of Massachusetts Institute of Technology professors published a book, *Limits to Growth,* which was a popularized version of computerized studies on the present and future predicament of man. They concluded that if the present growth trends in world population, industrialization, pollution, food production and resource depletion continue unchanged, the limits to growth on this planet will be reached sometime within the next 100 years.

Not since Thomas Malthus wrote his *Essay on the Principle of Population* in 1798, prophesying that population growth would bring disaster because we would run out of food, had such a cause for intellectual anxiety been presented or created such an enormous stir. The MIT professors' Systems Dynamics Group study was a project under the auspices of the Club of Rome, sometimes called "the invisible college." It came into existence in 1968 when a group of 30 scientists, educators, economists, humanists, industrialists and national and international civil servants from ten nations met in the Accademia dei Lincei in Rome and decided to promote a new public understanding of the global system in which we live and try to influence policymakers to take new world initiatives and actions.

Limits to Growth concluded that it is possible to alter its frightening forecast and to "establish a condition of ecological and economic stability that is sustainable far into the future." However, growth would have to be discarded in favor of "global equilibrium." How such equilibrium could be achieved before the 100-year deadline in a world community which finds it difficult to agree on when to hold an international meeting or the shape of the table around which the conferees sit was not spelled out. Nor did the computer or its information feeders come up with any answers about the potential of social, economic and political chaos resulting from zero growth and a declining world system.

The professors stated that the issues involved must be debated by a wider community than that of scientists alone and their purpose was "to open that debate." In this, they were highly successful. In the United States, the study was hailed with gloomy joy by the group of environmental and sociological doomsday prophets who had already captured a dismayed nation's attention. For the first time, we were aware of the problems our profligate consumption was creating. We were beginning to understand the implications of the phenomenon of "exponential growth" which was the basis of the assumptions made by the Club of Rome study.

The amount of annual world increase in population, food production, industrialization, pollution and consumption of nonrenewable natural resources—the study's five basic elements—follows a pattern that mathematicians call exponential growth. If you put $100 in a savings account and receive 7 percent interest, your money will double in ten years. The first year's interest is $7, which is added to the accounts, making it $107. The next year's interest is 7 percent of the new total, amounting to $7.49, making another new total on which to figure interest. In other words, the money grows exponentially. Exponential growth, when applied to such things as population and resource consumption, involves many other complex and changing elements but, in general, is the basis on which we make predictions of future supply and demand.

Predictions of the exponential growth requirements of the United States just between now and the year 2000 are enormous. The average age of the U.S. population is about twenty-eight. Life expectancy at that age is about forty-five years. Consequently, we have a forty-five year demand for everything, just to support people now living at present rates of consumption. However, by the year 2000, there will be from 40,000,000 to 90,000,000 more of us than there are today, to be consumers. Birthrates have greatly declined in the past few years, but the U.S. Census Bureau estimates that even if the decline continues, we will not reach the stage of zero population growth until sometime in the first half of the twenty-first century. The bureau now estimates that population will grow from our present more than 210,000,000 to somewhere between 251,000,000 and 300,000,000 by the end of the century. This means a tremendous expansion of houses, apartments, schools, hospitals, stores, factories, refineries, power plants, streets, roads, recreational facilities and all the other facilities, goods and services which a growing population requires and desires. Major urban centers have been expanding at the rate of 1,000 square miles per year, which is like adding a new Boston each year. We have been building 8,000 miles of new roads annually. Economic planning and development of metropolitan centers has been increasing at about 10,000 square miles a year, an area larger than the state of New Hampshire. At such rates, by 2000 urban areas already developed will be duplicated.

The amount of resources of all kinds required for this growth is staggering. "In the next twenty-six years we will create a Second America in the very real sense that we will mine, pump, manufacture and build at least as much as we did in all previous American history," says Dr. Vincent E. McKelvey, director of the U.S. Geological Survey and one of the world's foremost authorities on mineral resources. "The land areas that are expected to undergo development just in major urban centers and by highways and surface mining amount to more than 90,000 square miles by the end of the century, an area nearly equivalent to the state of Wyoming. Adding to this the need to replace worn-out buildings and roads, it is easy to see that we will have to more than duplicate the entire physical plant that now exists in this country. This construction will require prodigious amounts of resources, including energy, minerals, water and land. To illustrate just one aspect of this enormous task that lies ahead in these next twenty-six years, we will have to locate, excavate, move, process and put into place not less than a hundred billion tons of sand, gravel and stone."

Despite its magnitude, Dr. McKelvey does not find our growth prospects overly alarming or impossible to achieve. Nor does he consider that we will be putting our nation or our future at risk by doing so. He is one of many scientists who commend the Club of Rome for initiating new thinking about our potential problems, but strongly disagree with its conclusions and seriously criticize its assumptions. Dr. McKelvey points out that we are a mineral- and mineral-fuels-based society. While mineral fuels furnish energy for all our machines, the machines themselves and virtually all the things we use either have a mineral component or are in some way dependent on the use of minerals in their processing. Historically, our per capita gross national product has increased in nearly direct proportion to increasing consumption of energy and minerals, and for the past several decades in the United States, both have been increasing exponentially at the rate of a few percents per year. For many minerals, between now and the end of the century, projected needs would require amounts larger than the entire world has consumed in all previous history. However, we do not yet know the magnitude of undiscovered minerals and mineral fuels resources. No methods have been developed for a truly accurate long-range assessment of our mineral supplies. Nevertheless, the Club of Rome substituted for knowledge the general assumption that the resource supply is the equivalent of 250 years of consumption at present rates. It defined a fixed supply by assumption, so its conclusions are necessarily speculative. Other assumptions could support other conclusions. The fallacy of such an approach is further compounded by what Dr. McKelvey considers its two most serious errors. It made insufficient allowances for accelerated growth of the technology that can enlarge our resources and abate pollution. And it gave no consideration to human ingenuity.

"Crucial in the evaluation of potential resources is an understanding of what resources are and how they are created," Dr. McKelvey states. "Defining resources as materials usable by man, a little reflection reveals that whereas it is God who creates minerals and rocks, it is man who creates resources. To be sure, the earth as a planet is of fixed dimension. Perhaps the usable proportion of the earth and the energy it receives from the solar system is also fixed in an ultimate sense. But what is important to recognize is that the magnitude of resources that man may create with continued advance in science and technology is not discernible and may be many, many times larger than can be imagined now.

"Rather than living from and being limited by the bounty of nature, as Malthus thought, we are living from resources literally created by scientific research and technologic development. And rather than exhausting our natural resources by profligate use, as is often claimed, we have enormously expanded them by extending our ability to discover concealed deposits, by developing means to mine and process lower-grade materials, by finding ways to use new kinds of minerals and fuels, by using them more efficiently and by recycling some of them. These processes have not only increased the supply of usable materials but have made them available at progressively lower costs.

"What is most important about this is not merely that resources can be created and supply can be extended by continued research and technologic development, but the fact that human ingenuity is an integral part of the total system. Malthus essentially only considered two elements—people and food supply—and the MIT group was correct in recognizing other essential components of the total man-nature system. But to this list must be added human ingenuity, and it is perhaps the most important component of all.

And in terms of growth, its rate also has been exponential. As with population, resource consumption and other phenomena, perhaps exponential technologic growth cannot continue indefinitely. But certainly its limits are far beyond our imagination. Personally, I am confident that for millennia to come we can continue to develop the mineral supplies needed to maintain a high level of living for those who now enjoy it and to raise it for the impoverished people of our own country and the world."

Proponents of zero growth are more articulate and vociferous than they are numerous. However, the growing confrontation between energy use and environmental protection is making us reexamine our attitudes toward the *rate* of growth. We have blithely taken for granted the principle that more is always better and that there is always more to be had. We didn't have to pay the piper because we didn't know there was one, much less what his going rates were. Now we find ourselves dancing to a different tune, and the piper has turned into a bill collector. We are faced with the necessity of doing something entirely foreign to our character and experience: purposefully slowing our growth by conserving our energy resources.

We have not run out of energy resources, technology or ingenuity. But we have painted ourselves into a shortage corner. Until the paint dries and we can step out confidently once again, we are going to have to operate on a reduced scale of activities. Conservation is a state of mind and a state of pocketbook. Over the past few years I have been so keenly aware of the energy shortage that I have made it a point to turn out all unnecessary lights, radios, television sets and air conditioners. When I was in Saudi Arabia, just before the Arabs dropped the energy bomb, I found I was doing the same thing by force of habit. I felt a little foolish and asked myself, "What are you doing that for? This is where it's all coming from." Back in the United States, my habits were still the same, but my motivation had undergone a dramatic change. My electric utility bill had doubled.

In general, the public and industry were not aware of how much energy everybody was wasting until short supply and high prices forced us to take a new look. What we saw was a revelation. We responded so well to the exigencies of shortages and increased prices that, much to the distress of the petroleum-producing nations, whose sole aim is to keep petroleum production in short supply to maintain high prices, we created a counterforce against their goal to raise prices further by reducing our consumption to the point that by mid-1974 there was an excess of 2,000,000 barrels a day of oil production. Although this didn't solve our shortage problem or high prices, at least it proved what every kid on the block wants to demonstrate: We have muscle, and we can use it. Even a group of scientists and personnel in the isolated McMurdo Station of the U.S. Antarctic Research Program proved what could be done. Operating in year-round temperatures averaging 50 degrees below zero, they are totally dependent on air and ship lifts of all supplies to carry out their research. During the energy crisis, despite an increase in scientific programs, they cut their precious petroleum energy use by 20 percent over the year before. How did they do this? The same way you and I did! They turned down the heat, turned off the lights and cut down waste.

What we have to realize is that we must develop a total new *consistent* conservation ethic, in addition to making the right political decisions to increase our energy supplies. Energy conservation must be a national goal. Every energy user must become an energy conservationist. It is one thing to conserve energy in an emergency when we have to, but changing the American mental attitude toward energy use will be difficult. We are the most highly energized people on earth, consuming one-third of the world's energy with only 6 percent of its population. In the United States, human energy supplies less than 1 percent of all the energy we use to produce the nation's goods. Mechanical energy provides every American man, woman and child with the equivalent services of 1,350 full-time manual workers. Total U.S. energy use has more than doubled since 1950, while population has grown only slightly more than one-third.

Since 1965 energy *consumption* has been increasing by 4.5 percent annually. Domestic energy *production* grew at an annual rate of 3 percent between 1950 and 1970 but has been at a standstill since that year, which marked the beginning of environmental and energy legislative policy conflict. We have made up the difference between U.S. production and consumption by importing oil. We are now a net importer of about 15 percent of our total energy consumption. The rate at which we have been consuming our own energy and that of other countries is, of course, why we have developed such a high standard of living. We do not relish the thought of having to reduce it. However, we have learned a vitally important lesson from the energy crisis. There are ways to use far less energy and, at the same time, maintain our standard of living and continue to grow. But this is a job that can't be left up to the other fellow. Every energy user must shoulder his proportionate share of responsibility.

In eating our energy pie, the biggest slice is consumed by industry, using more than 40 percent of all energy. Transportation of all kinds consumes 25 percent. Residential use accounts for 20 percent. Commercial facilities, such as stores, office buildings, hotels, service stations, schools, hospitals, theaters and restaurants, use 15 percent. There is an incredible amount of energy waste in all these categories.

The biggest savings can come from industry, which until recently gave no more thought to energy conservation than the home user. Most manufacturers, including the energy industries themselves, have been guilty of taking abundant, cheap energy supplies for granted. American industries did not apply their technical and engineering skills to the problem of energy efficiency. No science of energy management was developed. Their plants and refineries had huge energy losses, simply because nobody knew they existed. Today it's a different story. Industry is taking the lead in efficient energy housekeeping and gearing its research and development programs to devise energy-saving methods, equipment and products.

Du Pont is an outstanding leader in energy efficiency management. Many years ago they began a systematic effort to ensure that their plants used energy with maximum efficiency. Their success is illustrated by the fact that from 1962 through 1971, the quantity of their output increased nearly 100 percent, but during the same period, the amount of energy they used increased only about 50 percent. Du Pont estimates that the average industrial plant can conserve 15 percent of its energy usage through proper energy management. If applied to all industry energy use, this is a potential energy savings equal to 1,500,000 barrels of oil a day. Assuming an average price of $8 a barrel, this represents a saving in energy costs of $4.3 billion a year. Normally, more than 50 percent of the savings can be achieved without significant new investment. This opens a new vista to all industry in terms of maintaining profits without having to increase prices to consumers. Du Pont recently established a consulting service in energy management which is servicing companies and municipalities whose energy bill is $500,000 or more annually.

In addition to improving the efficiency of its equipment and operations, industry has found that it can make savings like the homeowner. By reducing operating pressures and temperatures on several distillation towers, one Celanese chemical plant found it could save 600,000 cubic feet of fuel gas per day, worth more than $80,000 a year. One of its laboratories shut off air supply and exhaust systems in three buildings from 7 P.M. to 6 A.M. each workday, with estimated fuel savings of 25 percent of normal energy usage, worth $45,000 annually. In its New York office building it reduced energy consumption 30 percent by lowering thermostats and turning off lights.

Industry research has been increased to find ways to reduce the greatest energy loss of all. Although we think of electric utilities as energy *suppliers*, they are actually also energy *users*, consuming coal, gas, oil, nuclear fission products and using waterpower. Utilities convert one form of energy into another. In all stages of their operation—production, transmission and distribution—approximately two-thirds of the energy content of the fuels used is lost as waste heat. Electricity use more than doubled between 1960 and 1970. In 1972 the amount of coal, oil, natural gas and uranium used to generate electricity was 25 percent ofthe nation's total primary energy use. Consequently, when more efficient electricity conversion processes are developed, there is a potential for enormous resource savings.

An entirely new concept of energy saving by integrating electric power stations with industrial plants is being researched under the sponsorship of the National Science Foundation. It estimates the establishment of energy-industrial centers in the future could reduce fuel consumption by industry by as much as 30 to 40 percent. Electric utility consumption of fuel also could be reduced 30 percent. The foundation is also funding a research project on the concept of clustering power-generating facilities in what are called energy parks, rather than scattering new facilities around the country. The Atomic Energy Commission has made a preliminary analysis which indicates that there are a number of sites still available where such energy parks could be located.

For the past decade a number of industries have been developing the technology to recycle solid waste—garbage and trash—as a supplementary energy source. It would also solve one of our society's gravest problems: what to do with what we throw away, for we are running out of places to put it. The Environmental Protection Agency estimates that the energy value of the refuse generated every year in the United States is equivalent to 290,000,000 barrels of low-sulfur fuel oil, or 5 percent of current domestic oil consumption. If all municipal refuse collection could be converted into energy, it could generate 6 percent of America's total annual electric production. In addition, the EPA estimates that there is more than $1 billion worth of recoverage metals which could be "mined" annually from the nation's garbage. Solid waste plants have been operating in Europe for a number of years. Frankfurt, West Germany, produces 7 percent of its electrical energy from solid waste, and Amsterdam, the Netherlands, produces 6 percent.

Following the 1970 energy crisis, solid waste pilot plants were built on an experimental basis in various parts of the country, but the economics was not attractive. However, the 1973–74 oil shortage and steep increases in oil prices launched America's solid waste industry into spectacular orbit. It is our newest resource industry. Solid waste plants are being planned throughout the country, and companies are actually competing for garbage. The Union Electric Company of St. Louis began an experiment in 1972, with partial funding by the Environmental Protection Agency, recycling 350 tons of garbage daily and mixing one part garbage with nine parts coal to generate electricity. In March, 1974, Union Electric announced it was investing $70,000,000 of private capital in a solid waste plant, which will be the first in the nation to use all of a metropolitan area's solid waste as fuel. It will handle 2,500,000 to 3,000,000 tons of solid waste annually and generate 6 percent of Union's power, which services St. Louis and six adjoining Missouri and Illinois counties.

The Connecticut Resources Recovery Authority took a bold step and announced in May, 1974, that the state would construct a $290,000,000 system to convert all of the state's household and commercial garbage into low-sulfur fuels for power plants and commercially salable scrap iron, aluminum and glass. The system, the world's first, will funnel all 10,000 tons of refuse produced daily in the state's 169 towns and cities into ten regional treatment centers by 1980. The first two plants, modeled after the St. Louis plant, will begin operating in mid-1976 and will produce, at a profit, enough fuel to supply 10 percent of the electricity in their regions. The system is expected to reduce taxes, air pollution from garbage disposal and the need for new dump sites.

The idea of Oklahoma cow dung heating Chicago houses would have seemed preposterous before the energy crisis. Now the Natural Gas Pipeline Company of America has contracted with Calorific Recovery Anerobic Process, Inc., of Oklahoma City, for sufficient methane gas derived from feedlot manure to heat 3,500 Chicago houses. The price of $1.33 per thousand cubic feet is much higher than domestic natural gas, but it is much lower than prospective synthetic or imported liquefied natural gas prices. In Asia, I have seen water buffalo dung used on small farms to provide cooking gas and power, but the first use of manure in America on a large commercial scale by a utility illustrates how the new energy economics is prompting us to change our resource thinking. Other large feedlots are planning to initiate similar projects. Not only will converting manure to methane eliminate a large source of pollution, but after the manure is processed, the waste product can be used as a high-grade nitrogen fertilizer.

For a number of years we have been recycling about a fourth of our annual consumption of paper, metals, glass, textiles and rubber. The energy shortage has made us realize we have a much greater resource recovery potential and is spurring us to do more about it. We have been littering the countryside annually with 200,000,000 old tires, which don't decay or dissolve. Now the Oil Shale Company, which has been developing the first commercial oil shale plant, has applied its technology to the commercial recovery of petroleum and reusable materials from them. In partnership with the Goodyear Tire & Rubber Company, the shale company will build the first commercial scrap tire recycling plant to process 8,000,000 scrap tires annually. In addition to oil and carbon black, the plant will provide enough material to make an additional 2,000,000 new tires a year. If all scrap tires could be recycled, they could yield annually about 275,000,000 gallons of oil, almost 2 billion pounds of carbon black and 50,000,000 pounds of steel.

We throw away 60 billion disposable aluminum cans a year, but Alcoa has developed the technology to recycle used all-aluminum cars with just 5 percent of the energy it takes to make them the first time. It is buying back used cans from community reclamation centers. Recycling presently accounts for 30 percent of the aluminum, 40 percent of the copper and lead and 20 percent of the zinc now used annually in the United States. With the development of organized scrap reclamation, we will further decrease the drain on primary mineral resources.

A profound change in the American industrial attitude toward energy use is already under way with very little fanfare accompanying it. Industries have catered to our consumer-goods-oriented society by vying with one another to produce goods which encourage us to use more energy rather than less. Now, in our new state of energy consciousness, they are channeling their technological skills to produce appliances that will have a low energy cost for the consumer. General Electric has always been a research leader in developing electrical equipment, constantly redesigning appliances to improve their energy efficiency. In the 1930's it introduced fluorescent light bulbs which are four times more efficient than incandescents. Spurred by the energy crisis, it now has developed a new fluorescent lighting system for stores, offices and other buildings which uses 20 percent less electricity than its last model. It has added a power saver switch to room air conditioners which cuts off the fan while the compressor is idle. A similar feature has been added to refrigerators and dishwashers. You can put the machine on "natural dry" and save the power that would heat air to dry dishes. Robertshaw Controls Company has invented a new gas range igniter that eliminates the pilot light, which can burn 40 percent or more of all the fuel used in a range.

Such new developments are just a tiny sample of the avalanche of energy-saving equipment and devices which will be in the marketplace within the next five to seven years. In applied research, this is the period of time it generally takes for new products to be engineered and reach the consumer. A significant glimpse of what is coming is provided by a research project at the Massachusetts Institute of Technology, funded by the National Science Foundation and headed by Dr. J. Herbert Hollomon, former research director for General Electric and former Assistant Secretary of Commerce for Science and Technology. The study discovered that refrigerators, which rank first in residential electrical energy consumption costs, can be redesigned to cut their energy consumption by 50 percent. The saving would come from better insulation and more efficient motors, while the appliance kept the frost-free feature of recent models. Such refrigerators would cost 20 percent more but would pay for themselves in two years by reduced electricity bills. Dr. Hollomon estimates that gradual replacement of the nation's 60,000,000 refrigerators by the 1980's could cut their energy use from 2 percent of today's total energy budget, electric and nonelectric, to 1 percent.

A promising new energy-saving invention is a reactor, to attach to oil-burning units, which mixes water with oil and cuts fuel oil consumption by about 20 percent. It also eliminates many pollutants in the combustion process. Developed by Eric Cottell, a British-born inventor, it is being used successfully in the boiler rooms of a grade school and fifteen buildings of Adelphi University on Long Island. Cottell's reactor, which is about the size of a long loaf of bread, blends about three parts oil and one part water under extreme pressure. The mixture burns more cleanly and efficiently than regular fuel oil and produces almost no soot or ash. In addition to reactors for institutions, industry and apartment buildings, Cottell has developed a smaller model for homeowners which he plans to market for less than $100. He also has adapted a reactor for his automobile, which uses 18 percent water and the rest gasoline. It increased his fuel mileage by about 30 percent. It had such a low output of pollutants that he claims it makes automobile emission-control devices unnecessary. The cost of the reactor, mass-produced, would be between $100 and $200.

In the commercial sector, most of the energy consumed is for space heating and cooling, lighting and office equipment. Modern architecture is an energy consumption villain, wasting half the energy it consumes. Architects and engineers have gone back to their drawing boards to design energy-saving buildings, using new insulating materials, reflective glass, changing solar exposures, decreasing lighting intensity, using recycling heat systems and other innovations. New buildings can achieve 40 percent energy-consumption savings. We are on the threshold of an architectural revolution.

In the meantime, business is finding out that it can make tremendous savings in energy consumption in the buildings we already have. Furthermore, special new services have come into being. Several years ago, Grumman, whose lunar module delivered our astronauts to and from the moon, applied its aerospace-developed systems engineering to energy saving in its own plants and buildings as an economy measure. The results were so successful that it has entered the commercial field to improve buildings' energy efficiency use. It bases its fee on the money saved in energy consumption. Robertshaw Controls has devised a computer-automated building control system which automatically calculates and directs a building's heating, cooling and lighting to get the most efficient results. This system has been in use for the past six years at the International Monetary Fund's headquarters and has saved 27 percent annually in fuel and power bills.

The problem of achieving energy conservation in transportation directly affects the personal life-style and activities of almost every American. Eight out of 10 American households own at least one car, including half of all poor households. Three in 10 families have two cars, and 1 in 10 has three or more. Automobiles consume about 55 percent of transportation's one-fourth slice of our energy consumption pie. Since 1940 we have been doubling the total miles we drive every fifteen years. We have also steadily been getting fewer miles to the gallon of gasoline we use. One reason has been our increasing passion for ever-bigger cars. Gasoline consumption and the weight of a car go hand in hand. A 5,000-pound car consumes twice as much gasoline as a 2,500-pound car. We also like the luxuries of air conditioning, power steering and automatic transmission, which have added about 10 percent to decreased mileage. Antipollution devices have added another 10 percent penalty on 1973 and 1974 models. Consequently, the average American car, which got 14 miles to the gallon in 1958, gets about 12 miles today. This is why gasoline consumption has zoomed with America's 96,000,000 passenger cars driving 1 trillion miles in 1973. Not to mention the 275 billion miles driven by our 22,000,000 trucks and buses. We are the most highly mobile people on earth. Our private automobiles carry about 85 percent of all intercity traffic, whereas airplanes carry 10 percent and railroads and buses carry only 3 percent of the traffic.

How can we retain our freedom of movement at the least sacrifice and still conserve transportation energy consumption? This is the kind of problem we wish we could sweep under the rug and we are trying to. But it won't go away. Much as we hate it, we are going to have to retool our thinking about transportation habits while Detroit retools its factories to give us the lighter, smaller cars with less powerful engines which will help solve the problem. Obviously if we had small cars which would give us 24 miles to the gallon, we could cut gasoline consumption in half by 1985. But we haven't made up our minds yet that we really want them. At the beginning of the crucial gasoline shortage there was a rush to buy small cars. However, when gasoline became plentiful again, even at double the price, to Detroit's confusion customers switched back to buying bigger cars. There is wide agreement in the automobile industry that by 1980 smaller cars will account for 60 percent of the market, compared with 50 percent now. They also agree that the demand for big cars will never disappear, but that what consumers really want is a luxury small car. Consequently, automobile design engineers are concentrating on lighter cars to add more miles per gallon in fuel economy and also to halt the decline in overall sales.

The more horsepower we have under our automobile hoods, the faster we are tempted to drive, which also adds to our gasoline consumption. There is a fuel saving of 11 percent driving at 50 miles an hour instead of 60, or, in other words, you can save about 1 gallon in 7. We have the new energy-saving national 55-mile-an-hour legal speed limit, but as we all know, we aren't really observing it, although we have slowed down to an average of about 60 to 65 miles, whereas the year before we drove 75 against a 70 mph limit. On a recent long distance automobile trip, with deliberate, great effort I kept the speedometer at a steady 55. I never passed anybody, but everybody passed me. Yet I discovered a secret which more and more people are sharing and enjoying. It was the most relaxing and pleasant drive I ever made. The Federal Energy Administration estimates that if we all observed the new speed limit, we would save more than 5,000,000 gallons of oil products a day. Safety alone should make us want to do so. The combination of imperfectly observing lower speed limits and reducing our travel produced startling results in the first six months of 1974. The National Safety Council announced that all traffic deaths fell 23 percent to 20,460 from 26,600 in the first half of 1973. Mileage logged on the nation's turnpikes dropped 14 percent in the same period, while turnpike traffic deaths declined by 60 percent.

Much research is being carried out on modern electric cars, steam cars and gasoline-steam cars, but the technology is only in its infancy to do the job that Americans demand and require. What we really have to do is save transportation energy by improved mass transit, particularly in urban areas, where half the private automobile miles are driven. We have let our mass transit systems decay beyond reason and belief, as every frustrated person who uses them knows. Everybody wants better mass transit and agrees on the need for it as an answer to traffic congestion, pollution and energy saving. But nobody can agree on what kind or who is going to pay for the massive capital requirements to give us what we would like to have or need. Mass transit is one of our thorniest, most controversial political issues. Voters object violently to paying for what they consider somebody else's transportation. Municipalities, state governments and the federal government keep passing the buck to one another, and voters refuse to accept new taxes for public transportation. We have not yet made up our minds that it is necessary or advisable to make a national commitment to improved mass transit. We are still totally dedicated to the state of private automobile consciousness, and we have not realized the extent of our energy plight. Great advances have been made in mass transit technology and innovative approaches. Some communities are beginning to put new systems to work. But mass transit proponents see only conflict ahead before we reach national decisions to make efficient mass transit part of our life style.

Americans have unthinkingly been wasting tremendous amounts of energy in their homes. Since 20 percent of our total energy and 30 percent of our electric energy output is consumed in the home, if we would develop the same kind of efficiency mentality which industry is now exhibiting, we could achieve great national energy savings, as well as personal dollar savings. An American family spends about 7 percent of its average annual income on direct energy consumption. About half is for home uses, with the other half being spent on the family automobile. After the car, heating a home is the family's largest energy expense, totaling more than one-fourth of the family's energy consumption. Most homeowners do not realize that about 40 percent of their heating fuel bill goes to heating the outdoors rather than the home. Because energy has been cheap and abundant, building construction over the years has been progressively inefficient with inadequate insulation and the use of large quantities of glass. Installation of proper insulation, weatherstripping windows and doors, installing storm windows and doors and double-pane or insulating glass, can save up to 50 percent on the fuel bill. At today's energy prices, the investment would pay for itself in three to five years, and the homeowner would permanently save money and energy from then on. There is also a remarkable invention, called the heat pump, which many homeowners do not know about. Developed by General Electric in the 1930's, it can take the place of both a furnace and an air conditioner. It is basically a refrigeration unit and in summer collects heat inside the house and discharges it outside. In winter the process is automatically reversed. The heat pump collects solar heat outside the house and discharges it inside. The efficiency of a heat pump varies with the climate, but in average U.S. climates similar to St. Louis, Cincinnati, New York and Boston the efficiency of a heat pump compares favorably with that of a conventional furnace. In an all-electric home, it can save two-thirds of the energy requirements. If it is powered by oil or natural gas, it can cut fuel use in half.

As we have already learned, we keep our homes too hot or too cold and can save as much as 10 percent on our heating bills by turning down thermostats. Three degrees less, on a national scale would save more than 63,000,000 barrels of fuel oil and almost 760 billion cubic feet of natural gas annually. An estimated 30 percent of the national use of electricity in the summer months is for air-conditioning homes and apartments. Each degree that the thermostat is turned up saves about 5 percent of the energy used for cooling.

Throwing away your electric toothbrush will save you only 3 cents a year, but one 100-watt bulb burning around the clock for one year uses more than 60 gallons of oil and will add $56 to your electric bill. Consequently, you and I have to identify all the household energy villains, such as the water heater, which after the refrigerator and air conditioner, wears the biggest household appliance black hat. Most of all we have to realize that what each one of us saves not only is helping our own pocketbooks, but cumulatively amounts to great national energy savings because there are so many of us. Consolidated Edison calculates that if all 3,000,000 customers in New York City and Westchester County cut off a single 100-watt bulb that might burn six hours a day, the savings would be 1,500,000 barrels of oil a year, ten days' supply.

The big issue at stake in energy conservation is buying time to keep our economy going and enable us to make wise decisions in regard to long-range economic growth. We are at a serious turning point in our economic-political history. Economics and politics are inseparable. We have seen how hasty, ill-conceived environmental legislation has compounded our troubles and created shortages. Now environmental and consumer groups are pressing for legislation of all kinds which, in effect propose that the way out of the shortages is by more government regulations and controls. We don't have our heads on straight yet about cause and effect. We haven't learned Hardin's Law, formulated by the California biologist Garrett Hardin, which states, "You can never do merely one thing." Whatever decisions we make have got to be intelligent ones with full knowledge of the consequences and chain reaction, good or bad.

You and I are being pressured by everybody. Industrial leaders tell us that the private enterprise system is being threatened by the hostility and suspicion which has been generated against business. Consumer and environmentalist groups tell us we are being had by business. Politicians capitalize on this to try to restore some gloss to their tarnished images by promising to protect the consumer. The skeptical, investigative news media flits back and forth, giving us bits and pieces of sensationalism and shorthand about everything. We have been emotionally bruised and disillusioned by war, Watergate, crime, violence, the deterioration of our moral fabric and inflation. We have almost been pressured into believing that there is something fundamentally wrong with us. There isn't. We are simply suffering from a state of mental confusion. Our resistance is down, but we have what it takes to restore our mental health—national resilience. We need to take a moratorium on political overreaction until we catch our breath and all the facts are in so that we can understand what has happened and what our options are.

Economically, it has been a brand-new ball game since January 1, 1974, when the OPEC quadrupled oil prices. This has been both bad and good. It was a financial and emotional blockbuster. We felt that somebody had stuck a gun in our ribs and robbed us wholesale. On circumstantial evidence we loudly identified as the criminal the closest ones to our vision—oil and utilities companies—simply because nobody had been keeping us up to date on what was really happening. On the other hand, the increase in world oil prices which resulted in the U.S. government's permitting domestic oil prices to be increased has dramatically stimulated energy exploration and development and released our ingenuity and capabilities to achieve energy self-sufficiency once again. We are looking for and finding new oil and gas. We have initiated an energy-saving industrial revolution. We are creating more resources, developing new technology and learning how to use wisely what we have. If we can keep our cool and adjust to high energy prices temporarily, while lessening the financial burden on ourselves by voluntary conservation, both by industry and the individual, we've got it made in the long run. But if we let ourselves be pushed into the trap of trying to reduce raw material prices by government controls, price rollbacks and setting unrealistic legislative limits to our capacity for growth in order to obtain an illusory alleviation of our present financial pains and environmental fears, we will be exercising as much common-sense as trying to cure acne by committing suicide.

There is wide agreement in government, industrial, financial and academic circles that we must slow down our historic 4 to 5 percent growth rate while we are striving to achieve energy self-sufficiency to the fullest extent consistent with economic and environmental considerations. However, there is wide disagreement on how much we can and should slow down and how to go about it. Energy use is the key to growth. Even if the growth of energy demand in the United States can be slowed down to 3 percent per year, this country will still require about 25 percent more energy supply by 1980 and about 45 percent more by 1985. We are going to continue to grow, but high prices will automatically slow the rate of growth. High prices have already been the principal reason for a significant decline in petroleum consumption for the first six months of 1974. Demand was down an average of almost 6 percent from 1973 levels for the same period. Analysts forecast that domestic demand for the whole year would show a decline of more than 2 percent from 1973 consumption. This would be the first time in more than twenty years that Americans have failed to *increase* their annual consumption of petroleum, which normally has been increasing from 3 to 5 percent a year.

Economists agree that we must slow our overall growth rate—both by conservation and most efficient use of energy—in order to reduce our reliance on foreign supply and work toward our goal of self-sufficiency. But what a realistic growth rate *objective* should be will become an increasingly dominant national debate.

Currently, we are in the midst of a tremendous reassessment of new national and international economic facts. In order to make rational decisions affecting our economic future, we need to understand better how our options have changed. Irving S. Shapiro, chairman of Du Pont, has suggested that the government should be required to disclose the economic consequences of all federal programs and regulations, "including the benefits to be derived by one segment of society and foregone by the others." The idea of Economic Impact Statements would not be politically popular, but it points up our great need for coordinated thinking so that we can factually analyze the advantages and disadvantages of any proposed course of action.

The most ambitious private study of energy and national growth is the Ford Foundation's $4,000,000 Energy Policy Project, established two years ago, under the direction of S. David Freeman, an engineer and lawyer, formerly with the Tennessee Valley Authority and the Federal Power Commission, and from 1967 to 1972, head of the President's energy policy staff. A controversial preliminary report, *Exploring Energy Choices*, was published in April, 1974. The project's advisory board of businessmen, academicians and representatives of citizens' groups was sharply divided on the wisdom of issuing a report before detailed investigations were finished. However, Freeman's desire to enter the national policy debate as soon as possible prevailed. When the final report, *A Time to Choose*, was released six months later, it was equally controversial since it specifically recommended cutting energy growth consumption by more than half—from its historical rate of 4.5 percent annually to at least 2 percent. It maintained this could be done without hurting the economy or causing massive unemployment. It also recommended the desirability of moving toward a zero growth rate. The report sets forth ideas concerning three "scenarios" as a "framework for thinking about energy policy." They are based on historical growth trends, a "technical fix" lowered growth rate and a zero growth economy. The report is heavily weighted to favor conservation of energy resources over increasing production of energy. This reflects Freeman's strong personal views. In his speeches and writings he is an articulate advocate of government control of energy through pricing policies, new tax laws, federal regulation of energy consumption and increased federal participation in energy production.

The Ford Foundation report, like the Club of Rome's *Limits to Growth,* is useful for starting a debate or, as the report states, "to broaden today's energy dialogue." However, it has the same blind spots. It concentrates on environmental and technological problems without giving any accurate picture of what technology has done or is doing to solve them. And it ignores the exponential growth of human ingenuity.

No gospel has been developed to relieve us of the responsibility of making our own decisions. In the long run, we are the ones who have to make up our minds about what kind of world we want to live in and how to live in balance with our environment. We should not be asked to make hasty decisions, nor should we pressure our elected representatives to take hasty actions. We have unrealized social goals and unmet social needs to consider in whatever decisions we make concerning our future growth and progress. Fortunately, the nation has not taken out energy bankruptcy, nor are we faced with immediate disaster. We still have time to do our thinking. But time is running out.

7

Energy Abundance Through Technology: The Timetable

In November, 1973, a month after the Arabs dropped the energy bomb, President Nixon proposed that we "unite in committing the resources of the nation to a major new endeavor. An endeavor that in this bicentennial era we can appropriately call Project Independence. Let us set as our national goal, in the spirit of Apollo and with the determination of the Manhattan Project, that by the end of this decade, we will have developed the potential to meet our own energy needs without depending on any foreign energy sources."

The prospect of achieving such a goal by 1980 was unrealistic and impossible. As a matter of fact, Project Independence is having a hard time getting off the ground because, as yet, we have not generated any spirit of total national commitment to it. However, the Federal Energy Administration is beginning to put some flesh on the skeleton of the concept. It has been conducting extensive studies and holding nationwide hearings to prepare a blueprint, with options, of how to achieve energy self-sufficiency. In late 1974 it completed four comprehensive plans as guidelines for formulating federal policies. All the options were built on the assumption that the United States will still need to import 20 percent of its fuel energy needs in 1980. The options presented pros, cons, costs and environmental implications. They showed the range of choices between no change in current policies to heavy government intervention such as energy-use controls by taxes and regulations. They examined incentives and disincentives for increasing supplies and the government's role in research and development of long-term energy sources.

Achieving total national energy self-sufficiency, like nirvana, may be a state greatly to be desired, but the path to it will involve an equally arduous, disciplined effort. Furthermore, any possibility of getting there lies somewhere well into the next century. Now that

233

we are beginning to settle down and see what the problems are, our definition of "self-sufficiency" has changed. The rigid definition of the term implies zero energy imports, primarily oil. From a practical viewpoint, what we are shooting for is far less. As Federal Energy Administrator Sawhill said, in a recent Senate hearing, self-sufficiency does not mean the United States should "be totally independent of all other countries for oil supplies." Instead, it means that the United States "should not be vulnerable to embargoes or price increases." There is also a point where the benefits of reduced imports become unbalanced by the slowdown in economic activity. The FEA and Petroleum Industry Research Foundation studies are in agreement that an import level of 25 percent, as contrasted with our current 36 percent, is the cutoff point which would be a bearable risk. Even if we begin cutting import growth immediately, they do not expect that we could reach such a target before 1985.

We Americans are so psychologically geared to the idea of doing things quickly in a big way that it hardly seems possible that we can't have a crash program to get us out of our predicament. Nevertheless, the Manhattan and Apollo projects were kindergarten exercises compared to the technological, financial and political obstacles which Project Independence must overcome. It is next to impossible to draw up a specific timetable for how much energy and what kind we will be using just when, because too many unpredictable factors are involved concerning decisions we haven't made yet. That's why all energy studies today usually present multiple case histories. The numbers game now is so complex that it's a good thing we invented computers before the energy crisis, or we'd really be whistling in the dark. However, the majority of government and industry studies made to date agree in certain broad areas which give us a reasonably accurate view of our prospects for the near term, to the end of the 1970's; for the medium term, to 2000; and the long term—2000 and beyond.

In working toward a balance of energy supply and demand, our domestic supply cannot be increased very much in the next few years. This, of course, is because of the long lead times it takes to develop energy—four to five years to develop new offshore oil and gas after the discovery is made, four to six years to sink a new deep coal mine and eight to nine years to build a new nuclear plant. New supplies, already under development, will come into play, but the rate at which we increase future supplies depends on the rate at which we start new projects. We are currently dependent on oil and gas for three-fourths of our energy, and domestic sources will not be able to provide more than half the additional energy the United States will need between now and the early 1980's. The other half must come from increasing quantities of imported Middle East oil. However, about that time, the energy mix will start to change. Nuclear power supplies only less than 2 percent of our energy now, but plants under construction are expected to supply 20 percent of our electricity needs by then. Coal production will be increasing, but slowly, owing to its own special problems. If offshore oil development is well under way and we are cutting imports, as well as stepping up our conservation efforts, by the 1990's we should be approaching near self sufficiency. The breeder reactor, oil shale, solar power, and geothermal energy will not start making any significant contributions until after 2000. In the century ahead we hope to reach the end of the rainbow by mastering the technology of thermonuclear fusion—the ultimate solution to the world's energy problems. Before that happy day, we have nothing but hard work and hard decisions ahead of us.

The awesome magnitude of our immediate problems is dramatically pointed out by the task force on energy of the National Academy of Engineering, which was created by Congress to advise the federal government in matters of science and engineering and is composed of the nation's leading engineers. After the Arab oil embargo, the task force began a detailed study of what was necessary to close the demand-and-supply energy gap by 1985. Their report, published in May, 1974, estimated that energy demand for 1985 will be 58,000,000 barrels a day, in oil equivalent, if consumption is unrestrained; 51,000,000 barrels a day, if restrained. Even then, domestic energy supply will be only 40,000,000 barrels a day. To close this gap, using domestic energy resources, the task force concluded that we must do the following things:

- Increase oil and gas production by 25 percent. Specifically, we should drill an average of 58,000 wells annually until 1985—double the 1973 drilling rate.
- Double coal mining by 140 new eastern underground mines yielding 2,000,000 tons per year, 30 new Eastern surface mines with the same production, 100 new Western surface mines producing 5,000,000 tons per year.
- Increase nuclear power capacity to one-third of total electrical generation capacity.
- Produce 1,100,000 barrels a day of synthetic liquids from coal, and 500,000 barrels a day of shale oil by building, 20 new

methane-from-coal plants with capacity of 250,000,000 cubic feet a day; 8 new methanol-from-coal plants with 40,000-barrels-a-day capacity; 10 new medium-BTU gas-from-coal plants; 10 new 30,000-barrels-a-day coal-liquefaction plants; 50 new 5,000,000-tons-per-year shale mines and retorting plants; 10 new 50,000-barrels-per-day shale-oil-extraction and upgrading plants. New water supplies would have to be developed for all these operations.

• Achieve small increases in hydroelectric and geothermal power.

• These production goals would require $600 billion in private capital just for production facilities. Including working capital, dividends, debt service, and other financial operations, there would be a total capital need for $700 billion, averaging $60 billion a year, twice the amount currently invested by the energy industries.

• The energy-related work force would have to be increased by 30,000 additional engineers, 190,000 additional skilled construction workers, and 240,000 additional operators.

The task force considered that reaching these goals by 1985 was "improbable." It warned that even if we did, "the U.S. is buying time. For beyond 1985 looms an ominous prospect of even greater demands for energy from ever-increasing and ever-rising expectations at home and abroad. Unless innovative ways are developed for conserving and using energy and substantial new sources and new technologies are found for increasing energy supplies, the strategies presented by the task force would only postpone a grim future of energy scarcity."

The fact that we can't do the job by 1985 doesn't mean that we can't be well on our way to doing it. The study gives us a realistic appraisal of the enormousness of our task in the medium term and the importance of dedicating ourselves to it. The $700 billion capital requirements for Project Independence compare to $2.5 billion in 1945 dollars for the Manhattan Project and $25 billion spent on Project Apollo over a decade. The point is that energy supply must be tackled on many fronts and is not a single problem.

Where is all the money going to come from? The cost estimates do not even include the capital required for sustained research and development for new technology. Energy investment was about 2 percent of our gross national product in the 1960's and, to meet the new requirements, will have to rise to about 2.5 percent in the 1980's. The energy sector's share of total business capital expenditure, averaging about 20 percent in the 1960's, is projected to rise to between 30 and 35 percent in the period to 1985. The world's money supply is limited, and the energy industries have to compete successfully with other users of capital to get their job done. Investors and lenders look at the basic profitability of an industry before making financial decisions. If the return on investment is attractive enough, then the bulk of the vast sums necessary for our energy needs will be forthcoming from the existing, traditional private financial markets. However, investors and companies will not be able to take the business risks of expanded energy investments if punitive tax legislation or unrealistic price controls create an unfavorable profit picture.

The key to financing our energy future will be determined by the political decisions we make in the near term of the next few years. Either we can create a favorable financial climate for private energy industries to expand or we can stifle their growth. A question we have to ask ourselves is: "What can take their place and at what cost to the consumer?" A commonsense approach is to tighten our belts, conserve energy and encourage the private energy industries, which have the know-how, technological capabilities and the experience of efficient money management, to do the job which has to be done.

Although oil, gas, nuclear power, and coal will dominate the medium-term picture, to 2000, the groundwork is being laid both to expand their development and use through new technology and to develop entirely new energy sources.

The technology for synthetic oil and gas from oil shale and coal is well advanced. In addition, new technology is being developed to recover billions of barrels of oil which have been discovered but which it has not been technically feasible or economic to produce. The average recovery of oil in place today is only about 30 percent, but industry engineers predict that this will increase gradually to about 42 percent in 2000 and to 60 percent eventually. New technology and higher prices will make it feasible to rework abandoned oil fields. About 80 percent of gas originally in place is now recovered, but there are also large, unproducible reserves where the gas is locked so tightly in the rock formations that it cannot be economically recovered by conventional means. Low-yield nuclear underground explosions to fracture the rocks and free the gas have been tested successfully in New Mexico and Colorado. But there is great public opposition to their continued use. Hydraulic fracturing—pumping water in under high pressure—can be used, and depending on the economics of gas prices, the Federal Power Commission estimates its potential could be developed to between 2 and 5 trillion cubic feet annually by 1990.

The cost of recovering resources and the market price are the critical factors in estimating the amount of our available energy resources. The Atomic Energy Commission reports uranium reserves and resources in several cost-of-recovery categories from less than $8 to more than $100 per pound. Ore in the less than $8-per-pound class is minable now, and the AEC estimates reasonably assured reserves of around 300,000 tons, or just about enough to supply the lifetime needs of reactors in use or ordered in 1968, and only half that required for reactors expected to be in use by 1980. But they estimate that tens of millions of tons are prospective in the price range of $30 to $100 per pound. Uranium at such prices would be usable in the breeder reactor.

The newest energy boom is in putting to use one of the oldest forms of energy: the natural heat of the earth to generate power for electricity. Temperatures in the earth rise with increasing depth, but most of the heat is too deeply buried to be tapped for use. The depths from which heat might be extracted economically are unlikely to be more than 6 miles. The amount of heat in the earth's crust to this depth is estimated to be more than 2,000 times the heat represented by the total coal resources of the world. The catch is that this geothermal energy can't be used unless it is found in concentrated form called hot spots, similar to the concentration of mineral deposits. The thermal energy is stored both in the solid rock and in the water and steam filling pores and fractures. The first use of steam from natural geysers to generate electricity was in 1904 in Italy. Geothermal power plants around the world, primarily using wet steam, now generate less than 1 percent of the total world electrical capacity. The United States, with an abundance of oil and gas, never seriously considered developing geothermal power until the past decade. The first commercial generating plant was built in 1960 in the Geysers field, 90 miles north of San Francisco. Dry steam wells have been drilled which will be furnishing the Pacific Gas and Electric Company with about 5 percent of its power requirements in 1977.

Quantitatively, the largest geothermal resource potential is the energy in hot, dry rock. A technique to exploit this is now under development at the Atomic Energy Commission's Los Alamos Laboratory in New Mexico. In 1975 two holes will be drilled into a body of hot granite which will be fractured under water pressure. It is hoped that water injected down one hole will find its way through the fractures, become boiling hot, and then piped up as hot water or steam to drive a power plant. Another major hot spot has been discovered in Montana, and the National Science Foundation is funding a three-year exploration and drilling program to test the dry-rock technique further. If these experiments are successful, it may open up a new power vista for countries in many regions of the world which do not have conventional fuel resources, but which may have relatively shallow deposits of hot rock.

Presently, there are 1,800,000 acres in the United States, mostly in Western states, estimated to be proved geothermal-resource areas, of which 1,000,000 acres is owned by the federal government. An additional 95,000,000 acres, of which 54,000,000 are federally owned, are listed as "potential" geothermal areas. In January, 1974, federal proved geothermal lands were opened for the first time for competitive bids and $6,800,000 was bid for the California tracts offered. Oil companies are now the leaders in geothermal exploration because of their vast experience in drilling and solving drilling problems. Thousands of small entrepreneurs have made applications on the "potential" acreage which can be leased without bidding.

How great are our geothermal resources, and what role will they play in our energy future? There are no answers yet. "Guesstimates" range from their potential to provide from one-fourth to 100 times our present electricity consumption. There are tremendous technological problems to be solved before geothermal energy can become a major energy source. California's Imperial Valley is in an area with a vast subterranean reservoir of hot water, called rock soup because of the highly corrosive mixture of steam, water, salts, grit and dissolved metals that come from wells drilled there. New technology has to be developed to handle it. Conceivably, mineral by-products could be valuable. Also, more research is needed to determine the effect of withdrawing and reinjecting hot water in causing changes in the earth's crust, including earthquakes. However, as geothermal technology and its economics develop, the prospects of utilizing a source of inexhaustible energy rising from the earth's core will become an increasingly important factor in our energy supply during the twenty-first century.

The potential of using the sun, the source of all energy, to solve our problems is an ancient dream. Here again, research is being speeded up to put the sun to work for us commercially and economically. Man has been experimenting with harnessing the sun since the Greek physicist Archimedes, in 212 B.C., used huge metal mirrors to reflect the sun and set on fire the sails of the Roman fleet attacking Syracuse. Since then we have been trying to catch sunbeams and make them a power source. The simplest way is with a black surface that absorbs the sun's rays and heats up. If a fluid, such as air or water, is brought in contact with the heated surface, the energy can be transferred into the fluid and then used for practical purposes. By using this principle, we have developed solar hot-water heaters, steam generators and solar heating and cooling units for homes and buildings. Up until now such things have been mostly a curiosity because of the high cost of equipment. But high energy prices are changing that. During the next decade a mass market will be developed for solar devices. There are only a few dozen houses and buildings which now use solar energy on an experimental basis, but in mid-1974 Pittsburgh Plate Glass was the first major industrial concern to announce that it was beginning production of solar-heat collectors for the commercial market. The National Science Foundation is funding and testing solar heating systems in schools and houses in various parts of the country. One of these is the nation's largest solar project, a $747,000 solar plant, to be used to heat a 278,000-square-foot classroom center at Denver, Colorado, Community College. The total cost will be about $10,000,000 and is estimated to pay for itself in ten years through fuel savings. RCA is building a $6,000,000 solar-energy pilot project on top of its building at Rockefeller Center in New York, to meet part of its heating requirements. Commercial and residential use of solar energy is practical, and the technology is available; but the introduction of its use is expected to be gradual, and it will not have any significant impact on energy consumption until the next century.

The hopes of tapping the sun's energy for unlimited power generation are still paper projects and scientific research dreams. At the present state of technology it would require a mirror of about 30 square miles to boil enough water to supply the power needed by a city the size of Washington, D.C. Some scientists propose using large areas of the world's deserts to collect solar power. Our highest hopes of making a technological breakthrough is through photovoltaic energy conversion using solar cells. This method directly converts light to electricity in a semiconductor crystal such as silicon. This method has been used to produce power in spacecraft and telemeter signals back to earth, but until recently this method has been about 1,000 times more expensive than earthbound methods. Exxon research scientists have been able to reduce the cost of the cells by a factor of 10 over the past few years. This makes them economic in certain applications such as the charging of batteries in remote locations. They are being used on unmanned offshore oil platforms. Exxon has also introduced solar-cell equipment for boats, operating automatic bilge pumps. Scientists have advanced the concept of a system of satellite solar-power stations. The idea is not new, but the technology now available makes such suggestions practical in some future time. What mind can conceive man can achieve, despite the seeming immensities of the task. The realization that this limitless source of pollution-free energy does lie in the future is why many scientists and environmentalists object to our committing ourselves to nuclear energy objectives. However, no one has any idea of the billions of research dollars required for solar power or when technological breakthroughs will occur. While we are pursuing power in the sky, we must meet human needs on the ground by developing those energy sources which appear to be the most readily attainable.

For more than a hundred years, researchers have been trying to perfect the fuel cell so that electricity can be generated on the spot for power in houses, industry and vehicles without having to come from a central power station. A fuel cell is a silent pollution-free device with no moving parts, which produces electricity through a chemical reaction of hydrogen and oxygen. The hydrogen can come from natural gas or synthetic fuels, and the oxygen from the air. Fuel cells supplied electricity on the Apollo moon flights. They have been used experimentally in homes, trucks and tractors but have been too costly to be practical for large-scale use. Now, with the new energy economics, Pratt and Whitney Aircraft and nine electric utility companies are making a $42,000,000 research bet that by 1978 the fuel cell will be making an important contribution to energy supply, supplementing the utilities' traditional power-generating methods. The initial research program has been so successful that first deliveries to the nine utilities of units, valued in excess of $250,000,000 are targeted for 1978. Pratt and Whitney's demonstration fuel cells, no bigger than a television set, are already generating power in apartment buildings, office buildings, small factories and houses.

Another source of energy, as ancient as the earth, is its winds. In 1850, windmills provided almost 14 percent of America's energy. It is estimated that 6,500,000 windmills were made in the United States between 1880 and 1930. As recently as 1950, before rural electrification, there were 50,000 small wind generators in the

Midwest. Now the National Science Foundation is spending more than $1,000,000 in 1974, building the largest windmill in the country to test the feasibility of windmill power stations. Even windmill technology has problems. Winds are erratic, and we must learn to store electricity when they aren't blowing. Also, we must be able to mass-produce low-cost windmills. Five American universities have windmill research programs. Dr. William E. Heronemus, an engineering professor and windmill specialist at the University of Massachusetts, believes that large windmill complexes could be placed at sea on offshore platforms to use powerful ocean winds to generate electricity. Small windmills already are being used on many offshore oil platforms to produce power for warning lights and fog signals.

Energy research is expanding to almost every scientific field. Scientists are even putting microbes to work to create energy. Municipal land industrial sewage-treatment plants have used bacteria to consume waste for many years. In the process, methane—the principal component of natural gas—is produced. Using this principle, a new idea for electric power generation is being researched at the University of California at Berkeley by sanitary engineer W. J. Oswald and biologist C. G. Golueke. Algae, single-celled microscopic plants that convert sunlight into cellular energy, are grown in ponds, together with bacteria. The bacteria decompose sewage water into carbon dioxide, ammonia and other nutrients. Algae utilize these to store solar energy in their cells. They are harvested, placed in a digester where they become nutrients for bacteria which produce methane gas. Experiments to date demonstrate that the method could produce electric power for about twice the cost of conventional methods. Further research may lower the costs.

The boldest energy concept of all is to achieve limitless power by duplicating the thermonuclear fusion process which fires the sun and most of the billions of stars in the universe. A growing number of scientists believe that the time is near. The technology is based on that which developed the first hydrogen bomb explosion in 1952. The success of thermonuclear fusion depends on solving the problem of heating hydrogen fuel to 100,000,000 degrees Centigrade, nearly seven times hotter than the sun's interior, and holding it there long enough for the nuclei of light atoms to fuse and release tremendous quantities of energy. No materials on earth can withstand such temperatures. The process which scientists have been experimenting with is to confine the hot, dense hyperactive gas, called a plasma, to the center of a container by magnetic force. Unfortunately, their magnetic bottles have leaked, and continuous fusion could not be sustained. However, since 1970 the use of the laser beam has offered a radically new approach. A laser generates a powerful beam of light that can be focused on tiny hydrogen pellets in a vacuum chamber, turning them into miniature suns. The multiple mini-explosions create no danger of a big explosion, and there is no radioactive waste. The continuous heat energy released is extracted from the vacuum chamber and used to generate electricity. The work is still highly experimental and, like development of solar power satellites, requires billions of research dollars before nuclear fusion becomes a practical reality. However, once it is successfully developed, the world's energy problems are over for millions of years or as long as there is water on this planet. Fuel for fusion is deuterium and tritium, which are found in and easily extracted from water. The seas could supply the world's energy needs for billions of years.

As an abundance of new energy supplies are developed, low-cost energy will once more help pave the way to world progress. Our decreased dependence on oil and gas will release these resources for even more valuable uses. Chemically, they are the most versatile of all raw materials. There are about 10,000 different petrochemical products now and about 400 more are being added each year. Of their remarkable variety of uses, one of the most important is their capacity to increase the world's food supply. Natural gas already is a major world source for nitrogen fertilizers. The use of petroleum mulches on desert sands is making it possible to reclaim land for agricultural purposes and increase food production in arid areas. During the past decade, the petroleum industry has perfected processes to produce synthetic alcohols for use in food processing packaging and in food additives. It has also made the breakthrough in producing petroprotein, from the growth of bacteria on petroleum-derived foodstocks. We are beginning to use it for livestock feeds and for human consumption. The circle is coming full round. Man has been using petroleum as a substitute for his own muscle power. Now it can help provide power for his muscles.

Energy is the key to creating wealth, not just for the few, but the many. Today's energy problems and fears seem unnecessarily exaggerated when we contemplate the abundance of energy nature has placed here for our use. The energy potential of the atom is such that a handful of snow, if entirely converted to energy, could keep a home furnace running continuously for some 25,000 years.

We are living in a time period of the world's greatest knowledge explosion. Scientists tell us that by the mid-eighteenth century mankind's total fund of knowledge had doubled from what it was at the birth of Christ. It doubled again by 1900 and again by 1950. *However*, the next two *doublings* of mankind's knowledge took place in 1960 and 1968! If we continue to double our knowledge at this rate, perhaps we also can develop the talent to put it to use wisely to end world scarcities and create abundance for all.

Notes, Sources and Acknowledgments

Our current energy problem is of such recent origin that carrying out the detailed research for this book has been a jigsaw puzzle task of assembling and analyzing material and information from hundreds of books, newspapers, trade publications, scientific and specialized journals, Congressional hearings, studies made by government agencies, oil and energy companies, private and financial institutions and personal interviews. Just as we are entering a new energy era, so are we pioneering a new energy information era. We now face energy realities and economics which outmode most conclusions and ideas concerning energy published prior to 1970.

In this book, dealing primarily with today and the future, important source attributions are given in the text where they are pertinent. For those interested in knowing more details of the major topics discussed, I would like to mention some of the studies and books which I found most helpful, reliable or thought-provoking.

Unfortunately, from the layman's viewpoint, the nuts and bolts of today's energy are highly technical and scientific. The basic official documents are: *Future Petroleum Provinces of the United States,* National Petroleum Council report to the U.S. Department of the Interior, July, 1970; *U.S. Energy Outlook, An Initial Appraisal 1971–1985,* National Petroleum Council report to the U.S. Department of the Interior, July, 1971; *U.S. Energy Outlook,* National Petroleum Council full report to the U.S. Department of the Interior, December, 1972; *Understanding the National Energy Dilemma,* report of the Congressional Joint Committee on Atomic Energy (Washington, D. C., Center for Strategic and International Studies, Georgetown University, September, 1973); *United States Mineral Resources,* U.S. Geological Survey report (Washington, D.C., U.S. Government Printing Office, 1973); *U.S. Energy Prospects,* National Academy of Engineering study (Washington, D.C., National Academy of Science, May, 1974). An excellent new technical book covering all forms of energy is *Energy and the Future* by Allen L. Hammond, William D. Metz, Thomas H. Maugh II

(Washington, D.C., American Association for the Advancement of Science, 1973). A fascinating historical energy research study is *Energy in the American Economy 1850–1975* by Sam H. Schurr and Bruce C. Netschert (Baltimore, Resources for the Future, Inc., John Hopkins Press, 1960).

In the environmental and growth fields, the central issues are, of course, those discussed in this book in the two sections "Environment vs. Energy" and "Zero Growth vs. Building America Twice." These issues will provide a continuing national debate, and there is considerable recent literature expressing different views.

The most significant "prophets of doom" books concerning environment and growth are: *Silent Spring* by Rachel Carson (Boston, Houghton Mifflin, 1962); *The Population Bomb* by Paul R. Ehrlich (New York, Ballantine, 1968); Rene Dubos' *So Human an Animal* (New York, Scribner's, 1968) and *Reason Awake* (New York, Columbia University Press, 1970); Barry Commoner's *Science and Survival* (New York, Viking, 1967); and *The Closing Circle* (New York, Knopf, 1971); The Club of Rome's *The Limits to Growth* by Donnella H. Meadows, Dennis L. Meadows, Jorgen Randers, and William W. Behrens III (New York, Universe Books, 1972); and *Disaster by Oil* by Jeffrey Potter (New York, Macmillan, 1973). The preliminary report of the Ford Foundation Energy Policy Project, *Exploring Energy Choices* (Washington, D. C., Ford Foundation, April, 1974), the final Ford Foundation Energy Policy Project report, *A Time to Choose* (Cambridge, Mass., Ballinger, 1974), and *Energy: The New Era* by S. David Freeman, director of the Ford Foundation Energy Policy Project (Waler, 1974), all present a case for conservation of resources and reducing growth as the solution to our energy problem.

On the optimistic side of resource development and continued growth, I found enlightening material in *The Doomsday Syndrome* by John Maddox (New York, McGraw-Hill, 1972); *The Retreat from Riches* by Peter Passell and Leonard Ross (New York, Viking, 1973); and *The Disaster Lobby* by Melvin J. Grayson and Thomas R. Shepard, Jr. (Chicago, Follett, 1973). Also, there are three excellent, very readable new textbooks, containing collections of professional papers by leading scientists on the newest developments and thinking concerning natural resources. They are: *Man and His Physical Environment*, edited by Garry D. McKenzie and Russell O. Utgard, Ohio State University (Minneapolis, Burgess, 1972); *Man's Finite Earth*, edited by Russell O. Utgard and Garry D.

McKenzie, Ohio State University (Minneapolis, Burgess, 1974); and *Man and His Geologic Environment,* edited by David N. Cargo and Bob F. Mallory, Northwest Missouri State University (Reading, Mass., Addison-Wesley, 1974). A detailed scholarly report on environmental aspects of a national and international materials policy is the study *Man, Materials, and Environment,* by the National Academy of Sciences and National Academy of Engineering for the National Commission on Materials Policy (Cambridge, Mass, MIT Press, 1973).

My favorite source reference book for everything in connection with the past growth of America is the U. S. Bureau of the Census' *Historical Statistics of the United States: Colonial Times to 1957* (Washington, D. C., U. S. Government Printing Office, 1960). It may sound dull, but its statistical tables, showing how we got to where we are from where we started, make a stronger impact concerning our achievements than many of the polished summaries which our best historians give us.

There are many important books concerning the history of Middle East oil and international oil politics which are little known to most Americans because, up to now, this area has been of scant interest to us. The most comprehensive books, as an introduction to this field, are: *Oil in the Middle East* by Stephen Hensley Longrigg (New York and London, Oxford University Press, third edition, 1968); *Politics and World Oil Economics* by J. E. Hartshorn (New York, Praeger, 1962); *Americans and Oil in the Middle East* by Charles W. Hamilton (Houston, Gulf Publishing, 1962); and *The Kingdom of Oil* by Ray Vicker (New York, Scribner's, 1974).

Writing a book like this makes me realize the depth of my gratitude to the multitude of people all over the world who have made it possible for me to learn what I have tried to share. Many have been personal friends and teachers during my life's journey. Many I have never met, but appreciate equally. As one of these, Ralph Waldo Emerson, said, "We are all inlets and outlets of the same Divine Mind." So I thank the Creative Spirit, of which we are all a part, and most especially all those individualizing it who have enabled me to learn from them and those who have had the patience and wisdom to help guide me personally in my effort to report the story of this great challenge of our present time.

RUTH SHELDON KNOWLES

New York, New York
November, 1974

Index

250 *America's Oil Famine*

needs and population, 33, 49–53;
and oil import controls, 10; and oil
imports, 8–12; and oil needs, 8,
30, 49–53; and oil production, 9,
45–50; and projected oil needs,
30, 49–53
Engman, Lewis A., 59
Ente Nazionale Idrocarburi (ENI),
78, 85
Environmental Action, 172
Environmental Defense Fund, 37
Environmental policy, 33–40; and
air pollution, 28; and automotive
pollution, 39; and ecology move-
ment, 34–40; and energy policy,
171–213; and legislation, 35–41;
literature on, 38. *See also* Conser-
vation movement
Environmental Policy Act of 1970,
36
Environmental Protection Agency
(EPA), 53, 212–13 *passim;* crea-
tion of, 39; standards of, 213
Essay on the Principle of Population
(Malthus), 214
Esso, 85, 86, 105
Esso Standard of Libya, 81
European oil imports, 10
Exploring Energy Choices, 231
Exxon, 13, 37, 58, 71, 72, 147

Faisal, King, of Saudi Arabia, 7–8,
9–10, 13, 76, 102, 104, 108; and
Arab-U.S. relations, 9–11; atti-
tude toward Communism, 9; and
1973 energy crisis, 14; reaction to
U.S. pro-Israel policy, 16–17
Farmouts, 46–47
Federal Antiquities Act, 198
Federal Energy Administration
(FEA), creation of, 170
Federal Oil and Gas Co. (FOGCO),
157
Federal Power Commission (FPC),
27, 28, 53, 59–60, 61 *passim*
Federal Trade Commission (FTC),
55, 60; study of oil monopolies,
58–59
Federal Water Pollution Control Act
of 1965, 35

Ford, Gerald, 132
Freeman, S. David, 231
Friends of the Earth, 37, 172
*Future Petroleum Provinces of the
United States* (NPC), 41–42, 44

Gasoline: consumption, 225–27;
prices, 19, 21, 60, 136–39; ration-
ing, 17; supply of, 57. *See also*
Energy, oil
Gavin, Angus, 195–96
General Electric, 224, 228
Geothermal energy, 238–39
Golueke, C. G., 242
Grace Petroleum, 85
*Greatest Gamblers—the Epic of
American Oil Exploration, The*
(Knowles), 63
Growth, economic, 230–32
Growth, population, 214–32; and
energy conservation, 218–32
Gulf Oil Corp., 58, 69, 70, 72, 85,
126, 127, 131, 147

Halverson, James, 60
Hammer, Armand, 84, 86
Hardin, Garrett, 229
Hart, Philip A., 58, 59, 60
Heronemus, William E., 242
Hollomon, J. Herbert, 224
Holman, Eugene, 47
Hoover, Herbert, 68
Humphrey, Hubert H., 154
Hunt, Nelson Bunker, 90 91, 99,
100, 105, 106

Ibn Saud, King, of Saudi Arabia, 70
Idris, King of Libya, 82
Import quotas, abolition of, 54
Imports, oil, 26–33, 49, 52, 61–62,
119, 233; European, 10 *passim;*
Japanese, 10
Independent oil companies, 151–54
Independent Petroleum Association
of America, 49, 151, 156
Indonesia, 68, 79, 129–30; oil crisis
of 1963, 79
Inflation, 135, 136, 141
Inouye, Daniel K., 149

Oil shortages, remedies for, 20–23
Oil spills, 36–37, 173, 175, 176–94; containment of, 183; and refineries, 193–94; and supertankers, 184–91. *See also* Santa Barbara spill; Torrey Canyon spill
OPEC. *See* Organization of Petroleum Exporting Countries
Organization of African Unity, 121
Organization of Petroleum Exporting Countries (OPEC), 63–66, 80–81, 108–12, 116, 117, 118, 129, 130, 132; 135, 142, 147, 149, 159, 164–67
Oswald, W. J., 242

Pacific Gas and Electric Co., 238
Page, Howard W., 72
Pan American Oil Co., 78
Panarctic Oils Ltd., 124
Perez Alfonso, Juan Pablo, 63–65, 126
Pertamina, 129, 130
Peterson, Peter G., 11–12, 118
Peterson, Russell W., 22
Petroleum-exporting countries, development of, 63–105
Petroleum shortage, 54–62. *See also* Energy crisis; Gasoline; Oil
Phelan, James D., 68
Phillips Petroleum Co., 128
Piercy, George T., 94, 163
Pipelines, oil, 37–38, 56, 59, 126–27, 168, 194–98
Pittsburgh Plate Glass, 240
Pole, Jean, 124
Pollution. *See* Conservation movement; Environmental policy
Population Bomb, The (Ehrlich), 38
Pratt and Whitney Aircraft, 241
President's Advisory Committee on Energy Research and Development, 24
Prices: of gasoline, 19, 21, 60, 136–39; of natural gas, 25–26, 56, 60, 155–56; of oil, 17, 20, 25–26, 66–67, 77–96, 107–10, 111–12, 122–23, 131–32, 136–39, 148, 149, 159; alleged fixing of, 55–56; auctions, 130–31; proposed roll-back, 149–52. *See also* Teheran agreement
"Pricing of Middle East Crude Oil and Refined Products, The" (Tariki), 66
Profits, 57, 135–68
Project Independence, 18, 192, 203, 233, 234, 236

Qaddafi, Muammar, 14, 82–83, 84, 86, 88, 98, 99, 105, 106, 117, 159; anti-British policy, 88, 100; anti-Israel policy, 88; nationalization of oil companies, 106–7
Qatar, 71

Rasmussen, Norman C., 204
Rationing, 17
Ray, Dixy Lee, 205
Reason Awake (Dubos), 38
Recycling, 221–23
Reed, James, 172
Refineries, 193–94
Ribicoff, Abraham, 147
Robertshaw Controls Co., 224
Rockefeller, Nelson, 39
Rogers, Will, 19
Rogers, William, 92
Royal Dutch Shell, 58, 68, 72, 77, 79, 85, 139, 179

SIRIP, 78
Sadat, Anwar el, 14, 105
Saito, Rokuro, 185
Santa Barbara oil spill, 34, 36, 173, 182. *See also* oil spills
Saud, Prince, 10–11
Saudi Arabia, 9, 16–17, 63, 65, 70–71, 75–76, 81, 91, 110–11; relations with Iran, 108
Sawhill, John C., 168, 192, 234
Schmertz, Herbert, 144
Schmidt, Helmut, 115
Schuler, G. H. M., 91
Science and Survival (Commoner), 38
Shah of Iran, 15, 93, 104, 108–9, 119 *passim*
Shakhbut, Sheikh, 73